371·26 (S)

LB
3056
·G7
SHO

ISSUES IN ASSESSMENT AND TESTING

Series Editors: Donald McLeod and Ingrid Lunt

# NATIONAL TESTING
## Past, Present and Future

**Diane Shorrocks-Taylor**

*School of Education*
*University of Leeds*

BPS
BOOKS

Published by The British Psychological Society

First published in 1999 by BPS Books (The British Psychological Society), St Andrews House, 48 Princess Road East, Leicester LE1 7DR, UK, and 22883 Quicksilver Drive, Stirling, VA 20166, USA.

A catalogue record for this book is available from the British Library.

Library of Congress Cataloguing-in-Publication Data on file.

ISBN 1 85433 286 4

Typeset by Book Production Services, London.
Printed in Great Britain by MPG Books Limited

***Issues in Assessment and Testing series***
*Understanding Psychological Testing* by Charles Jackson
ISBN 1 85433 200 7
*Getting to Grips With Psychological Testing* by Geoff Trickey
(forthcoming)

# Contents

## 3 The development of the tasks and tests: background and summary

# List of tables and figures

All figures in *Chapter 3* are reproduced by kind permisison of the Qualifications and Curriculum Authority.

# Acknowledgements

The thoughts and information presented in this book are the result of a decade of involvement with the National Curriculum and, before that, many years of work in the fields of developmental and educational psychology. It is therefore not easy to acknowledge all those who have helped to shape the thinking that has gone into it. These include my colleagues here in the School of Education at the University of Leeds and the staff of SEAC/SCAA/QCA in its various manifestations. However, particular people have commented on various drafts of the chapters and I would like to thank them. They are Melanie Hargreaves, Peter Pool and John Threlfall from this department, Chris Whetton from NFER and Wendy Chisholme from Bradford LEA. Special thanks also go to Robat Powell from NFER Swansea and to Ella Owens and Rolant Wynne from the University of Wales, Bangor, for providing me with the information about testing in Welsh. I am also much indebted to the series editors, Donald McLeod and Ingrid Lunt, for their helpful comments, challenging questions and only very mild cracking of the whip. Any errors that remain are my own.

Diane Shorrocks-Taylor
School of Education
The University of Leeds

# Series Preface: Issues in assessment and testing

Psychological testing has been around for a long time. It is here to stay, and the use of tests in some form or another is going to continue to expand. So what is it all about? That is one of the questions that we are setting out to try to answer in this series. And at whom is it aimed? Anyone who is at all interested in finding out about tests and other forms of psychological assessment, for whatever reason.

For almost the whole of the twentieth century psychologists have been devising ways of assessing all manner of human attributes – feelings and fears, skills and aptitudes, beliefs and attitudes, wants and needs, insights and interests. Their quest has had two main aims. One, the theoretical, has been the advancement of knowledge about the psychology of the human species. The other, the practical, is about finding ways of helping to put that knowledge into effect. Our interest focuses in large measure on the latter, the principles-into-practice side, but not so intently as to exclude some of the more interesting theoretical and philosophical issues that surround and underpin psychological assessment.

Assessment in some shape or form pervades just about everything that we do. Formally or informally, we find assessments being made during the course of our education, in our working lives, when we get ill, and even if and when we offend against society's codes of behaviour. Children are assessed in a variety of ways, ideally – though maybe not always – as a means of ensuring that their development follows its most effective path to the full development of their individual capabilities. Young people and adults are assessed for their suitability for a particular line of work or for their potential to develop into it. People in work are increasingly involved in assessment for career development purposes, for promotion, for succession planning, for the purposes of putting together effective working teams, and so on. If our mental health falters, there will be assessments aimed at finding ways of helping us back to a state where we are at the very least better able to cope. Those who offend against the law may on occasion be assessed to determine their fitness to plead, and assessment will form an integral part of any programme of rehabilitation for the inmates of our prisons. It is all around us, and psychological testing is one of the forms that it typically takes.

Tests come in an extraordinarily wide array of forms, styles, content and purpose. But underneath it all there are really only two main kinds. One of them centres on ability – on knowledge, skills and aptitudes. The focus of the other is on our 'personality' – what kind of people we are, how we typically respond to the world around us and how we make that world respond to us. Although the technical terms 'psychometrics' or 'psychometric test' are often used, they imply nothing more than 'psychological test' – the term that we will use throughout the series.

There is already a great deal in print that is aimed at the specialist, at the testing and assessment professional. Issues in Assessment and Testing is not that kind of series. It does not set out to compete with specialist volumes in test construction. Rather, its aim is to try to meet the needs of the 'lay' practitioner, or of the interested observer with a healthy but unmet interest in the issues that surround psychological assessment and testing. We aim not so much to promote psychological testing and assessment as to help shed as much light as possible on the whole area. We hope to open up discussion, to enhance understanding of what tests and other formal assessment methods can achieve, and to foster a better educated use of methods and procedures of these sorts.

*Donald McLeod and Ingrid Lunt*
Series Editors, Issues in Assessment and Testing

# Introduction

In considering the present character of the state schooling system in the United Kingdom, particularly in England and Wales, the sentiment often expressed by educationists is one of disbelief. This disbelief arises from the fact that at the time of writing, in the late 1990s, a statutory, centrally determined National Curriculum is now in place in our schools and alongside it a comprehensive system of statutory national testing. The term 'statutory' implies that there are legal requirements for schools. Viewed from earlier years, say the early 1980s, such a situation would never have been thought possible, by teachers and politicians alike.

At this point, however, it is necessary to make an important point. I have just referred to the 'state schooling system in the United Kingdom', implying that the changes apply equally and are the same in all four countries of the union. This is not entirely the case. In general terms, there are many parallels, but both Scotland and Northern Ireland have their own versions of a National Curriculum which are rather different from that in existence in England and Wales and, even in Wales, the curriculum has its own character. In terms of testing, England and Wales work to broadly the same system, although from 1999 testing in Wales will become independent from that in England. However, both Scotland and Northern Ireland have a different approach to both the curriculum and its assessment, with much less reliance on centrally provided national tests. In the main, this book focuses on testing in England and Wales, but reference is made to developments in Scotland and Northern Ireland where interesting comparisons arise.

One of the main purposes of this book, therefore, is to chart the course of these considerable educational changes and to throw some light on the influences and reasoning behind them. The other major purpose is to provide some insight and information into the nature of the tests themselves, how they are constructed and used and some of the controversies that surround them. National testing currently applies (in England and Wales) to 7-year-olds, 11-year-olds and 14-year-olds and all three of these age groups will be dealt with. The statutory tests cover the core subjects of the National Curriculum, namely English (and

Welsh in Wales), mathematics and science (except for 7-year-olds), and these subjects will be considered in the chapters that follow.

All the test materials relate to the relevant aspects of the National Curriculum; that is, they are based on the detailed curriculum outlines for each subject. Because of this, charting the changes and examining the nature of the tests requires background information about the politics of the curriculum and the government agendas that have been in play. If war is just an extension of politics, in this case education certainly is, and no full understanding of the present situation is possible without this information. It is also necessary to draw on some technical and statistical information, bearing in mind the needs of non-specialist readers.

*Chapter 1* looks in more detail at the origins of the National Curriculum and its testing programme, and relates these to national debates about 'standards' in schools, an increasing call for accountability in the education system and the rights of parents and the community to know what is going on in schools. *Chapter 2* asks the question, 'What are the national tests like, and why?' Going back to the major report on the national testing system (the TGAT Report, DES/WO, 1988) the main characteristics of the tests are outlined, with all the changes that have occurred since, and issues such as the 'ages and stages' debate and the role of teachers' own assessments addressed. To complete this group of chapters providing background information, *Chapter 3* describes the overall structure of the tests and gives some examples of the tests for all three age groups and across subjects. *Chapter 4* is more technical in nature and covers such aspects as criterion-referencing, the dependability and validity of the scores derived from the test materials and progression across the stages of the curriculum.

In *Chapters 5, 6* and *7*, the testing carried out at each of the three age groups is examined in more detail, outlining further the content of the test materials and giving some of the history of the developments and changes that have occurred at each phase. Thus, *Chapter 5* deals with 7-year-olds (Key Stage 1), *Chapter 6* deals with 11-year-olds (Key Stage 2) and *Chapter 7* deals with 14-year-olds (Key Stage 3). The final chapter essentially tries to draw the discussion together and looks to how the testing system could develop and change in the future.

This is clearly a great deal of material to cover in comparatively few pages, but it is to be hoped that the end result is sufficiently comprehensive and informative to provoke thought and generate further debate on these very important matters.

Diane Shorrocks-Taylor
February 1999
Leeds

# 1 The origins of the national tests

This chapter presents an account of the origins of the National Curriculum in the United Kingdom and in so doing, acts in a preparatory way for the chapters that follow. By introducing and summarizing some of the main points at this stage, the more detailed information and arguments in subsequent chapters will be set in their wider context. The National Curriculum has two dimensions: the subjects and the specifications within them, and the assessment system that fits alongside. The focus here is on the development of both of these, so as to provide the broad setting for the focus on assessment that is the main emphasis of the book. It should also be emphasized that although the curriculum and its assessment are considered for the full 5 to 16 years age range, this book will really only address Key Stages 1, 2 and 3 (ages 5 to 14 years), the focus of National Curriculum testing.

## Some background discussion: falling standards and centralized control of the curriculum

The forces for the recent educational reform in the United Kingdom can be traced back to the 1960s and 1970s, when rumblings began to be heard about the fragmented nature of much of the curriculum in both primary and secondary schools, and the fact that each school was virtually free to devise its own. The only legal requirements were for a daily act of worship and an agreed form of non-compulsory religious education for all pupils. The results of this *laissez-faire* situation were highlighted in the controversial Black Papers of the 1960s (for example, Cox and Dyson, 1969), a series of polemical publications about poor schooling and falling standards emanating from the conservative right-wing, blaming 'progressivism' for the declining state of education. Perhaps most tellingly, however, the clarion call for considered educational reform is often dated to James Callaghan's well-known 'Ruskin' speech in 1976 (Callaghan, 1976) in which he expressed worries about schooling and called for a 'Great Debate'.

But from any rational point of view, there was very little evidence either way to indicate reliably whether or not educational standards were rising or falling. This is a line argued by Caroline Gipps (1990), who points out that ever since the nineteenth century the cry has been heard that 'standards' were falling in schools. Even with the advent of public examinations, it is not possible to argue the case either way, since syllabuses have changed in various ways, and there are few retained scripts to carry out re-marks over time. However, the desire to improve what goes on in our schools does not have to be based on the assertion that standards are falling.

Surveys by HMI (Her Majesty's Inspectorate) during the 1970s had revealed enormous variation in the quality of what was going on in schools and suggested the need for intervention. Although it is usually acknowledged that the term 'National Curriculum' was not used before 1985, an official publication (DES, 1980) had suggested the need for a curriculum of a broad character for pupils in secondary schools. When the Conservative government came to power in 1979, led by Margaret Thatcher, the debate intensified, especially with the appointment of Kenneth Baker as Secretary of State for Education in 1981. An article by Taylor (1995) provides some fascinating insights into the struggles within government in the years leading up to the Educational Reform Act of 1988. He suggests that there was fundamental conflict between the main protagonists, with Margaret Thatcher wanting to focus only on the 'core' subjects (a 'back-to-basics' kind of stance) through regulation rather than legislation, and Kenneth Baker advocating a broad curriculum (in line with the ideas of HMI) enforced in legislation. The crunch came in December 1986, when Kenneth Baker announced the idea of a statutory National Curriculum in the course of a TV interview.

In the apparently heated discussions that followed this pre-emptive strike, the focus was on the size and scope of the curriculum that was to be put in place: broad or narrow? The rest is history, as they say, since the result was the English/Welsh ten-subject curriculum (eleven in Wales), with three (four in Wales) 'core' subjects and seven other 'foundation' subjects plus religious education. This outcome is worthy of further comment, not least since a fully subject-based curriculum was not the response in either Scotland or Northern Ireland, as we shall see later in this chapter.

Curriculum theory is a distinct branch of educational study in its own right, and there are many possible ways of delineating the different kinds of knowledge and skills that need to be acquired by pupils: the framework does not have to focus on the conventional 'subjects'. The present subject-based National Curriculum in England and Wales has direct links back to turn-of-the-century ideas and to the kinds of curriculum used in traditional grammar schools (Moon, 1990). In many ways, a very different curriculum, one with a more vocational slant, would have been more in keeping with the 'market' notions of the government of the time (Elliott, 1991). However, the traditional, subject-based approach could not be abandoned for political reasons, namely the powerful myth that traditional subjects are the source of educational excellence.

The important matter of assessment, however, was yet to be fought over. As an issue, it did not really figure in the debate until the 1980s, with two publications *Better Schools* (DES, 1985) and *The Curriculum from 5 to 16* (HMI, 1985), both of which advocated a new emphasis. It was at this point that 'accountability' and an assessment-led agenda began to emerge in the context of a National Curriculum (Daugherty, 1995), which could of course easily have been put in place without any formal monitoring of this kind.

The theme of evaluation and monitoring on a national scale (and for age groups under the age of 16) had been raised earlier, however. In 1974, the Assessment of Performance Unit (APU) was set up, and later provided national monitoring of performance over time in English, mathematics and science. This was achieved through the assessment of national samples of pupils, using specially prepared banks of assessment materials and, in this way, it generated national evaluation data. However, by definition, not all pupils needed to take part each year, so the monitoring of the performance of **all** children and **all** schools could not be achieved. There will be more discussion of this in the next chapter. The APU was ended once the changed political agenda dictated the new National Curriculum and the assessment of all children in all schools.

## The development and provisions of the National Curriculum: the curriculum dimension

Kenneth Baker set up a Task Group on Assessment and Testing (TGAT) in the summer of 1987, a group briefed to advise the Secretary of State on the 'practical considerations which should govern all assessment including testing of attainment at age (approximately) 7, 11, 14 and 16' (DES/WO, 1988, Appendix A). The group was made up largely of 'educational establishment' members, a clever means of selling the ideas to sceptical professionals, and it was allowed a fairly free rein (Ball, 1990) until shortly before it was due to report. At this point it was made clear that the assessment system should serve four key purposes, namely **formative, diagnostic, summative** and **evaluative**. These terms will be discussed in more detail later on, but briefly they mean that the assessments should provide sound feedback to teachers in order to support the learning process (a formative purpose), they should help teachers to diagnose gaps and problems in pupils' learning (a diagnostic purpose) and they should provide an overview of pupils' learning (a summative purpose). The final 'evaluative' purpose implies that the assessments should generate national monitoring information, a purpose now formally stated for the first time.

The TGAT proposals were broadly accepted and set the framework for the assessment system and for the specifications to the subject working groups, who then went on to outline (for each curriculum subject) the precise content of the curriculum. Each Working Group was required to define the 'attainment targets' for their subject and to group these into broader 'profile components' – the major dimensions of the subject. They were also to consider the question of whether all 'attainment targets' and 'profile components' were appropriate for all age groups and to tailor the curriculum requirements accordingly (DES/WO, 1988,para 176).

It has to be said that the first curriculum documents produced, especially in the core subjects, did not necessarily reflect this advice. The 'profile components' were delineated in rather strange and complex ways, especially in mathematics and science, and the advice to make the lower levels in the (then) 10-Level scale more broad and general was not always achieved. The report also recommended that the working groups should devise the curriculum so that:

> *Attainment for each profile component should be described in terms of a set of staged criteria, in relationship to which the diverse performances of the children can be classified. The levels and corresponding criteria should form a single spectrum irrespective of age, but be so constructed that normal performance of pupils would correspond to the second level at age 7 (for profile components appropriate at that age) and would involve the use of a larger number up to 10 at later ages. These would span the complete range of GCSE grades as specified in Section XI.*
>
> (DES/WO, 1998, para 177)

This gave rise to the Attainment Targets and Profile Components in the early versions of the National Curriculum, each divided into 10 levels and the many 'criteria' within each level.

By way of summary, *Table 1.1* shows the timing for the Working Groups, the production of the first consultative reports from the groups, and the dates of the publication of the Statutory Orders for each subject. In each subject, a draft Order was published first, a short time before the final Order, to allow scope for comments. The many files and folders filling school bookshelves are testimony to the breadth and detail of what was produced.

What is clear from this table are two things: the speed at which the whole curriculum was devised and put into statute, and the very short time allowed to the Working Groups for their detailed and important work, especially in the core subjects. It also proved to be a recipe for fragmentation, setting in motion a process of curriculum development by disparate groups of professionals, working to an overall structure but without the vital ingredient of a picture of the whole curriculum and the values it was seeking to embody. Many have subsequently blamed these factors for the problems experienced both with the curriculum content and its assessment.

To complete this background information about the National Curriculum, *Table 1.2* shows the years in which the curriculum subjects were introduced into schools (primary and secondary, Key Stages 1, 2 and 3) and the years in which the first statutory tests were used in the core subjects. By 1992, the content of the full curriculum was mostly prepared, and by 1994 most of it was being delivered in schools. Its main characteristics, as we have seen, were that each subject was divided into its major sub-areas of knowledge and skills (say Reading within English), referred to as the *Profile Components* and *Attainment Targets* and the content should fit within a 10-Level scale of increasing difficulty within each of these Attainment Targets. The problems that emerged in relation to these requirements will be dealt with in more detail in later chapters.

It is not easy to summarize such a massive piece of legislation, but some of the key characteristics of the 1988 version of the curriculum are as follow.

- It was **subject-based** (10/11 subjects), seeking to offer a 'broad and balanced' curriculum to all pupils. However, what was specified was the **content** of what was to be taught, in great detail, not the **methods** of teaching.

- In the wide range of prescribed subjects, some were designated 'core subjects' (English, Mathematics, Science, and Welsh for Welsh-speaking schools in Wales) and the rest, 'other foundation subjects'. Religious education was not formally included in the National Curriculum, although it had to be taught. These subjects were not intended to represent the whole curriculum in schools: time was to be left for important aspects of learning, such as personal and social skills and the development of economic and industrial understanding.

- It contained some **innovative** conceptions, for instance in its inclusion of Technology as an important subject in the curriculum for all age groups, and also the introduction of Science into primary schools.

- It was an **entitlement** curriculum, requiring all schools to ensure that each child received the full range of the curriculum as specified. The curriculum applied to all state schools but not to private, independent schools, although many of these acknowledged and applied the National Curriculum.

- It included an **assessment system**, based directly on the detailed specifications within each subject of the curriculum, and to be carried out through a combination of teachers' own assessments and the use of nationally devised and provided assessment materials.

**Table 1.1:** The timing of the developments and finalizing of the Statutory Orders in each National Curriculum subject

| Date | | Core Subjects | | | | Foundation Subjects | | | | |
|---|---|---|---|---|---|---|---|---|---|---|
| Year | Month | English | Mathematics | Science | Welsh | Technology | History | Geography | Modern Foreign Langs. | Art/Music/PE |
| 1987 | Jul | | Working Group | Working Group | | | | | | |
| 1988 | Apr | Working Group | | | | Working Group | | | | |
| | Aug | | Report | Report | | | | | | |
| | Nov | Report (1)* | | | Working Group | | | | | |
| 1989 | Jan | | | | | | Working Group | | | |
| | Mar | Order (1)* | Order*** | Order*** | | | | | | |
| | Apr | | | | Report | | | | | |
| | May | | | | | | | Working Group | | |
| | Jun | Report (2)** | | | | | | | | |
| | Aug | | | | | Report | | | | |
| 1990 | Mar | Order (2)** | | | | | | | | |
| | May | | | | | Order | | | | |
| | Jun | | | | Order | | | | | |
| | Jul | | | | | | Report | | | |
| | Oct | | | | | | | Report | | |
| 1991 | Mar | | | | | | Order | Order | | |
| | Aug | | | | | | | | | Working Group |
| | Nov | | | | | | | | | Report |
| 1992 | Mar | | | | | | | | | Order |

Key: *English 5–11
**English 5–16
***These Orders were revised in 1991, to take effect in schools from August 1992

- It therefore embodied the principle of on-going **evaluation of each child's learning** in other words, not only a focus on what was to be **taught** but also an emphasis on what the child had **learned**.

- Across all subjects, the curriculum spanned the full statutory school **age range of 5 to 16**. For the first time, this provided all schools, secondary, middle and primary alike, with a common framework for planning and delivery of the curriculum. It was intended to generate **coherence** across the different phases of education and a more effective exchange of information between them.

- The 10-level scale, covering the whole age range from 5 to 16 also emphasized **differentiation**. In other words, even within the same age-group, not all children have the same learning needs or attain at the same level. As importantly, it potentially highlighted the fact that an individual child could attain at different levels in different subjects or parts of subjects.

- The rights of parents in the education system were emphasized in the Act – their rights to information about their child's progress in schools in relation to each Attainment Target.

- New bodies were set up with particular responsibilities, namely the National Curriculum Council (England), the Curriculum Council for Wales and the Schools Examination and Assessment Council with responsibility for assessment in both England and Wales.

As might be predicted, such massive changes received a mixed response from teachers, particularly those in primary schools, who had little experience of formal syllabuses and externally imposed requirements, at least since the virtual demise of the 11-plus system. It was also especially significant for primary schools because 7-year-olds would be the first group to be assessed, in 1991. As Campbell (1993) pointed out, many of the critics seemed to be mourning the loss of an apparently 'golden age' of primary education, where rich experiences abounded and creativity and integrated learning were to the fore. However, the problem was that such schools and learning environments were hard to find in 1970s and 1980s Britain. In fact, many studies (for example, Alexander, 1984; 1992; Bennett *et al.*, 1984; Galton and Simon, 1980) had provided sound evidence that all was not well in primary schools. These studies revealed a rather haphazard approach to curriculum planning and delivery, much repetition, lack of appropriate matching of learning activities to the learning needs of individual children and little continuity and progression within primary schools or with receiving secondary schools. All this does not necessarily imply criticism of the teachers involved; rather, it highlights the need for just such an agreed and shared curriculum.

**Table 1.2:** The introduction of National Curriculum subjects into schools and the first years of formal national testing (core subjects only)

| Key Stage | Maths | Science | English | Welsh (1) | Welsh (2) | Technology | History | Geog. | Art/Music/P.E. | Modern Languages |
|---|---|---|---|---|---|---|---|---|---|---|
| **KS1** | 1989 | 1989 | 1989 | 1990 | 1992 | 1990 | 1991 | 1991 | 1992 | N/A |
| **Tests** | 1991 | 1991 | 1991 | 1991 | 1993 | | | | | |
| **KS2** | 1990 | 1990 | 1990 | 1990 | 1994 | 1990 | 1991 | 1991 | 1992 | N/A |
| **Tests** | 1994 | 1994 | 1994 | 1994 | 1997 | | | | | |
| **KS3** | 1989 | 1989 | 1990 | 1990 | 1992 | 1990 | 1991 | 1991 | 1992 | 1992 |
| **Tests** | 1991 | 1991 | 1992 | 1992 | 1994 | | | | | |

Key:   Welsh (1)   Schools where Welsh was already being taught
       Welsh (2)   Other schools in Wales

This original version of the curriculum did not specify the amount of time to be devoted to each subject, either in primary or secondary schools, for the reason that it was thought this would be unacceptable to schools. The general sense was, however, that the core subjects would be the predominant focus in primary schools, but less so as pupils got older. In many ways this reflected the emphasis on 'basics' already prevalent in primary schools, where roughly 50 per cent of teaching time seemed to have been devoted to basic literacy and numeracy (Alexander, 1992), with correspondingly less time for all the other subjects. Interestingly, similar findings have more recently been reported (Colwill, 1996) as part of the school monitoring exercise being carried out by the School Curriculum and Assessment Authority. All this, of course, raises the question of exactly what balance should be achieved in the face of a need for a broad curriculum experience for children, and how should this balance change as they get older? It would also be naïve to assume that the tests themselves, focusing as they do on the core subjects, do not exert a considerable influence on the amount of time spent on each curriculum subject.

From the beginning, problems were recognized in relation to Key Stage 4, that is, pupils aged 14 to 16. The curriculum required all children to study all these subjects to the age of 16, with the end-of-Key-Stage assessments taking the form of (revised) GCSE exams and other, more vocational, qualifications. This gave rise to two problems: an overcrowded and over-demanding curriculum for some pupils, and insufficient scope for others (for instance, the higher attainers) to take a wider range of subjects. The result has been the development of more flexible approaches at this Key Stage. There is provision for pupils to drop some subjects after Key Stage 3 and to focus on new ones or, alternatively, to take vocational qualifications which have been dovetailed in alongside some of the National Curriculum subjects. Some of the more recent official publications on the matter have emphasized the wide range of possibilities available for this age range, including GNVQ and NVQ courses (SCAA, 1996a). Since 1988, there have also taken place detailed negotiations with Examining Boards and other qualification-awarding bodies to bring existing syllabuses and assessment in line with the requirements of the National Curriculum for Key Stage 4.

Bringing together some of these issues, it is clear that the curriculum was wide-ranging and developed at speed, driven largely, but not entirely, by political motives. The legislation governing it was similarly broad in scope, resulting in shelves of curriculum documents in school staff-rooms throughout the land.

## Pupils with special educational needs (SEN)

There was a mixed response from those working with pupils identified as having special educational needs (SEN). In terms of the principles and structure of the curriculum, there was, in general, a welcome for the idea of entitlement to a broadly based and well-planned curriculum for all pupils (Sebba and Byers, 1992). Also welcomed were the ideas of continuity and progression and the focus on the learning needs and achievements of the individual child. Sharing clear information with parents was an aspect already better established with this professional group. However, the negative aspects of the curriculum were perceived as being the emphasis on raising standards and the competition between schools which this could generate.

Most children identified as having special educational needs are in mainstream schools, with only a minority in special schools, and even prior to the National Curriculum, much work had been done on devising an appropriate curriculum for them. As Sebba and Byers point out, this had often focused on the **how** of teaching (that is, teaching methods) rather than on the **what** (the content of the curriculum). Such work had included behavioural approaches to teaching, so the idea of having clear teaching and learning objectives was well established.

It is worth stressing the fact that the National Curriculum was not intended to be the whole curriculum for any school, mainstream or special. The body formally responsible for it, the National Curriculum Council (NCC), published several pamphlets (for example, 1990a, 1990b) pointing out that other important issues needed to be covered, such as personal and social skills, and other cross-curricular themes. In many ways, therefore, this provided an impetus to consider the whole curriculum in a new way, especially among those dealing with children with special educational needs. There was provision in the legislation for the National Curriculum (both the curriculum and the assessments) to be *disapplied* for some pupils, at the judgement of their headteacher. In this process, the main question must always be the needs of the pupil and whether it is judged that they could benefit from the curriculum. In the context of entitlement, many teachers of children with special educational needs were reluctant to disapply their pupils.

Assessment, however, was mostly viewed by this group (SEN professionals) in a more negative way, notwithstanding the fact that the TGAT Report had advised that:

> *The national tests should be designed to be appropriate to children across the whole ability range, modified as necessary for children with particular sensory problems (i.e. blind and partially sighted children, deaf and partially hearing children) and those with communication difficulties.*

(DES/WO, 1988, para 171)

Clearly anticipating some of the testing problems that might emerge, the TGAT Report also advised that:

> *Some children with special educational needs might be entered for the national tests but might not prove capable of coping with them adequately. To avoid any possibility of such children perceiving themselves as failures, the national tests should be designed in such a way as to permit the teacher to curtail the test discreetly without the child being aware that this was being done, or to give assistance, the extent of this being recorded.*
>
> (DES/WO, 1988, para 173)

These were supportive suggestions, but the complex structure of levels presented difficulties for many of these pupils. It was a common complaint that the Level 1 requirements were often too high, an issue that led many SEN teachers to devise their own 'pre-Level 1' objectives or criteria. The assessments themselves, when they arrived on the scene from 1991 onwards, also posed many professional dilemmas: teachers working with children with learning or other difficulties wanted their pupils to show the positive things they could do and achieve, but at the same time recognized that the national requirements were beyond many of these children.

To summarize, in terms of the overall structure and content of the curriculum, teachers working with pupils with special educational needs could see the advantages and disadvantages, and their reception of the curriculum and its assessment reflected this.

## The development and provisions of the National Curriculum: the assessment dimension

We have already seen the origins of the assessment system in the political agendas of the 1970s and 1980s, involving all children and all schools. The TGAT Report set the framework of the four Key Stages, formative assessment within each of these stages, and summative assessment at the end of each Key Stage, as well as the 10 Levels that were to be the focus of the reported results for each child.

In each subject, however, the curriculum specification made a distinction between two aspects, as shown in *Table 1.3*. The Statements of Attainment (SoAs) became the basis for the detailed recording of children's progress, providing information for the teacher in an on-going, formative way, but also information on which to base their summative assessments at the end of each Key Stage. The SoAs also provided the content for the development of the national tests and tasks at the end of each Key Stage. *Table 1.4* gives an indication of how many Attainment Targets there were in each subject (using the

**Table 1.3:** The overall structure of the National Curriculum in each core subject

| Programmes of Study | Profile Components and Attainment Targets |
|---|---|
| The Programmes of Study set out the knowledge, skills and processes that must be taught at each Key Stage in a detailed but general way. | The range of Profile Components and their Attainment Targets in each subject set out the knowledge, skills and understandings pupils should have attained by the end of each Key Stage, arranged as a 10-level scale and with the required Statements of Attainment (SoAs) specified at each level. In summary form, this can be depicted as follows in Mathematics (1991 version): Profile Components: 2 Attainment Targets: 8 6 10 Levels in each AT Statements of Attainment at each of these 10 Levels |

**Table 1.4:** The number of Attainment Targets and Statements of Attainment in some National Curriculum subjects (1991 version)

| Subject | Number of ATs | Number of SoAs |
|---|---|---|
| English | 5 | 158 |
| Mathematics | 5 | 145 |
| Science | 4 | 176 |
| Welsh (core) | 3/4 | 147 |
| Welsh (second language) | 3 | 134 |
| Technology | 5 | 157 |
| History | 3 | 45 |
| Geography | 5 | 183 |
| Modern Foreign Language | 4 | 142 |

1991 revised versions of the Mathematics and Science Orders when some of the worst excesses had been removed) together with the number of SoAs.

The result of this complexity, even after revision of the curriculum, was not only a desperately broad curriculum for teachers to plan and deliver, but also an enormous recording task. Most schools, under the guidance of their Local Education Authority (LEA) staff, developed labyrinthine systems of checklists, until it became almost a case of death by a thousand tick-boxes! The situation was especially difficult in primary schools, where it was frequently one teacher who had to plan, teach and assess the whole curriculum for a class, and also to report to parents. Almost by definition, one teacher could not be a specialist in every National Curriculum subject.

It is not surprising therefore that when the first Standard Assessment Tasks ('SATs', although this term is no longer officially used) were used in schools with 7-year-olds in the summer of 1991, there was something of an outcry. Newspaper headlines of the 'Top marks for wasting time and money' or 'New tests fail the grade' variety were plentiful, only to be repeated the next year, when some of the Key Stage 3 tests were also introduced into schools. The crunch seemed to come in 1993, when Key Stage 3 teachers boycotted the tests and called for change. The response to this boycott together with pressure from other sources gave rise to the Dearing review (Dearing, 1993).

### The Dearing review: a summary of the main points

The Dearing Report, whose recommendations were accepted by the government of the day, advocated some important changes to both the curriculum and its assessment. Very broadly, these can be summarized as follows.

- A streamlining of the curriculum for 5- to 14-year-olds (Key Stages 1, 2 and 3) to free more time for schools to use for other aspects of children's education. This was to be done rapidly, so that it could be in place for September 1995.

- A reduction of the curriculum content for these Key Stages, to be focused on the non-core subjects.

- Greater flexibility in the curriculum for 14- to 16-year-olds, so that schools could offer more options, including vocational opportunities for pupils.

- A reduction in the demands on teachers both by simplifying the curriculum and by reducing recording and testing demands.

- The 10-Level assessment scale was to be kept, but used only up to the end of Key Stage 3.

- The replacement of the listings of Statements of Attainment at each of the 10 levels in each Attainment Target by Level Descriptions, with consequent effects for both recording systems and assessment procedures.

- Better provision for pupils with special educational needs, in the form of including Level 1 and 2 specifications in all subjects and broadening the assessments at Key Stages 2 and 3.

- A period of five years when there would be no further changes to the curriculum.

These proposals were not only accepted by the government, they were welcomed by angry and beleaguered teachers, struggling in the face of unreasonable complexity and demands.

The 1993 curriculum review, like the original development work, did not begin from first principles of curriculum thinking, but was instead determined by practical expediency. However, as Golby (1994) argues, it nevertheless represented a continuing debate on the curriculum which is important in a democratic society.

In curriculum terms, the new emphasis on post-14 education (in fact seen as the 14–19 years age sector) was significant in wider educational and political terms, giving the potential for greater diversity and flexibility of provision, academic, technical and vocational. Those working with children identified as having special educational needs also gave a cautious welcome to some of the changes (Byers, 1994), particularly the emphasis on Level 1 provision for all age groups in all subjects.

In assessment terms, perhaps the two most significant factors were the much reduced recording demands for teachers and the retention of the 10-level scale. The simplification of the curriculum, even in the core subjects, was to be achieved through a reduction in the content of the Programmes of Study and by losing the notion of Statement of Attainment (SoAs) at each level in each Attainment Target. In itself, this very much reduced the need for teachers to devise and maintain checklists and sets of tick-boxes. Instead, what was now suggested were 'Level Descriptions' for each level in each Attainment Target which were to be used in a 'best-fit' way by teachers. These will be explained in later chapters. The new curriculum also attempted to clarify the role and status of two kinds of assessment, those made by teachers themselves (Teacher Assessment) and those provided by the results of the national tests. These were now to be reported separately to parents, and the difference between them explained.

## Some comparisons with Wales, Scotland and Northern Ireland

In the introduction, it was stressed that the main focus of discussion in this book would be the system in England and Wales since the situation in Scotland and in Northern Ireland is rather different. In this first background chapter, it is important to summarize the major differences in both the curriculum and its assessment; and to begin we will consider Wales, since there are some important differences here, even though the systems in England and Wales are usually viewed in a parallel way.

### The curriculum and its assessment in Wales

Historically, Wales has never had the autonomous institutional framework found in Scotland and this placed it in rather a different position when the idea of a National Curriculum was being mooted in the 1980s. There appeared to be little by way of a coherent strategy to prepare to deal with this in Wales (Jones, 1994). Perhaps because of this, the TGAT proposals for the overall structure of the curriculum and its assessment were accepted for Wales (the Welsh Office had been involved), to be administered through the School Examinations and Assessment Council in England. The Act did, however, also set up the Curriculum Council for Wales as an advisory body.

In 1987, Wales published its own document on the curriculum in which it was suggested that Welsh language and literature should be a compulsory part of the curriculum; hence the inclusion of Welsh in the core subjects. Or rather, to be more precise, it is only a core subject in schools where Welsh is the main medium of instruction; in the rest it is a foundation subject taken by all pupils. All children in Wales now learn Welsh from the age of 5.

However, far from being exactly parallel in England and Wales, various subjects in the curriculum for Wales have a distinctive character, reflecting a background of considerable discussion and negotiation. The two classic battlegrounds in England, namely English and history, proved strong discussion points in Wales too, with the result that the history curriculum in Wales reflects Welsh history, while the English curriculum in Wales is different from that in England. There were also clashes over art and music, again leading to different emphases in Wales. The final result is that only science, mathematics and PE are the same in terms of curriculum content.

In relation to assessment, the two systems are parallel, bearing in mind the fact that the content of the assessments in English and history in particular are different because the curriculum content is different. As of the year 2000, however, Wales will establish its own assessment system, producing its own tests in the core subjects for Key Stages 1 to 3.

### The curriculum and its assessment in Scotland

Responsibility for education in Scotland is devolved to the Scottish Office and this has meant that the Scottish education system has always retained a considerable degree of autonomy. This notwithstanding, changes to both the curriculum and its assessment were put in place alongside those in England and Wales, and with some parallels. However, there are also many significant differences.

The curriculum relates to the age range 5 to14 (Primary 1 to Secondary 2 inclusive) but is conceived of in a very different way from that in England. As Harlen and Malcolm (1994) point out, the Scottish Consultative Council on the Curriculum (SCCC) had been issuing guidance to teachers for a very long time by 1987, when the idea of a National Curriculum was being developed, and primary schools were the initial focus. A 1983 paper (SCCC, 1983) suggested the following framework for primary schools:

| Subject | Further additions for secondary schools |
|---|---|
| language arts | |
| mathematics | |
| environmental studies | *scientific studies and applications* <br> *social and environmental studies* <br> *technological activities and* <br> *applications;* |
| expressive arts | *creative and aesthetic activities* <br> *physical education;* |
| religious and moral education | |

This became the basis for the new curriculum but developed in more detailed ways for secondary schools, as shown in italics in the list. It is clear that this represents a more cross-curricular approach to curriculum design, with the potential for greater flexibility. Another difference in the structure of the curriculum is that it is based upon a 5-Level scale across the 5 to 14 years age range (not 10 levels as in England and Wales). Both the curriculum and the assessments were non-statutory in the beginning, but the poor response by teachers led to them being made a requirement.

The assessment and reporting system is also very different. Originally, testing was to take place in Primary 4 and in Primary 7, the final primary year, and was to concentrate on English and mathematics only. Since only primary schools were involved initially, the assessment materials were developed by the

Primary Assessment Unit of the Scottish Examination Board (SEB), using mainly experienced teachers for the development work. As in England and Wales, it was the assessment system that caused most controversy, so that in 1994 new arrangements were put in place. Under this revised system, formal testing must happen each year from Primary 1 to Secondary 2 and must cover reading, writing and mathematics. The test materials can be used by teachers when they judge it to be most appropriate for the children; the testing is intended to give teachers the means of verifying their own assessments and ensuring that their judgements are in line with the agreed standards.

### The curriculum and its assessment in Northern Ireland

Several writers on the topic of the curriculum and assessments in Northern Ireland (for example, Wallace, 1994; D'Arcy, 1994a) emphasize the deliberate policy in the province of keeping in line with the system in England and Wales. Being geographically small in size, with a comparatively small number of schools, calibrating standards and having test results that bear comparison with the other countries in the Union is seen as important. Most significantly, the province is one of the few areas left that still has a selective secondary school system, and this was perceived as having undue influence on the curriculum in primary schools.

Similar problems of curriculum fragmentation and lack of central control were noted in the 1980s and various curriculum initiatives were begun, both in the primary and secondary sectors. As in Scotland, these initiatives and the thinking that had gone into them were not abandoned when it came to devising a new curriculum; instead, they were built upon, giving rise to a curriculum with a cross-curricular character. The cross-curricular themes were such aspects as 'education for mutual understanding' or 'information technology', and they became embodied into six major 'Areas of Study", grouping cognate subjects together. These are:

English
mathematics
science and technology
environment and society
creative and expressive studies
language studies
religious education

The curriculum applies to all children up to the age of 14 and is monitored by the Northern Ireland Curriculum Council (NICC).

Assessment is in the hands of the Northern Ireland Examinations and Assessment Council (NISEAC) and is, once again, different from England and Wales. Originally, the idea was to focus on teachers' own assessments, but influence from London led to this being changed so that, in addition, 'Common Assessment Instruments' (CAIs) were included; in other words, externally administered testing. As in the rest of the United Kingdom, there was considerable teacher protest, and low participation in the national piloting of the tests, leading to a re-think in 1993. At this point, the Department for Education and Science (DES, London) announced that piloting would continue for another year and that the CAIs would be replaced by 'Assessment Units' designed to 'assist' teachers' own assessments, not replace them.

## Summary

- The origins of the National Curriculum were both educational and political, responding to great diversity of provision in schools (both primary and secondary), and to the perception that standards were falling.

- The structure of the new curriculum followed very traditional, subject-based lines, and contained a significant assessment dimension.

- The development of the curriculum content specifications for the individual subjects was a fragmented process, with each subject Working Group following a general brief but with no overall plan or vision.

- The result was a series of highly detailed and complex curriculum specifications, housed in the famous 'files' to be found on all school bookshelves.

- The first years of national testing, beginning in 1991, brought complaint and boycott from teachers and many of their professional associations, the response to which was the Dearing review in 1993.

- This review maintained the essential structure of the curriculum, but with considerable simplification and changes of emphasis.

- The curriculum provision in Wales, Scotland and Northern Ireland contain some significant differences from that in England and have provided interesting points of comparison and contrast over the years.

# 2 Influences on the structure of the national tests

The last chapter traced some of the origins of the National Curriculum in England and Wales, in particular the framework within which the national tests were conceived and which determined their character and purposes. It is the aim of this chapter to go into more detail about the assessment aspects of the National Curriculum and to outline the influences on the nature of the tests themselves.

The Task Group on Assessment and Testing (TGAT) set up by the government in 1987 had been briefed to do the following:

- offer advice on a coherent system of assessment, including testing, to cover the whole period of compulsory schooling;

- suggest approaches that would be practicable and cost effective;

- address the range or purposes to which assessment, including testing, could be put;

- focus on the issue of agreed attainment targets, in line with advice also given to the subject Working Groups;

- consider a range of assessment approaches, including written, practical and oral tests;

- address the issues of the overall volume of assessment and the arrangements for administration, marking and moderation;

- work on the assumption that testing at the age of 16 would be covered by GCSE and other public examinations;

- advise on the most appropriate form of testing for each of the Key Stages;

- avoid, if possible, setting qualitatively different targets for children of different abilities;

- suggest ways in which the assessment information could best be communicated to parents and the wider public;

- offer advice on the development, piloting and standardization of the assessment instruments and on quality control matters.

In order to understand their recommendations, it is necessary to understand the assessment ideas and initiatives of that time which had an influence on the content and spirit of the new proposals.

## Some background influences on the development of the assessments in the National Curriculum

The TGAT Group was set up at a time when there had already been considerable re-thinking of the nature and purposes of assessment in education. Beginning with the broadest kind of influence, the 1960s and 1970s had seen a very fundamental questioning of the **psychometric** tradition in testing, often associated with IQ measures and so on. This approach focused on 'ability' measures, individual differences, selection and prediction, but had proved less than helpful to educators (Wood, 1988). Perhaps one of the most familiar applications of this kind of approach is the 11-plus type of testing, used for selection (and by implication for prediction). The tests used were, and are, mostly a combination of general verbal reasoning tests and achievement tests in mathematics and English. The argument against straightforward psychometrics was that the information gained from, say, an IQ test was of little use in planning the next steps in teaching or in helping to detect gaps in a child's understanding of a topic or idea. Yet these are precisely the issues the teacher must address. Perhaps the worst dimensions of psychometric approaches and measurement were displayed in the arguments about race and IQ, arguments that are irrelevant in the context of classroom teaching.

Glaser (1963) is often credited with drawing most attention to the problems in the psychometric approach and to suggesting that such *norm-referencing* in testing should be replaced by *criterion-referencing*, where one child's performance is not compared to the performance of others (norm-referencing) but to some stated aim or objective that the child does or does not achieve (the 'criterion' in a criterion-referenced system). So each person is tested against an agreed standard of achievement on a particular question or activity, and in theory, if the standard is met, everyone can pass. As we shall see in later chapters, the two are not always clearly distinguishable, but, nevertheless, these new approaches seemed to have much more educational relevance than earlier ones and offered the prospect of being able to measure performance in more absolute terms.

Both kinds of testing have not had an easy time in terms of litigation, however, especially in the USA. The Civil Rights and equal opportunities legislation put in statute there has given rise to legal action against test results and their implications for personal opportunities and life chances. This is especially the case with norm-referenced tests but also happens with criterion-referenced testing, where individuals claim that the authorities are infringing their civil rights because the tests make them reveal their ignorance! Others have claimed a similar breach of their rights because, having failed to pass examinations, the state is withholding certificates and diplomas (Guy and Chambers, 1974).

Apart from this important change of approach and attitude, four particular themes/initiatives in the United Kingdom seem to be of special relevance in influencing the TGAT proposals. Each of these will be dealt with in turn:

- the new GCSE examinations;

- graded/modular tests;

- profiling and Records of Achievement;

- the work of the Assessment of Performance Unit (APU).

### The new GCSE examinations

The late 1980s saw the introduction of a new system of examination for16-year-olds. It had been discussed for many years and was intended to replace the dual system, of GCE 'O' Levels and CSE (Certificate of Secondary Education) qualifications. Together, these exams had been intended to cater for different sectors of the age group: 'O' Levels for the top 20 per cent and CSE for the next 40 per cent (Robinson, 1988). The intention was that the new exam would cover and extend this range by introducing a different kind of assessment. The idea of criterion-referencing was seen as appropriate, since it potentially allows the measurement of pupils' achievements in a more direct way. The approach also allows for the measurement of changes in scores from year to year, since different numbers of pupils may literally make the grade (criteria) from year to year. In fully norm-referenced examinations, however, there may be 'fixed' proportions for each grade each year, so absolute improvement cannot be ascertained.

There was therefore much discussion about making the new GCSE exams criterion-referenced. Murphy (1988) outlines the detail of the arguments and decisions and points up an important distinction between true criterion-referencing and 'grade descriptions'. As we have seen, strict criterion-referencing requires learning outcomes (what pupils should know and be able to do) to be specified in detail and then the pupils' performance judged in order to see if these requirements have been met. Trying to achieve this in the new GCSE examinations proved too much of a challenge (Murphy (1988, p.11) says it 'led many teachers a merry song and dance' before it was abandoned) and instead the approach adopted was a kind of half-way house, using more general 'grade descriptions' rather than detailed and specific attainment criteria. These grade descriptions exemplify in a more general way what attainment should look like for each grade. However, all the detailed criteria do not have to be specified or met. These two interpretations are very different, and they are mirrored almost exactly in changes within National Curriculum assessment over the first few years of its existence, as we shall see later. A truly criterion-referenced system had never been put in place anywhere (at that time) in the context of a national examination system, and it was not even implemented in 1988, the first year of the new GCSE. The implications for teaching and for assessment in secondary schools would have been enormous. However, the focus was still firmly on certification (and selection) in mostly academic terms, although some discussion was also given to the issues of the assessment of practical skills as well as the more formal academic ones (Goldstein and Nuttall, 1986).

The idea of a criterion-referenced approach had clearly taken hold and was still very much under discussion at the time of the TGAT deliberations. Perhaps the legacy of the GCSE initiative left its mark in the idea that, in principle, a whole age cohort could be assessed in this way if the appropriate training and time were available, even in high stakes testing and certification.

### Graded and modular testing

As an approach to assessment, graded testing has existed in Britain for over a century, with perhaps its best known form being the graded music examinations developed by the Associated Board of the Royal Schools of Music. They are graded in the sense that the total syllabus (and performance requirement) is divided into a sequence of units, each of which has a limited focus and is more difficult than the earlier ones. Most of the grades have a theory requirement, a performance component and aural tests, so that, for instance, Grade 1 for piano requires the playing of major and minor scales, broken chords and the performance of three pieces played at sight. At the higher Grades, these requirements gradually become more demanding. The precise assessment criteria are something of a closed book.

Graded examination systems have also been used widely in some sporting activities, such as gymnastics. In the late 1970s, however, the idea began to be extended into the school curriculum, most notably in modern languages, for example Graded Objectives in Modern Languages (Harding and Naylor, 1980). However, the Cockcroft Report (DES/WO, 1982) had also suggested 'graduated' testing in mathematics.

The idea began to take on even more significance in relation to the growing CSE/'0' Level problem and the 40 per cent of pupils who were leaving school with no formal qualifications. The nature of graded tests in the school curriculum, it is argued, makes them especially appropriate for lower-attaining pupils, since the syllabus gets divided into manageable sections or units, each with clear learning objectives and short-term, achievable learning goals. Since, in principle, assessment can occur at any time, when it is appropriate for the pupil, this approach seems to link more closely to the learning process and can be highly motivating for pupils (Mortimore and Mortimore, 1986).

One of the most significant initiatives came from the Inner London Education Authority (ILEA) and the University of London Schools Examination Board with the development of materials in modern languages, mathematics, science and English. This proved to be a considerable task because of the need to agree the content of the 'units' and link these in to existing syllabuses but also because of the training needs of teachers. They were (and are) seen as successful educational initiatives, although the graded test approach could lead to an almost permanent state of assessment in classrooms, with potential problems for classroom organization and sustained curriculum experience and delivery.

The fact that they were in some ways an improved approach to assessment should not prevent a clear analysis of their short-comings in technical terms, as Nuttall and Goldstein (1984) point out. The fact that pupils can, in principle, re-take a particular grade test until they succeed (or give up) has considerable implications for the structure and development of the materials. In the case of graded music tests, practice may indeed make perfect, but the problem lies in judging how far the performance generalizes. Would the candidate perform as well if faced with another test piece of equivalent difficulty that had not been so drilled?

If the test questions or tasks remain the same, there is a danger of teachers teaching (and pupils revising) directly to the questions in order to enhance the possibility of success. Trying to eliminate this by producing sets of parallel tests that can be used interchangeably at each grade makes enormous demands on the test developers that probably could not be justified in resource terms. The choice of content for the grades or modules also needs careful consideration to try to ensure coherence within each unit of learning and obvious links between them. It is worth emphasizing that *progression* is often the major principle and selling point for graded tests, but unless this can be clearly demonstrated and justified throughout a sequence of graded units and tests, then they are more appropriately regarded as modular tests that can be taken in more or less any order. Issues of reliability also arise, as they did later in National Curriculum testing, and for the same reasons. Assessment requirements need to be agreed between a wide range of teachers, all of whom need to be shown to be applying exactly the same assessment criteria and standards, otherwise the fundamental reliability of the outcomes is brought into question.

## Profiling and Records of Achievement

Since the early 1940s, suggestions had been made about the need for a broad-based assessment and report for each pupil, reflecting the detail of their competence and the wider aspects of their achievements in school. As the decades moved on, this idea took on even more importance in the face of a significant proportion of pupils leaving school without formal examination qualifications. For these pupils especially, there was an urgent need for some more formal recognition of their achievements, so that employers could make judgements on their capabilities. However, it was emphasized that all pupils would gain from having these wider achievements acknowledged in a systematic and formal way (Mortimore and Mortimore, 1986).

Broadfoot (1986) has referred to the profiling initiatives that took place in the late 1970s and early 1980s as an 'assessment revolution' (p.1). She argues that they represent more comprehensive and relevant assessment procedures and are a form of assessment in which pupils can be equal partners. Formal tests and examinations have limitations, and it is most important to recognize this, not least if a balanced view is to be presented. Broadfoot suggests the following points. Test results:

- will always contain errors because there is no such thing as perfect reliability;
- are not necessarily a valid indicator of what a pupil can do;
- may measure only a small sample of achievement;
- may encourage extrinsic motivation;
- may discourage co-operative learning;
- may conceal vital differences between different kinds of competencies.

In contrast, it is claimed that profiling approaches support the learning process, show respect for the learner and include reports on skills, aptitudes and capabilities that are useful for pupils. In profiling, the outcomes are not conveyed as a single, aggregated score, but, instead, the aspects of the learning or assessment are reported separately, so more of the diversity and richness of performance are retained.

Many school and LEA (Local Education Authority) initiatives were begun in the late 1970s and early 1980s, embodying a range of approaches and pur-

poses, but all with the broad aim of profiling the attainments and characteristics of each pupil. They were given different names (for example, 'Record
of Personal Achievement', 'Record of Attainment') and they varied in the
main focus points used in the record and who was responsible for completing it, pupils or teachers. The Schools Council surveyed the scene in 1982
(Balogh, 1982) and drew attention to the great diversity of approach to be
found, and to both positive points and problems.

The positive aspects of profiling were (and are) the recognition they gave
to many different kinds of achievements and qualities and the motivation
this often generated for pupils, especially the lower-attaining ones. At best,
they had encouraged schools to re-evaluate the curriculum needs of all their
pupils and had given rise to effective forms of pupil self-assessment in some
cases. Because the records were gradually accumulated over a number of
years, they often contained rich information from a wide variety of teachers
and focused in a constructive way on pupil weaknesses as well as strengths.

But they were, and are, not without their disadvantages. In schools
where they were used only with the non-examination pupils, they could be
seen as second-rate school outcomes and, most importantly, teachers are
not necessarily qualified to judge and report on the personal qualities of
their pupils. Such judgements were liable to 'halo' effects (generalizing the
positive attributes of some pupils or their opposite) and could be highly sub-
jective. An individual teacher may have seen very little of the full
personality or characteristics of a pupil, so what was the basis for such
judgements? Different teachers might assess the same child very differently.
Unless considerable training was provided for teachers then such problems
could not be acknowledged and rectified, but this had significant cost implications. There was also a need for a clear and shared understanding of the
purpose of the records, so that only appropriate and relevant information
was collected. But perhaps the most problematic of all were the technical
issues raised about the approach, questioning the comparability and reliability of the assessments being made by hundreds of teachers in hundreds of
schools, in aspects of pupil behaviour that may be notoriously difficult to
assess (personality characteristics, for instance).

As Goldstein and Nuttall (1986) suggest, the key aspects are the accurate
defining of the 'elements' of the profile, academic and personal, and achieving comparability of judgement across individuals. The dimensions of
behaviour or personality that are included need detailed specification so as
to maximize the reliability of the judgements made, acknowledging that not
all these elements should be rated along the same kind of scale. However,
such scales contain measurement error, as do all assessment instruments. It
is salutary to note that profiling (and records of achievement) measures,
often perceived as straightforward and appropriate for teacher use, in real-

ity need a great deal of additional information and training if they are to work effectively.

Pole (1993) points out that the 'profiling' rhetoric was well established by the late 1980s, but there had been little detailed research into their precise effects in particular schools. His case-study of one school showed that, in practice, records of achievement could have many beneficial effects, but their influence would not necessarily be the same in all schools. A crucial factor seemed to be the commitment of the senior management of a school to provide the necessary impetus and resources to sustain the programme. In reality, also, the early idealism of more equal relationships and 'negotiation' between teachers and pupils could become subverted to the point of the 'record' being used as a way of controlling pupils.

In sum then, the use of profiles and records of achievement in schools made progress during the 1980s, mostly as a response to the 'qualification gap' of many pupils but also as a movement to improve assessment. This was an attempt to focus more closely on the quality of teaching and learning in classrooms and the problem of capturing the range of pupils' achievements in school. Profiles and records of achievement were also seen as potential motivators for disaffected pupils. In 1991, a National Record of Achievement was introduced by the then Secretary of State for Education (Kenneth Clarke) as a way of linking the National Curriculum to broader achievements in school.

### The work of the Assessment of Performance Unit

The final strand of influences on the development of thinking about assessment in the National Curriculum is the work done by the Assessment of Performance Unit (APU). In some ways, the link is a direct one, since one of the leading members of one of the research teams (Professor Paul Black, Kings College, London) also chaired the TGAT committee.

The APU was set up in the mid-1970s, although its roots went back to the earlier debates on the need for better national monitoring of standards of attainment in schools. Its initial terms of reference were:

1. to identify and appraise existing assessment instruments and methods of assessment which may be relevant for these purposes;

2. to sponsor the creation of new assessment instruments and techniques for assessment, having due regard to statistical and sampling methods;

3. to promote the conduct of assessment in co-operation with local education authorities and teachers;

4. to identify significant differences in achievement related to the circum-

stances in which children learn, including the incidence of underachievement, and to make the findings available to those concerned with resource allocation within government departments, local education authorities and schools (DES/WO, 1974).

This initiative was related to similar moves in the USA, where the National Assessment of Educational Progress (NAEP) was set up to address issues of educational disadvantage and falling standards. Forbes (1982) linked this to the 'extraordinary surge' (p.70) in Minimum Competency Testing (MCT) in the USA since 1976. This set minimum levels of performance in a skill or area of knowledge, often with the aim of screening out potential problems for some pupils. However, the levels set may well be misinterpreted and lead to lower expectations.

The NAEP was created to try to monitor standards across the USA and met with similar problems from the education community to those encountered by the APU here. Teachers on both sides of the Atlantic saw the initiatives as a threat to the breadth of the curriculum delivered to pupils and to the autonomy of schools. This influenced the overall character and approach adopted by the NAEP in important ways. It addressed ten learning areas rather than just the 'basics' and focused on the performance of groups of pupils not linked to any individual schools or school districts. It was a voluntary programme, not controlled by the federal government but rather supported in a co-operative way by the wider educational community, who agreed the appropriate learning goals and objectives.

The links to the early approach of the APU in this country are clear, and in fact the first Director of the APU (Brian Kay) visited the USA to discuss their programmes. One major difference emerged between the two programmes, however, namely the extent to which they were overtly intended to influence the nature and delivery of the curriculum. As some of its critics had feared, the NAEP aimed to have an effect on the curriculum. Forbes (1982) wrote:

*Furthermore, NAEP is involved in educational theory and is dedicated to innovation and experimentation to a degree that state and local agencies are unable to match. It seeks to raise educational standards by improving the educational objectives on which they are based. In summary, it tests what should be taught as well as what is taught.*

(p.76)

This was not the case in the UK, where the topic of control of the curriculum was assiduously avoided. However, some of the most important characteristics of the approach to assessment adopted by the APU in this country can be related to work in America For instance, the Working Group on the Measurement of Educational Attainment (WGMET), adopted a **sampling**

**approach** to the monitoring of achievement and the idea of **item banking** (Gipps and Goldstein, 1983). Interestingly, however, the original focus on monitoring 'underachievement' rapidly became translated into monitoring 'standards' more widely and in 1978 the newly appointed monitoring team began the work on mathematics. This was closely followed by a team for Language in 1979 and then by a team for science in 1980. The mathematics and language teams were located at the National Foundation for Educational Research (NFER) and the science team at Kings College, London and the University of Leeds. The original plan (Simon, 1979) had been to widen this focus by including, additionally, 'Physical Development', 'Aesthetic Development' and 'Personal and Social Development', but these were never fully pursued.

The work advanced well and according to plan in all three subjects: high quality and imaginative assessment materials and approaches were developed for the nominated age groups (11-year-olds and 15-year-olds in all three subjects and additionally 13-year-olds in science), useful reports were written and much progress made. But some fundamental problems began to occur in the discussions about how best to monitor statistically trends over time (Gipps and Goldstein,1983). The Statistics Advisory Group, established very early, was the forum for this debate and the main problem was the appropriateness of using the **Rasch** approach (a form of statistical analysis) to measuring trends over time. These are topics to which we will return later in this book, but a brief summary of some of the main points may be helpful here.

The approach of the APU, as we saw earlier, was to create a large bank of questions and assessment activities (including practical activities), so that at any point in time when assessments needed to be carried out, a test could be created from an appropriate selection of these questions. This meant that different tests could be constructed for different purposes, so pupils could not become familiar with a particular set of questions. It seems to allow more effective monitoring of performance from one occasion to the next. However, this approach only works if the characteristics of each question used in any test are known in statistical terms (its relationship to a particular domain of knowledge, its level of difficulty and so on). If this is the case, then the characteristics of a whole test can be worked out and compared to performance on earlier tests, thus allowing the comparison of performance over time. This seemed fine, in principle, until serious questions were raised about the validity of the Rasch technique being used, especially the kinds of assumptions implicit within it.

The other important characteristic of the APU approach was its emphasis on **light sampling** of the population of pupils in an age-cohort for purposes of monitoring national standards. This is in marked contrast to the approach of the National Curriculum, where every child in the age group is included, unless specifically disapplied. In the APU model, a representative sample of pupils was to be assessed and national trends inferred from this. It was argued that this placed less of a burden on schools and had the additional benefit of allowing more in-depth investigation of performance, since only a small number of pupils were involved. However, the APU fell victim to changing political agendas and radically different terms of reference, as well as controversies from within. The new requirements were for an assessment system which also allowed each individual school to be judged through the performance of its pupils in the national tests: a sampling approach does not allow this. In addition, a sampling approach to monitoring standards does not directly inform decisions about the allocation of resources, at a national or local level (Nuttall, 1980).

It is not easy to evaluate the APU initiative as a whole, although the assessment materials produced in all three subjects were innovative and exemplary. Despite this, the materials and reports were not circulated or known widely and did not therefore have the impact that might have been expected. They had no formal link to the secondary school examination system which also reduced their relevance in many teachers' eyes. Over time, the original brief became changed, moving away from trying to account for low attainment by some pupils to monitoring performance over time. Since it was never clearly resolved how this could be achieved in technical terms, its potential claim to provide a model for monitoring the new National Curriculum was considerably weakened.

One of the key players in the research teams, Paul Black, summarized the achievements of the APU (Black, 1990), particularly in relation to science. He argued that the initial suspicion for the venture became transformed when the materials and reports were published. The materials helped to establish a process approach in science teaching and made a significant contribution to the assessment of practical skills. He also suggested that the research generated by the programme has proved valuable throughout the world. The conclusion can only be that many positive achievements in both curriculum and assessment terms have clearly accrued that have had wide subsequent influence, not least in the National Curriculum and its assessment.

## Four strands of influence: a summary

In summary, therefore, four strands of influence on the emerging curriculum and its assessment have been traced. There were undoubtedly more, but these convey something of the scene as the assessment system was being developed in 1988. The main points are as follows.

- The idea of criterion-referencing in a national assessment context had taken hold and been tried in the new GCSE examinations and to some extent in graded tests. Notwithstanding some of the technical problems, the idea was a powerful one and seen as having educational relevance.

- In making the educational case for profiling, many of the pitfalls of traditional examinations were highlighted, and suggested important aspects of assessment that should be considered.

- Graded tests had raised the issues of sequence and progression in learning that was also to exert an influence.

- The innovative approaches to devising assessment tasks and questions embodied in the APU materials provided significant models for possible ways forward in assessment.

### The key proposals in the TGAT Report

These were some of the influences on the approach to assessment in the National Curriculum, but what emerged as the main proposals from the TGAT group? Paragraph 13 of the report makes explicit the fact that it represents a new approach to a national assessment system, although naturally grounded in much of what had gone before:

> *Whilst present practices, both in this country and in others, give many examples of positive uses of assessment, no system has yet been constructed that meets all the criteria of* **progression, moderation, formative** *and* **criterion-referenced** *assessment set out in paragraph 5 above. Our task has therefore been to seek to devise such a system afresh. We believe that the model of assessment put forward in this report builds on some existing good practice and represents an advance on assessment practices in other countries.*

> (DES/WO, 1988 , para 13)

In a long report, with 226 paragraphs of discussion, 44 recommendations and over 120 pages of Appendices, certain messages and emphases stand out, perhaps the most well documented of which are the four key principles for the assessment system (the 'paragraph 5' referred to above). These will provide the main points of discussion for the remainder of this chapter, and are that:

1. the assessment results should give direct information about pupils' achievement in relation to objectives: they should be **criterion-referenced**;

2. the results should provide a basis for decisions about pupils' further learning needs: they should be **formative**;

3. the scales or grades should be capable of comparison across classes and schools if teachers, pupils and parents are to share a common language and common standards: so the assessments should be calibrated or **moderated**;

4. the ways in which criteria and scales are set up and used should relate to expected routes of educational development, giving some continuity to a pupil's assessment at different ages: the assessments should relate to **progression.**

## 1) 'THE ASSESSMENTS SHOULD BE CRITERION-REFERENCED'

This approach to assessment has already been mentioned, but this now needs to be looked at more closely. All assessment in education is about making informed judgements, based on good evidence, and using these judgements to support appropriate educational decisions. It serves important functions if the results can be shown to be appropriate for their purpose and generally trustworthy. It is also important to remember that there will always be *error* in any assessment: the perfect system has not yet been devised and is probably not possible. When we assess, we are essentially making inferences about what the behaviour or outcome really indicates and how validly and reliably any task is tapping what a pupil knows, understands or can do.

Even when we have come up with a result or score for any task, it is meaningless unless it is given significance by comparing it, either with the results from other people or with a specified set of behaviours or knowledge. This is the basic distinction between *norm-referenced* and *criterion-referenced* assessment, mentioned earlier (pp. 23–24). The national assessment system, as first outlined in the TGAT Report, was to be criterion-referenced and attainment-based: in other words, the results should show what a pupil knows and can do, not just rank order them in relation to others or predict what that child will be capable of in the future, as most tests of *ability* imply.

In any assessment or testing process of this kind, it has first to be decided exactly which attributes, knowledge and skills are to be measured, then activities or questions have to be devised which allow these to become 'visible' in order to judge the performance or understanding of the child. One potential criticism in this situation is that because some knowledge or qualities are easier to measure than others, we may be in danger of choosing a narrow (and maybe irrelevant) range of outcomes and missing out on some central ideas and qualities which are difficult to pin down for assessment purposes.

This is not necessarily a criticism that can be levelled at the **original specifications** in the Attainment Targets of the National Curriculum: many of them were a clear attempt to incorporate some quite complex and subtle kinds of knowledge and insights, perhaps too subtle in some cases. However, they did not all seem to have been devised with assessment in mind. Even in their revised versions (as in mathematics and science) they still contained a great deal of ambiguity and imprecision, as we shall see in detail later. The paradox here is that the qualities that made them credible in curriculum terms were the very qualities that make them so difficult as starting points for assessment. In the revised mathematics and science Statements of Attainment, fewer Attainment Targets and Statements were achieved by building even more content into many of them and by making others very general. Neither of these was helpful in terms of assessment, and teachers clearly found enormous difficulties coming to terms with the Statements, in all their versions.

## 2) 'THE ASSESSMENTS SHOULD BE FORMATIVE'

It has by now become almost a cliché to say that effective teaching is based on accurate assessment of what children already know and can do and where any 'gaps' exist. Teachers aim to achieve this by a judicious use of observation, questioning and analysis of the child's work and errors. These, ideally, are carefully recorded and each child's progress monitored so that teaching can be focused on their learning needs. This is *formative assessment* at its most valid and useful, and it is this quality that the national system encouraged in the original TGAT proposals. Prior to the development of the National Curriculum proposals, much work had been done in Scotland on using formative assessment in productive ways in the classroom (Black, 1982) which also influenced the thinking of the group. Of course, these ongoing assessments made by the teacher can be summarized as required, in order to provide a *summative* score or level, so in the context of teacher assessments both possibilities exist.

But how should the summative scores arrived at through teacher assessment be related to the summative scores reached via the national tests? From the beginning, it has always been suggested that the two sets of scores can be combined (DES/WO, 1988) and that the extent of the curriculum to be covered in fact required this. The summative assessment of the tests provides a 'snapshot' of a child's performance at one point in time and is clearly of a rather different nature to the teacher assessments.

Teacher assessments are based on long-term, detailed consideration of a child's performance in a wide variety of contexts, a quality that is likely to be especially important with young children. When they are summarized into a summative score, it could be argued that this makes such assessments more trustworthy and valid than a single Standard Assessment Task administered at one point in time (Owen, 1991). This argument would only hold for the national assessments if it could be clearly demonstrated that all teachers were applying the same interpretations and mastery criteria in all their assessments. Questions raised earlier throw considerable doubt on this, at least in the short term.

### 3) 'The assessments should be moderated'

The comments in the previous section indicate both the need for, and the difficulties of, moderation. The original TGAT proposals were for varied approaches to assessment, including tasks and activities, all of which would need standardizing as closely as possible through moderation.

A national assessment system that is criterion-referenced requires effective training procedures so that teachers can reach agreed definitions and interpretations and apply the same standards. The need for a more practical approach to assessment was especially great at Key Stage 1, since 7-year-olds may not have the skills to work with more formal pencil-and-paper tests. Moderation was therefore necessary, but even with older pupils at Key Stages 2 and 3, the kinds of assessment originally envisaged (often task-based) required teachers to understand exactly what the performance criteria should be. It could also be argued that moderation procedures themselves (teacher meetings, agreement trials, exemplification of the required standards) might play a significant role in both clarifying the meaning of some parts of the curriculum and also in enhancing the professional development of teachers. There is, however, a 'bottomless pit' problem with all moderation procedures. How do we decide when sufficient agreement has been reached in this very costly enterprise? Clearly, it could go on indefinitely, but some balance has to be struck between resourcing and the requirements of effective assessment.

### 4) 'The assessments should relate to progression'

A central plank of the original TGAT proposals was that progression in all the Attainment Targets should be demonstrated via a **10-Level, age-independent scale**, covering the school years from age 5 to 16. Such a scale would be age-independent since it would in theory be possible for a 7-year-old to be demonstrating attainment at, say, Level 6 and a 14-year-old attaining at Level 2.

Some of the origins of this approach can be seen in the graded tests mentioned earlier, but the precise number of grades or levels varies according to the age-range covered and the nature and extent of the curriculum to be taught and assessed. For a single age cohort (for example, all 11- year-olds), a five- or six-point scale seemed to be most common, so, averaging this across the four Key Stage assessment points, ten levels seemed appropriate to the TGAT committee. In the TGAT Report, this was outlined in a famous graph, showing **expected attainments** at the different Key Stages on this 10-Level scale.

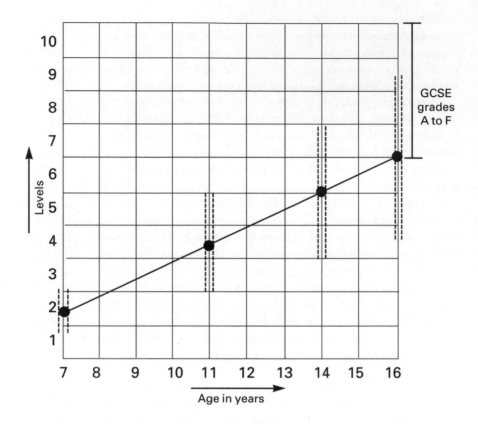

**Figure 2.1:** Expected attainments at Key Stages

This is a useful graph when it comes to understanding more about the assessment system of the National Curriculum. Assessment takes place at the end of each Key Stage, at ages 7, 11, 14 ( and then 16), and at each Key Stage the tests or tasks must address a particular range of levels. At the higher Key Stages, the range of levels to be covered becomes broader. For example, for 7-year-olds at Key Stage 1, there are three expected levels of attainment that should be attained by approximately 80 per cent of the age group, but most pupils will be expected to attain Level 2. This is the meaning of the dotted lines on the graph. By Key Stage 3, however, most pupils will be expected to attain Level 5 or Level 6, although some will attain above or below this. The approach to assessment at age 16 (Key Stage 4) no longer follows this suggested pattern and is not dealt with in any detail in this book. However, for the rest, this graph is the source of the general understanding of what the 'expected' level of attainment should be for each Key Stage and is the basis for judging the performance of schools in the context of the 'league tables'. This is a topic that will be dealt with in more detail in later chapters.

In practice, this means that the tests or tasks at each Key Stage must cover a progressively wider range of levels, either through level-specific tasks or tests or through packages of tasks or tests that cover several levels. Later chapters, which discuss each Key Stage in turn, will say more on these points.

The merit of the 10-Level scale is that it provides a common framework for the discussion of a child's progress across schools and phases. Its age-independence also allows pupils to be monitored at their own rate, irrespective of their chronological age. But once again this has not proved so ideal in practice and the matter was taken up in the review of the curriculum carried out in 1994 (Dearing, 1993). No changes were suggested, even though the problems of a limited number of points on the scale for an 11-year span of schooling and the problem of age-independence were mentioned at length. This will be discussed later in *Chapter 4*.

## The Attainment Targets and their assessment

Not only do the National Curriculum tests have to address particular levels at particular Key Stages, they also have to address most aspects of the curriculum: in effect, most of the **Attainment Targets** specified for each Key Stage. However, these have changed over the years since the first Order was published in 1988 and these major changes are shown in *Table 2.1*. The most striking changes occurred in 1990/91 when the overwhelming scale and unwieldiness of the first curriculum specification were recognized. Looking at the number of Attainment Targets in the first legislation, it is even clearer why the first national tests could cover only some of the list, with the remainder assessed through teacher assessment. As we shall see in *Chapter 5*, this generated some interesting problems in the early Key Stage 1 assessments. Pruning the number of Attainment Targets back to four or five in each subject meant that most could be covered through the testing programme.

However, two further matters need to be raised in relation to the Attainment Targets. The 1990/91 versions still contained the 'process' aspects (for example Ma.1 and Sc. 1 and En.1, the 'Speaking and Listening' aspect of English) but it was judged that these were inappropriate for assessment via the national tests or tasks. From that point on, it was recognized that these too would continue to be assessed through teacher assessment. The later revisions to the curriculum also acknowledged the fact that not all Attainment Targets were appropriate for all Key Stages, so some are not included at the first or second Key Stages. These cannot then be included in the assessments either.

**Table 2.1:** The Attainment Targets in the core subjects and changes in them over time

| Subject | 1989 | |
|---------|------|--|
| English | En1 | Speaking and Listening |
| | En2 | Reading |
| | En3 | Writing |
| | En4 | Spelling |
| | En5 | Handwriting |
| Mathematics | Ma1 | Using and applying mathematics |
| | Ma2 | Number |
| | Ma3 | Number (Operations) |
| | Ma4 | Number (Estimation) |
| | Ma5 | Number/Algebra |
| | Ma6 | Algebra |
| | Ma7 | Algebra (Graphical representation) |
| | Ma8 | Measures |
| | Ma9 | Using and applying mathematics |
| | Ma10 | Shape and space (Shapes) |
| | Ma11 | Shape and space (Location) |
| | Ma12 | Handling data (Collecting and recording) |
| | Ma13 | Handling data (Representing and interpreting) |
| | Ma14 | Handling data (Probabilities) |
| Science | Sc1 | Exploration of science |
| | Sc2 | The variety of life |
| | Sc3 | Processes of life |
| | Sc4 | Genetics and evolution |
| | Sc5 | Human influences on the Earth |
| | Sc6 | Types and uses of materials |
| | Sc7 | Making new materials |
| | Sc8 | Explaining how materials behave |
| | Sc9 | Earth and atmosphere |
| | Sc10 | Forces |
| | Sc11 | Electricity and magnetism |
| | Sc12 | Information technology / microelectronics |
| | Sc13 | Energy |
| | Sc14 | Sound and music |
| | Sc15 | Using light and electromagnetic radiation |
| | Sc16 | The Earth in space |
| | Sc17 | The nature of science |

| 1990/91 | 1995 |
|---|---|
| En1 Speaking and Listening<br>En2 Reading<br>En3 Writing<br>En4 Spelling ] Presentation<br>En5 Handwriting ] | PoS Speaking and Listening<br>Reading<br>Writing |
| Ma1 Using and applying mathematics<br>Ma2 Number<br>Ma3 Algebra<br>Ma4 Shape and space<br>Ma5 Handling data | PoS Using and applying<br>mathematics<br>Number<br>Shape and space<br>Handling data (Key<br>Stage 2 and Key<br>Stage 3 only)<br>Algebra (Key Stage<br>3 only) |
| Sc1 Scientific investigation<br>Sc2 Life and living processes<br>Sc3 Materials and their properties<br>Sc4 Physical processes | PoS Experimental and<br>investigative science<br>Life processes and<br>living things<br>Materials and their<br>properties<br>Physical processes |

## From Statements of Attainment to Level Descriptions

The 1995 revised versions produced other changes too in the way the curriculum was specified. Whereas the earlier legislation had maintained formal criterion-referencing and specified the criteria at each level (the Statements of Attainment), the 1995 version outlined the curriculum (Programmes of Study) in a Key Stage by Key Stage way, and set out the attainment expectations through Level Descriptions rather than listings of criteria to be attained at each level. True criterion-referencing was therefore lost: instead the approach became known as a criterion-*related* one. The intention was that the national tests and tasks should be based on the Programmes of Study for each Key Stage but that teachers, for their own teacher assessments, should use the Level Descriptions in each Attainment Target to locate each pupil in a 'best fit' kind of way. This change was made (Dearing, 1993) in order to ease the job of assessing, so that teachers could now be freed of the endless lists of 'Statements' and instead make more global judgements about their pupils' performance. The difference between the two, the listings of Statements of Attainment and the equivalent Level Descriptions, are exemplified in *Table 2.2*, and it may be worth asking: which provides the more accurate form of assessment both for planning and teaching and for making summative assessment judgements?

It is also worth pointing out that this change had considerable implications for the nature of the national tests. The listings of Statements of Attainment, although difficult to work with as starting points for assessment, had nevertheless acted as the 'criteria' in a criterion-referenced system. Losing them meant that the starting points for the assessment questions and activities had to move to the Programmes of Study which were set out in paragraphs of continuous prose and were much more 'loose'. Clearly, these more general specifications can be used as the basis for assessment and, in fact, they could be said to allow more freedom to the test writers. However, it can be argued that the idea of strict criterion-referencing became rather submerged at this point in the history of national testing.

## Summary

- The Task Group on Assessment and Testing was briefed to offer advice on a coherent system of assessment that met a range of varied requirements.

- Their deliberations and recommendations were influenced by the then current views of best practice in assessment, beyond traditional psychometric approaches.

**Table 2.2:** Some examples of the Statements of Attainment (SoAs) in one Attainment Target (AT), En2 Reading in comparison with Level Descriptions at selected levels in the National Curriculum, English

| Level | Statements of Attainment (1990) | Level Description (1995) |
|---|---|---|
| *Level 2* | a) read accurately and understand straightforward signs, labels and notices.<br>b) demonstrate knowledge of the alphabet in using word books and simple dictionaries.<br>c) use picture and context cues, words recognised on sight and phonic cues in reading.<br>d) describe what has happened in a story and predict what may happen next.<br>e) listen and respond to stories, poems and other material read aloud, expressing opinions informed by what has been read.<br>f) read a range of material with some independence, fluency, accuracy and understanding. | *Pupils' reading of simple text shows understanding and is generally accurate. They express opinions about major events or ideas in stories, poems and non-fiction. They use more than one strategy, such as phonic, graphic, syntactic and contextual in reading unfamiliar words and establishing meaning.* |
| *Level 4* | a) read aloud expressively, fluently and with increased confidence from a range of familiar literature.<br>b) demonstrate, in talking about a range of stories and poems which they have read, an ability to explore preferences.<br>c) demonstrate, in talking about stories, poems, non-fiction and other texts, that they are developing their abilities to use inference, deduction and previous reading experience.<br>d) find books or magazines in the class or school library by using the classification system, catalogue or database and use appropriate methods of finding information, when pursuing a line of inquiry. | *In responding to a range of texts, pupils show understanding of significant ideas, themes, events and characters, beginning to use inferences and deduction. They refer to the text when explaining their views. They locate and use ideas and information.* |
| *Level 6* | a) read a range of fiction and poetry, explaining their preferences through talking and writing, with reference to details.<br>b) demonstrate, in talking and writing about literature, non-fiction and other texts that they are developing their own insights and can sustain them by reference to the text.<br>c) show in discussion or in writing that they can recognise whether subject matter in non-literary and media texts is presented as fact or opinion, identifying some of the ways in which the distinction can be made.<br>d) select from a range of reference materials, using appropriate methods to identify key points.<br>e) show in discussion of their reading an awareness that words can change in use and meaning over time and demonstrate some of the reasons why. | *In reading and discussing a range of texts, pupils identify different layers of meaning and comment on their significance and effect. They give personal responses to literary texts, referring to aspects of language, structure and themes in justifying their views. They summarise a range of information from different sources.* |

- Assessment initiatives put in place during the 1970s and 1980s clearly influenced the thinking of the group, especially the work done on the new GCSE examinations, graded tests and profiling.

- The work of the APU also had a considerable influence on their deliberations, not least because of some of the innovative approaches to assessment to be found in the APU assessment materials.

- The central proposals of the TGAT Report were those of criterion-referencing, formative assessment linked to summative assessment, moderation and progression.

- These principles, although adopted to a large extent at the beginning, became changed and re-interpreted with time, especially in the Dearing review of the curriculum and its assessment.

- The latest versions of the legislation in the core subjects are very different from those of the earlier ones, and they pose different challenges for assessment.

# 3 The development of the tasks and tests: background, summary and examples

The last chapter summarized some of the influences on the National Curriculum tests and set out the major characteristics of the approach suggested by the Test Group on Assessment and Testing (TGAT). This chapter will now explore how the recommendations were put into practice in the tests for the three age groups, 7-, 11- and 14-year-olds. The aim will be to describe, briefly, the structure of the tasks and tests for each of the three Key Stages and to give some examples of the assessment task activities and test questions. The curriculum, and therefore the tests based upon them, have changed since 1988 and this will also be summarized. The focus will be on the test materials in English, mathematics and science.

## The timetable for the development of the tests

In chronological terms, it has already been mentioned (see *Table 1.2*) that both the curriculum and the testing programme were not implemented at the same time for the three Key Stages. The Key Stage 1 tests came on-stream in 1991, the Key Stage 3 tests in 1991 and 1992 (pilots) and finally the Key Stage 2 tests in 1993 and 1994 (again, pilots). The reason for this staggered approach was the length of the Key Stage involved: Key Stage 1 lasts for only two years and could therefore be implemented and assessed first; Key Stage 3 lasts for three years and Key Stage 2 for four years. Hence the sequence of implementation.

Naturally, each set of tests in each of the core subjects required a lead-in time for development to take place. This was a radical new venture in assessment, since it was the first time a national assessment system had been put in place that was criterion-referenced and classroom-based. Many new issues had therefore to be addressed or old principles revisited in this new context. The decision was taken at an early stage that the tests would not be developed by a single national body, but that the work would be put out to competitive tender for each of the core subjects at each Key Stage, as they came on stream. The research and development groups awarded the contracts were, and are, known as the Test Development Agencies.

*Figure 3.1* summarizes the sequence of test development times. For each of the core subjects (in England), it shows when the Test Development Agencies began their work and when the first sets of materials were formally pre-tested. Naturally, in the years leading up to the first full pilot, preliminary versions of the tasks and tests were trialled and evaluated. By 1994, the assessments were in place at all Key Stages, although they have continued to develop since.

It is worth noting two things about the information in *Figure 3.1*. The first is that at Key Stage 3, mathematics and science have not been developed in direct parallel with English: the second is that the development time for the tests at the different Key Stages was not the same.

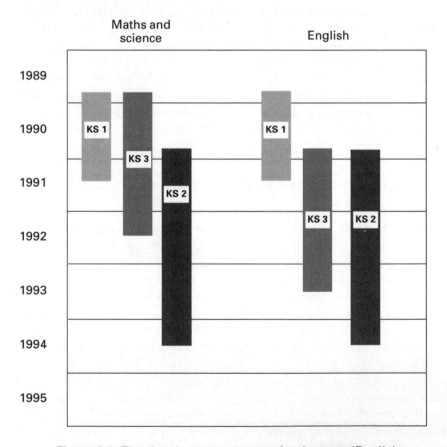

**Figure 3.1**: The development process for the tests (English, mathematics and science) at the three Key Stages

Over time, as lessons were learned about assessment and testing issues and as political agendas changed, the nature and content of the tests also changed. Perhaps the biggest change occurred as a result of the Dearing review in 1993, when the curriculum and testing process became more streamlined. (Further details are provided about developments at each separate Key Stage in *Chapters 5, 6* and *7*.) For now, however, *Table 3.1* summarizes the changing structure of the assessments since 1991, not charting every detail but giving a general sense of what the testing has been like at different points in time and for the different Key Stages.

## Some examples of task activities and test questions from the Key Stage 1 assessments

It is not possible or appropriate to present numerous or detailed examples of task activities and test questions from the assessments for 7-year-olds, given limited space and extensive material to cover. Nevertheless, it is important to try to convey something of the nature of the activities and questions used between 1991 and the present.

From the many that could be chosen, it seems helpful to exemplify some of the most significant landmarks at this Key Stage. This suggests the following examples:

one of the science task activities from the first year of testing;
- examples of questions from the Reading Comprehension Test;
- examples from the Levels 2–3 Mathematics Test;
- one of the more recent task activities at Level 1.

### Part of the 'Floating and Sinking' assessment activity: 1991

This activity was used in the first run of the Key Stage 1 assessments and was intended to assess the 'process' aspects of the science curriculum, Sc1. The page shown here (*Figure 3. 2*) shows only a part of the total activity and was intended to be carried out with a small group of four children. The page (a left-hand page from the Teacher's Book) is set out in three columns, while the right-hand page contains the scoring grid for each child in the group. As a teaching activity it was thought to be an interesting one, but as an assessment activity it had many flaws (see Shorrocks *et al.*, 1992). Significant questions were raised about the 'standard' nature of the task in a situation where the teacher could choose the materials to be used for floating and sinking (this would radically affect the results) and where the responses from the children in the group might be influenced by what the other children had said.

**Table 3.1:** The structure of the tasks and tests (core subjects) at the three Key Stages since 1991

| Key Stage | Versions of the National Curriculum and the kinds of assessment based upon them: general characteristics | | | Comments |
|---|---|---|---|---|
| | 1989 | 1990/1 | 1995 | |
| Key Stage 1 | In **all core subjects**, assessments based on practical activities used mostly with small groups of children. Some of these included the use of worksheets. | **English:** mostly task-based, including reading text aloud, but with an optional Comprehension test for Levels 2–3. **Mathematics** and **Science:** task-based with some worksheets. | **English:** task-based at Levels 1–2. Tests of Reading Comprehension, Writing and Spelling for Levels 2–3/4. **Mathematics:** task-based at Level 1 with Mathematics Test at Levels 2–3. **Science:** no formal testing: assessments done through Teacher Assessment. | At this Key Stage, a gradual move from small group, practically based assessment, to a situation of task-based assessments at the lower levels and formal pencil and paper tests at the higher levels. From 1994, Science was no longer assessed through formal testing. |
| Key Stage 2 | No tasks or tests for this version of the curriculum. | **English:** task-based at Levels 1–2, with practical activities. Tests at Levels 3–6, in Reading Comprehension, Writing and Spelling. **Mathematics** and **Science:** task-based at Levels 1–2, pencil and paper tests at Levels 3–6. | **English:** task-based at Levels 1–2, with practical activities. Tests at levels 3–6, in Reading Comprehension, Writing and Spelling. **Mathematics** and **Science:** task-based at Levels 1–2, pencil and paper tests at Levels 3–6. | This was the last Key Stage to come on stream, and a pattern of more formal pencil and paper tests for most pupils in the age group had become established. Practical tasks used for pupils attaining at the lowest levels. |
| Key Stage 3 | Task-based assessment for pupils at lowest levels. Pencil and paper tests for the others. | **English:** tasks at Levels 1–3, with tests for Levels 4–10. **Mathematics** and **Science:** task-based at Levels 1–2. Tiered tests at Levels 3–10. | **English:** tasks at Levels 1–3, with tests for Levels 4–10 (8). **Mathematics** and **Science:** task-based at Levels 1–2. Tiered tests at Levels 3–8. Mental Arithmetic test in 1998. | Very early assessments used a more task-based approach, but this rapidly changed to pencil and paper tests. General pattern of tasks for lowest levels and tiered tests for higher levels. |

| Sc 1 — What to do | SoA | Evidence of Attainment |
|---|---|---|
| **PART B: Exploring Floating and Sinking**<br>♦ Set out all the apparatus and give each child four objects<br>♦ Present this part of the Activity to the children as a challenge to find out as much as they can about why some objects float and some sink<br>♦ Ask the children to tell you *what* they think will happen if one of their objects, which you name, is placed in the container of water. Then ask *why* they think this will happen. With each child, repeat this with a second object<br>♦ Give each child a copy of the chart – Sc 1 *Pupil Sheet 1* and four sheets of A4 paper<br>♦ Explain to the children that they are to draw, weigh, make a prediction whether each object will float or sink and then test each object to see if it will float or sink. On the supplied chart they have to record their predictions and the outcomes of the tests to see whether each object will float or sink. They also have to record the weight of each object<br>♦ Explain to the children that they should observe and begin to draw each object without using a hand lens and then finish the detail of their drawing of each object with the use of a hand lens<br>♦ Allow the children to carry out their practical work and complete their charts and drawings | Sc 1/2a  Ask questions and suggest ideas of the 'how', 'why', and 'what will happen if' variety<br><br>Sc 1/3a  Formulate hypotheses | ② When questioned, says *what* they think will happen if the *two* objects named are separately put into a container of water (correctness of prediction is not important)<br>*or*<br>③ In addition to ②, is able to give a *reasoned* explanation of *why* they think each object will float or sink. This is an 'I think... because...' type statement of their ideas, for example, links weight or colour or texture with floating or sinking<br><br>*The relationship does not have to be 'correct' but it must involve reasoning* |
| | Sc 1/2f  Record findings in charts, drawings and other appropriate forms | ② Completes chart and drawings with reasonable accuracy, showing appearance, weight, predictions and outcomes of tests for floating and sinking for each of the four objects |
| | Sc 1/2b  Identify simple differences<br><br>Sc 1/3d  Select and use simple instruments to enhance observations | ② Drawings and/or results of weighing show that the child can identify simple differences between the objects<br>*or*<br>③ Drawings and/or oral responses show that the child can observe *greater detail* of one or more of the objects using a hand lens |
| | Sc 1/2c  Use non-standard and standard measures | ② Finds and records the weights of *three* of the *four* objects by comparison to standard or non-standard units using balance scales (comparison using 'feel' is not sufficient) |

**Figure 3.2:** Part of the 'Floating and Sinking' assessment activity: 1991

### *Examples of questions from the Reading Comprehension Test: 1995*

By 1995, the assessments in English at Key Stage 1 had become more formalized in the sense of including pencil and paper tests. *Figure 3.3 a and b* shows part of the Level 2–3 Reading Comprehension Test. The presentation was an imaginative one, where the children read their reading booklet, which contained narrative and non-narrative passages (in colour), and then answered questions about what they had read. To convey some of the nature of the test, two pages are reproduced here, one from the reading booklets and the other from the test booklet based upon it.

It was while Vicky was munching on an apple from the tree that something funny happened in her mouth. Something she'd been waiting for.

A tooth came loose. It was at the bottom of her mouth near the front – just in the place where her tongue had to go when it had nothing to do.

Vicky quickly pushed the apple into her pocket.

Tom was watching her, of course. "What are you doing?" he asked.

"Nothing," Vicky said. But it wasn't true. She *was* doing something. She was wobbling her loose tooth with her tongue. She was trying to do it secretly so that Tom wouldn't notice.

"Then why are you pulling faces?" Tom demanded.

## Vicky's Wobbly Tooth

1  What made Vicky's tooth come loose?

☐ Sucking a lollipop.  ☐ Bumping into Tom.

☐ Falling over.  ☐ Eating an apple.

☐ Jumping off the wall.

2  Why did Vicky have to rescue her tooth quickly?

_____

_____

3  Is Tom Vicky's brother?  ☐ Yes  ☐ No

How do you know?

_____

_____

**Figure 3.3 a and b:** Examples of questions from the Reading Comprehension Test: 1995

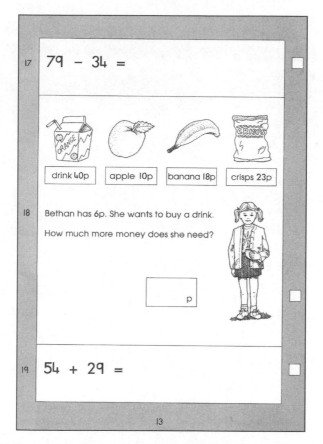

**Figure 3.4:** Examples of questions from the Mathematics Test (Levels 2–3): 1996

## Examples of questions from the Mathematics Test (Levels 2–3): 1996

As with English, the Key Stage 1 mathematics assessments had also become more formalized, with a Levels 2–3 Mathematics Test. The page shown in *Figure 3.4* is a question located towards the end of the booklet and shows a combination of direct calculation questions (Questions 17 and 19) and a question set in a context.

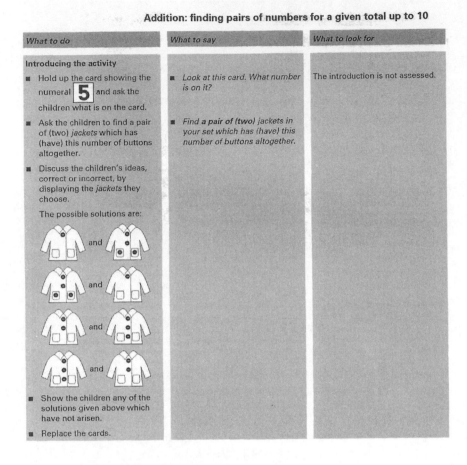

**Addition: finding pairs of numbers for a given total up to 10**

| What to do | What to say | What to look for |
| --- | --- | --- |
| **Introducing the activity**<br><br>■ Hold up the card showing the numeral **5** and ask the children what is on the card.<br><br>■ Ask the children to find a pair of (two) *jackets* which has (have) this number of buttons altogether.<br><br>■ Discuss the children's ideas, correct or incorrect, by displaying the *jackets* they choose.<br><br>The possible solutions are:<br><br>■ Show the children any of the solutions given above which have not arisen.<br><br>■ Replace the cards. | ■ *Look at this card. What number is on it?*<br><br>■ *Find a pair of (two) jackets in your set which has (have) this number of buttons altogether.* | The introduction is not assessed. |

**Figure 3.5:** Part of the Level 1 task activity: 1997

## Part of the Level 1 task activity: 1997

The final example from Key Stage 1 is part of the Level 1 task in mathematics. The task was intended to be orally administered and practically-based, with a small group of children. Each child had their own set of materials (the 'Jacket' cards) and responded with these as they were asked various questions. The main assessment issues with an activity such as this are the manageability and appropriateness of the materials provided for both the teacher and the children, and the problem of ensuring that each child is asked a question of comparable difficulty but not exactly the same as any of the questions the other children have been asked. This is an extremely taxing requirement for the developers when the numbers used (according to the specifications of the curriculum) must not exceed 10. The page shows another important aspect of assessment at this level (the lowest level assessed), namely the need to establish the procedure very clearly and to try a 'practice' attempt before beginning the proper assessment.

## Some examples of task activities and test questions from the Key Stage 2 assessments

In a similar way to Key Stage 1, choosing examples from the many possible task activities and test questions at Key Stage 2 is not an easy one. The best way of proceeding appears to be to exemplify the major characteristics of the approach Key Stage 2, so in this section the following will be included:

- part of the reading assessment activity at Levels 1–2 in English;
- an example of a question from the science test (Levels 3–5);
- an example of a page from the mathematics test (Levels 3–5);
- part of the Spelling Test (Levels 3–5) in English.

### *Part of the reading assessment activity in English (Levels 1–2): 1994*

At Levels 1–2 the Key Stage 2 assessment in English was similar to the reading assessment task for Levels 1–2 at Key Stage 1, at least in the earlier version of the curriculum. Choosing this activity serves a dual purpose since it is still the form of assessment used at present. The task is grounded in a series of published books (available in bookshops and in school libraries) which have been selected for their interest and appropriateness for the age group. In each of these books, each chosen to provide equivalent reading aloud contexts irrespective of which book the child or teacher chose, a set passage is selected. The story/information in the book is first discussed with the child and then the nominated section is read aloud. As the child reads, the teacher annotates (discreetly) a separate version of the text, noting the child's strategies and errors. This scoring system then provides the basis for judging the accuracy and fluency of the reading. Understanding of the passage is assessed through questioning about the content.

From the beginning, when this kind of 'running record' approach to the assessment of reading was introduced (in the first Key Stage 1 assessments in 1991), it was welcomed as a valid and innovative approach to assessment, one that also provided a good model for effective classroom practice for teachers.

| What to do | What to look for |
|---|---|

**SoA addressed   En2/2b**   *demonstrate knowledge of the alphabet in using word books and simple dictionaries*

| | |
|---|---|
| • Give the child the classroom dictionary. Choose **three** words from the opening lines of the child's reading book which begin with letters from the beginning, middle and end of the alphabet. Point to each word in turn and ask the child where to find the words in the dictionary. Indicate to the child that you are looking for the approximate place in the dictionary. | Satisfy yourself that the child is turning to the approximate section of the dictionary in all cases; to the beginning, middle or end. You do not need to insist that the exact entry be found. All **three** answers should, however, be correct to show evidence of attainment. |

▶ *Record assessment of En2/2b on the Assessment Record Sheet*

**SoA addressed   En2/2f**   *read a range of material with some independence, fluency, accuracy and understanding*

| | |
|---|---|
| With your guidance a child selects a book from the *Booklist and Running Records*. The choice of book should take account of the child's interests and tastes but you should avoid any that are particularly familiar. A child may have heard or read the book in the past, but should not be assessed on a book he or she already knows well.<br><br>Read through the beginning of the book with the child. This reading assessment should be as relaxed and enjoyable as your normal experience of sharing a book with a child.<br><br>None of the *Running Record* passages are taken from the very beginning of the books. Therefore use the initial reading to make sure that the child knows any names or distinctive vocabulary in the opening section of the chosen book. | For this Level 2 activity, children should be reading the text independently, rather than remembering what it says.<br><br><br><br><br><br><br><br>You should give whatever help is needed to familiarise the child with the book, reading it with the child up to the point where the *Running Record* passage begins. |

**Figure 3.6:** Part of the reading assessment activity in English
(Levels 1–2): 1994

### Example of a question from the Science Test: 1995

From the formal beginning in 1994, the pattern of the Key Stage 2 assessments in science has been similar: Levels 1–2 being assessed through tasks, and the higher levels through tests, including an Extension test for the highest attainers in the year group. The example given shows a question from the 1995 main tests. It demonstrates the emphasis placed on explaining scientific phenomena as well as questions using more 'closed' approaches. The problem with such 'open' questions in national tests is, of course, marking them, even when there is external marking by trained markers. In this case, the mark scheme for this question is almost one page long and attempts to give the **principles** for marking the vast range of explanations pupils produce. The responses must refer in some way to *heat* being needed in the process, although the word 'microbe' was not needed. In the second part, reference had to be made to the absence of oxygen. All the explanations could be expressed in any way as long as the key aspects were there.

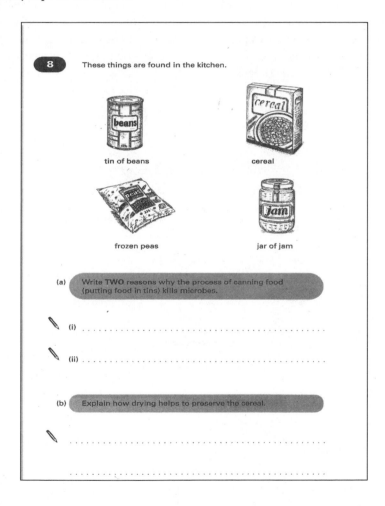

**Figure 3.7**: Example of a question from the Science Test: 1995

*Example of a question from the Mathematics Test (Levels 3–5): 1996*

As with the science assessments, the pattern in testing mathematics was also established quite early. In the example given here, the two questions on the page show the difference between 'contextualized' and 'non-contextualized' items. The use of real-life contexts, in this case a sponsored walk, is thought to give meaning and relevance to the calculation as well as demonstrate the significance of mathematics in everyday life. It is also worth commenting on the format of the page. The 'answer boxes' focus the pupil on where to write the answer and what form the answer should take, supported by the pencil icon by the box. Question 7 on this page exemplifies another important principle: it appears to be a closed question but there are several possible answers, requiring the pupils to think strategically.

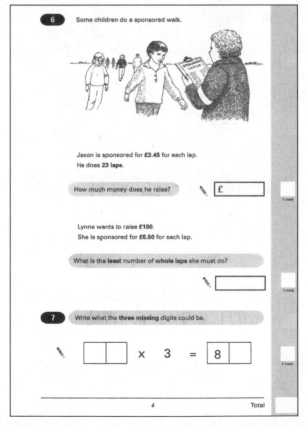

**Figure 3.8:** Example of a question from the Mathematics Test (Levels 3–5): 1996

*Example of the Spelling Test in English: 1997*

It is commonly accepted that one of the most difficult areas to assess is spelling, partly because of the vagaries of the English spelling system, but also because the domain is so large and complex that any individual's experience of it will be partial. This makes choosing the sample of words to assess fraught with difficulties. Finding an appropriate method of assessing it, especially for younger children, is also not without its problems. The format at Key Stage 2 has been to create a passage of prose, with certain words left out. The passage is read aloud to the pupils and they fill in the words in the gaps, once they have heard them spoken by the teacher. The example below shows the first section of the 1997 test passage, with the missing words being, in order: *still, moment, shook, remained* and *silence*. The early words are more straightforward, while the later ones become more difficult.

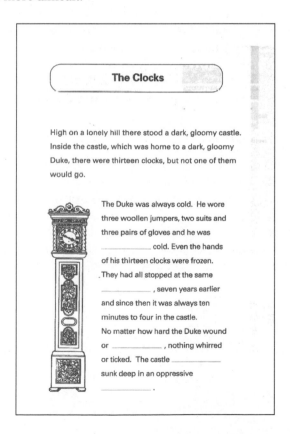

**The Clocks**

High on a lonely hill there stood a dark, gloomy castle. Inside the castle, which was home to a dark, gloomy Duke, there were thirteen clocks, but not one of them would go.

The Duke was always cold. He wore three woollen jumpers, two suits and three pairs of gloves and he was _____ cold. Even the hands of his thirteen clocks were frozen. They had all stopped at the same _____ , seven years earlier and since then it was always ten minutes to four in the castle. No matter how hard the Duke wound or _____ , nothing whirred or ticked. The castle _____ sunk deep in an oppressive _____ .

**Figure 3.9**: Example of the Spelling Test in English: 1997

## Some examples of task activities and test questions from the Key Stage 3 assessments

The choice of examples from the Key Stage 3 tasks and tests will be made for similar reasons as for Key Stage 2. They will be chosen to represent the overall character of the assessments, some of which was established from an early point. However, unlike the other Key Stages, the subject distinctions are especially important here. In mathematics and science, the approach was agreed early and there have been few major changes. In English, however, the situation has been much more controversial and changing, so some of this must also be conveyed.

The following will therefore be chosen from the Key Stage 3 assessments:

- part of an assessment activity at Levels 1–2/3 in mathematics;
- an example of a question from the Science Test (Tier 5–7);
- an example of a question from the Mathematics Test (Tier 4–6);
- part of one of the task activities in English (Levels 1–3);
- an example from the Shakespeare Paper in English (Levels 3–5);
- examples from the new 'assessment materials for English'.

### *Part of the assessment activity at Levels 1–2 in mathematics: 1993*

As in the other Key Stages, the lowest attainers at Key Stage 3 are assessed through practically-based tasks, delivered orally and administered in small groups. The same general problems of such assessment apply here as at the other Key Stages, although the overall presentation of this (early 1993) task activity is perhaps not so easy to follow for the teacher as later ones. This example is assessing the ability to continue and to devise a repeating pattern (Level 1) and marks were awarded for patterns of different kinds of complexity.

**Small Group Strategy**

Pupils may be asked to draw the patterns they have continued or devised.

Pupils working in a group should be given different patterns.

Some pupils will make one complex pattern while others whose first pattern is simpler will need to make more than one pattern. Pupils who have finished before others may be asked to make different patterns. Some may be asked to use the same set of counters which they used in their pattern to make as many different patterns as they can and to record these.

**Assessment**          **Maximum 6 marks**                          **B**

| SoA | Mark | Requirements | Additional guidance |
|---|---|---|---|
| 3/1a<br>Devise repeating patterns. | 3m | 1m for continuing the teacher's colour pattern for at least 2 cycles (simplest).<br><br>1m for continuing the teacher's size pattern for at least 2 cycles (harder).<br><br>1m for continuing the teacher's 3-type pattern for at least 2 cycles (hardest). | Patterns must be continued for at least 2 cycles, but may finish in the middle of a cycle or have subsequent errors. .<br><br>Pupils who obtain the mark for a pattern automatically also obtain the mark(s) for any simpler pattern. |
| | 3m | 1m for devising the simplest pattern:<br>* cycle of 2<br>ie<br>a b a b a b type.<br><br>1m for devising a harder pattern:<br>* cycle of 3 with 2 or 3 types;<br>* cycle of 4 with 2 or 4 types;<br>eg<br>a b b a b b a b b type;<br>a b c a b c a b c type;<br>a a b b a a b b a a b b type;<br>a b c d a b c d a b c d type.<br><br>1m for devising a complex pattern:<br>* cycle of ≥ 4;<br>* 3 or 4 types of counter;<br>* one type at least twice in cycle;<br>eg<br>a b b c a b b c a b b c type;<br>a a b b c c a a b b c c a a b b c c type;<br>a a b c c d a a b c c d a a b c c d type. | Patterns must contain at least 3 correct cycles, but may finish in the middle of a cycle or have errors on both sides of the 3 cycles<br>eg a b c a b c a b c a;<br>a a b a b a b a b b.<br><br>Patterns must differ from other visible ones.<br><br>Pupils who obtain the mark for a pattern automatically also obtain the mark(s) for any simpler pattern. |

**Figure 3.10:** Part of the assessment activity at Levels 1–2
in mathematics: 1993

### *Example of a question from the Science Test (Tier 3–6): 1995*

Parallel issues arise in the science assessments at Key Stage 3 as at Key Stage 2 and in many ways the questions for the two age groups have some similarities of presentation. The example given here is of completing a table of explanations of pollination methods. The mark scheme for the question requires that both the pollen transfer method and the explanation must be correct for the mark to be awarded and that appropriate terminology must be used.

13. Most pollen grains are transferred from one flower to another either by **wind** or by **insects**.

Look at the drawings below which show pollen grains from three different plants.

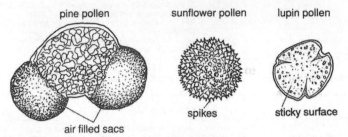

pine pollen   sunflower pollen   lupin pollen

spikes   sticky surface

air filled sacs

(a) Using your observations:

 1. State the method by which each of these pollen grains is transferred.

 2. Give a careful explanation for the method you have chosen each time.

 Write your answers in the table.

*3 marks*

| name of plant | method by which pollen is transferred | explanation for method chosen |
|---|---|---|
| pine | | |
| sunflower | | |
| lupin | | |

**Figure 3.11**: Example of a question from the Science Test
(Tier 3–6): 1995

*Examples of questions from the Mathematics Test (Tier 4–6): 1997*

Again, there are similarities between the tests in mathematics at Key Stages 2 and 3, although the questions at Key Stage 3 tend to be longer, sometimes spanning three pages on a single topic. This would be considered unacceptable with the younger pupils at Key Stage 2, since the concentration required would be too great for many children and too many marks could be associated with a single theme, which some pupils may or may not engage with. The example given here shows an algebra question in which the pupils must complete the sequence of 'bricks' in a wall by writing in the appropriate algebraic expressions.

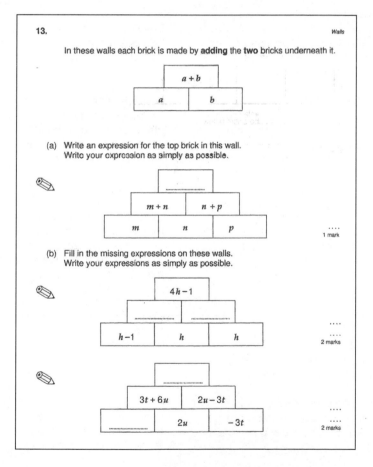

**Figure 3.12:** Examples of questions from the Mathematics Test (Tier 4–6): 1997

## Writing Task Record Sheet

Name of Pupil........................................ Pupil Number...............................

Teacher............................................... Teaching Group Number ☐

Tick the boxes which correspond to the pupil's performance

| Statement of Attainment | Assessment Criteria |
| --- | --- |
| **Task 1: Story** | |
| **Section A**<br><br>**En 3/1a** Use pictures, symbols or isolated letters, words or phrases to communicate meaning.<br><br>**En 3/2a** Produce, independently, pieces of writing using complete sentences, some of them demarcated with capital letters and full stops or question marks.<br><br>**En 3/3a** Produce, independently, pieces of writing using complete sentences, mainly demarcated with capital letters and full stops or question marks. | **Level 1**<br>Writes isolated letters/words and tells you what they say. ☐<br><br>**Level 2**<br>Writes independently; separate 'ideas' or sentences can be identified; at least two of these sentences begin with a capital letter and end with a full stop. ☐<br><br>**Level 3**<br>Writes independently; ideas expressed in recognisable sentences; at least half the sentences correctly punctuated; in a long piece, any passage of 10 sentences may be assessed for punctuation ☐ |
| **Section B**<br><br>**En 3/2b** Structure sequences of real or imagined events coherently in chronological accounts.<br><br>**En 3/3b** Shape chronological writing, beginning to use a wider range of sentence connectives than 'and' and 'then' | **Level 2**<br>Order of events is plausibly chronological ☐<br><br>**Level 3**<br>In addition to the requirement for level 2, a range of at least three different sentence connectives or phrases is used to relate one event to another. ☐ |

**Figure 3.13:** Part of one of the task activities in English (Levels 1–3): 1995

## Part of one of the task activities in English (Levels 1–3): 1995

At Levels 1–3, the 1995 assessment of En3 (*Writing*) took the form of two activities: writing a story and producing a piece of non-chronological writing (for example, a notice or invitation ). They were to be prepared for this by discussion with the teacher and each piece of writing was to take 20–30 minutes. Deciding the 'level' of the products was judged in relation to the information given in the example. It is interesting to ask how 'standard' such teacher judgements would be, based only on this kind of approach.

## Example from the Shakespeare Paper in English (Levels 4–7): 1996

By 1996, a pattern of assessment had also been established in English, namely assessment tasks for Levels 1–3 and parallel written 'main' tests for Levels 4–7. These comprised Paper 1, covering reading comprehension and an assessment of writing, and Paper 2, a 'Shakespeare' paper. In Paper 2, certain scenes from Shakespeare were selected and pupils had to answer extended questions on one scene from the choice provided (see the example given).

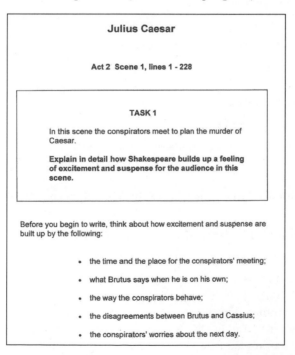

**Julius Caesar**

**Act 2  Scene 1, lines 1 - 228**

**TASK 1**

In this scene the conspirators meet to plan the murder of Caesar.

**Explain in detail how Shakespeare builds up a feeling of excitement and suspense for the audience in this scene.**

Before you begin to write, think about how excitement and suspense are built up by the following:

- the time and the place for the conspirators' meeting;
- what Brutus says when he is on his own;
- the way the conspirators behave;
- the disagreements between Brutus and Cassius;
- the conspirators' worries about the next day.

**Figure 3.14:** Example from the Shakespeare Paper in English (Levels 4–7):1996

### *Example of the new English assessment: 1998*

The final example comes from the new materials introduced into the Key Stage 3 English assessments in 1998. This represents a drive towards the testing (and teaching) of the 'basics' in the language, and the example shown here gives a flavour of the kinds of questions asked and of the assessment approach.

---

Read the following text in which a boy describes an incident involving his mother. It was written down as the boy said it.

'We had some coal delivered, and er it got some rocks and bits of scale in it and she said er get a, get a, we had a bag it was a, quite a strong bag she said fill it up with some of the coal and stuff and we got it on the bus and we went all the way to the bottom of Hills Road Bridge, the coal office and inside was an old table and er I didn't know what she was going to do with it, just take it back and probably tell them you know the coal's not very good and as she went she bent down picked it up and WHOOSH! straight across the counter dust coal everywhere take it back she said and come back and get the rest of it they couldn't believe it'

Imagine you are a police officer that has been called to the scene. You have to write a report of what the boy (Ken) said had happened.

In the report you should:

*   Arrange and summarise the facts into a sensible order.

*   Write in an appropriate way for a formal report, including using the third person, the past tense and reported speech.

Read the passage again before you begin to write.

The opening has been done for you:

*Ken, the woman's son, said that they had some coal delivered ...*

*11 marks*

---

**Figure 3.15**: Example of the new English assessment: 1998

## Some conclusions about the tasks and tests at the three Key Stages

We have seen that the test development process was put in place at speed, especially at Key Stage 1, ironically perhaps the most technically difficult of the testing programmes. This was followed by the tests at Key Stage 3 in mathematics and science and finally in English. When this full Key Stage 3 testing programme was implemented, in 1993, the result was large-scale protest from teachers, but this time from the more powerful secondary school lobbies, and it was listened to. Teachers at Key Stage 1 had worked valiantly to put the assessment system in place in 1991 and 1992, and had voiced their protest, but it was apparently only when Key Stage 3 teachers made their voices heard that any notice was taken. This in itself is a very interesting comment on the power structures within the educational system of the UK. The result, as we have seen, was the Dearing review and the changes it brought.

As the testing programmes gradually came on stream, problems and issues emerged whose resolution gradually shaped the form and scale of the assessment system, influenced also by political agendas. This chapter has exemplified the move away from the early TGAT principles with their broad and innovative approach to assessment towards pencil and paper tests for most pupils in each age group. Practically-based and orally delivered tasks were and are used (now optionally for Key Stages 2 and 3) for lower attaining pupils.

## Special arrangements in the testing

Special arrangements are allowed, even in the written tests, for pupils with particular difficulties. This is important in the context of an entitlement curriculum and educational equality arguments. These are set out in the official documentation for the tests (for example, SCAA, 1997d) and state exactly what is allowed and not allowed by way of support during the testing. The pupils for whom the special arrangements apply are:

- pupils with statements of special educational needs;

- pupils without such a statement who are affected by a disability or a specific learning difficulty which makes access to the tests difficult;

- pupils not yet fluent in English or Welsh.

Some of these do not need official permission, for instance, the use of a separate room for the testing, 'sectioning' the test and allowing such pupils to take it in smaller sections at a time and the use of mechanical or technological aids. These include such things as the use of brailled answers for pupils with visual impairments or the use of an amanuensis for pupils who can only dictate an answer, not write it. However, even in these cases, the regulations require that if this support is given, the nature of the information provided does not change the assessment demand of the questions. Special arrangements that may require permission include varying the timing of the tests or using 'signers' for pupils with hearing impairments. All details of these procedures are outlined in the documentation produced officially (*op. cit.*).

## External marking of the tests

A significant result of the Dearing review (Dearing, 1993) was the recommendation of external marking of the tests. It was introduced in 1995 as a response to teacher complaints about the time demands of the testing and it applied to Key Stages 2 and 3 only. At Key Stage 1 the written test papers are not marked externally but are marked by the teachers themselves and audited by the Local Education Authorities. Financial support is provided in the form of supply cover to cover some of the time taken for administering the tests.

At Key Stages 2 and 3, however, all written test papers are marked by trained markers, a system operated by the various examining boards who also devise and mark the GCSE and A Level exams. Instructions are provided to schools about where to send their papers for marking and the marked tests are then returned to the schools. Some important points about this external marking are that:

- all markers have teaching and subject experience;

- they are all trained for a full day in preparation for the marking and are provided with detailed mark-scheme materials, over and above those provided to the schools themselves;

- each marker's marking is checked, usually at the beginning and again at the end of the marking;

- each marker must arrange for a clerical checker to review all their paperwork and entries on the forms;

- the scripts of pupils whose marks fall close to the Level borderlines are double-checked.

Schools have a right of appeal if they feel they can demonstrate mistakes in the marking and each year a significant number of appeals are made. However, even this system cannot eliminate all errors or disagreements about pupil responses and how they should be credited.

## Summary

- The tests and tasks were developed at different points in time, in a sequence dictated by the length of the Key Stages.

- The assessments at Key Stage 1 were very much the 'guinea pigs' of the system, with the added constraint of the challenges posed by the testing of 7-year-olds.

- The first Standard Assessment Tasks (then referred to as 'SATs') at Key Stage 1 were detailed, had a strong 'practical' aspect to them and were devised mostly for small group delivery. In many ways this was highly appropriate and valid for the age group but manageability and time problems raised protest, not least because of the potentially negative effects on the delivery of the rest of the curriculum.

- The result at Key Stage 1 has been a gradual streamlining of the assessments in terms of time, mode and range. Formal assessments now only take place for English and mathematics, and largely take the form of written test papers.

- At Key Stage 3, the next on stream, the original intentions to have varied and broad-based approaches to assessment in the three core subjects rapidly became transformed into straightforward pencil and paper tests for the vast majority of the age cohort.

- A sticking point throughout the testing at Key Stage 3 has been the testing in English. We will trace some of this controversy in a later chapter, but it was protest in this arena that precipitated the full review of the curriculum and its assessment in 1993 (Dearing, 1993).

- Key Stage 2 testing was the last to be put in place and by then it was more or less established that the assessments should mainly take the form of written pencil and paper tests.

- At all Key Stages, special arrangements can be made for pupils who have statements of special educational need or who have particular disabilities. These include the use of special apparatus, the use of braille or British Sign Language, and the use of amanuenses for pupils who cannot write their own answers.

- External marking of the written test papers (not the assessment tasks) was introduced in 1995 at Key Stages 2 and 3.

# 4 Developing the tasks and tests: some technical issues

In the previous chapter, a sample of the materials used in national testing were reproduced. As we saw, at all three Key Stages, the testing now includes both assessment tasks/activities for lower attaining children, and pencil and paper tests for the higher attainers in each age group. The technical issues surrounding both these forms of assessment are important for evaluating the overall effectiveness of the national testing programme and it is these technical issues that are the focus of this chapter.

However, certain important points from earlier chapters should be reiterated here. Assessment is about making informed judgements, based on good evidence, and using these judgements to make appropriate educational, selection or vocational decisions. But it must be remembered that there will always be error in *any* assessment, since we are always making inferences about what the behaviour or outcomes indicate. As Wood (1982) suggests:

> *The test form interposes itself between knowledge or ability and judgement, and to the extent that it is an imperfect transducer of what the student knows or is able to do, so will the judgement be distorted.*

(p. 125)

Also, the results only gain significance when we locate them in a context, either by comparing them with the results from other people or with a specified set of behaviours or knowledge. The national assessment system, as we have seen, was devised to be criterion-referenced and attainment-based, and the results are therefore *descriptions* of what a child knows and can do, not *prescriptions* of what that child will be capable of doing in the future. This is an important distinction and one that does not always sit easily in the minds of some educators and teachers, especially in the UK, where tests and examinations have mostly been experienced in the context of selection in what has been judged, at least in the past, to be an elitist education system.

Whatever the nature and purpose of the assessment, however, many of the basic principles are the same, and can be summarized in the general model of the assessment process shown in *Figure 4.1*. It applies particularly in relation to creating more formalized assessments (tests, rating scales, teacher-devised classroom tests and so on).

**1. Decide the purpose of the assessment and what is to be assessed**
Are the assessments for selection purposes, summative certification, diagnosis?
What needs to be assessed? the qualities of a person; a body of knowledge and understanding; a 'construct' such as intelligence; practical skills etc.?

**2. Operationalize this decision**
What kinds of questions, activity, problems to solve, items, equipment etc.?

**3. Implement these measures**
What is the best delivery mode, response mode, or scale, to be used in the assessment?
What are acceptable performance criteria or mastery levels for the responses?

**4. Gather the evidence**
What kind of evidence? Will they be written responses, oral responses, behaviours, drawings, practical outcomes, artefacts, ephemeral responses etc. ?

**5. Make the assessment judgement**
Do the responses meet the performance criteria or mastery requirements?
Can they be aligned in a particular category; mastery definition?

**6. Interpret the results and act on them**
The results need to be seen in the context of the kind of referencing involved and the wider purpose, context and consequences of the assessment.

**Figure 4.1:** A general model of the assessment process

This process is essentially the same irrespective of the type of test or assessment, whether they involve the assessment of fine motor skills, IQ, personality, attitudes, or knowledge and understanding of a particular set of concepts or body of information.

In the National Curriculum, as we saw in *Chapter 3*, the assessments take the form of tasks and written tests, so this model will now be used to explore these two forms of assessment.

## The assessment tasks

### Some general considerations

These kinds of tasks have been referred to as *'practical activity-based assessments'*, a phrase that needs clarification. We must distinguish between assessments that are delivered through the medium of a practical task, often on a one-to-one basis or in a small group, and the assessment of practical skills in their own right. In the first, the one that is the focus here, the aim is to test knowledge and understanding by using an activity as the context for the assessment and eliciting a response from the pupil such as carrying out an instruction or activity, or completing a game. The questions may, in principle, be delivered in the written mode or orally, depending on the purpose of the assessment and the skills of those being assessed. Of course, if it is oral skills themselves that are the focus of the assessment, then it is the oral mode that must be used in asking or answering the questions, or responding in other ways to demonstrate, for instance, comprehension.

However, practical skills themselves may be the focus of some kinds of assessment: it may be important to establish that a candidate can make an electrical circuit, carry out an experiment, assemble a piece of equipment, type 60 words per minute or sew a straight seam. The assessment principles outlined in *Figure 4.1* still apply, but they have this particular purpose.

### Assessment tasks in the National Curriculum

*Chapter 3* made it clear that assessment tasks have been, and are, used with the younger age groups and with lower attaining children in the older cohorts. In the early days of the Key Stage 1 assessments, it was intended that most of the assessments for 7-year-olds should be of this kind, but manageability considerations soon gave rise to more formal pencil and paper tests. These tasks are not now statutory for the lower attainers at Key Stages 2 and 3, although it is expected that teachers will use the task materials provided earlier (or similar activities of their own devising) to make their summative teacher assessments for the lower attaining pupils.

### Oral delivery of the questions and oral responses by the pupils

At all three Key Stages, the tasks rely on the teacher asking questions orally and the pupils responding orally. Written responses are not expected, although in the past (for example at Key Stage 2 in 1995) answer booklets were provided for pupils who were able to write their answers.

This oral delivery and response mode is not without its problems, however. While oral questioning is often seen as the mainstay of much classroom teaching (not least in the new guidelines from the National Numeracy and Literacy Projects in the UK), it is also the case that many teachers are not given specific training in questioning pupils in any depth. It is a complex and difficult skill. There is a wide literature on problems of interpersonal communication, both with adults and with children (Light, 1979; Harris and Coulthart, 1986). For children of school age, these problems include misinterpretation of what the other person has said, the notorious difficulty of understanding such terms as 'more than', 'less than', 'before', 'after', 'between' (and many more), and the tendency to respond with what they think the teacher wants to hear rather than to give a genuine, personal response (Donaldson, 1987).

Given this background, oral questioning in an assessment situation is fraught with difficulties. The actual wording of the questions and the interpretation of the response become vital and can influence the validity and reliability of the whole enterprise. The questions must be carefully planned and structured and be appropriate to the assessment purpose: questions that elicit higher order thinking skills must be used if this is required, or very clear and straightforward questions if this is more appropriate (Ebel, 1991). There is often a tendency for the teacher to step in too soon if there is no immediate response from the pupil, where increasing the wait time may elicit more. There should also be the flexibility to ask for clarification or for a re-statement, bearing in mind that some children may become more confused by this.

### Assessment on a one-to-one basis and in a small group

On the surface, assessment on a one-to-one basis, with just the teacher/examiner and a single pupil seems an ideal situation for making assessments. However, it is wise to consider the stress this may place on a pupil who may not be used to such focused attention and detailed questioning for a sustained length of time. They may not possess the listening skills and experience necessary in this situation. Paradoxically, this may militate against effective assessment unless the pupil is put at their ease and given breaks. Of course, for some pupils, for instance those with particular learning difficulties or disabilities, this may be the very best, and indeed only, viable assessment context. If the pupils need to communicate through a special keyboard, sign system or amanuensis, one-to-one discussion may be an vital support for them. This is allowed in the National Curriculum assessments.

More usually, however, the assessment tasks are administered with small groups of pupils (two, three or four at most) and here the problem is a different one. The challenge is to devise questions so that no two pupils are asked the same question but the cognitive demand is of the same order of difficulty for each. This is not easy but it is very important. If each pupil is asked the *same* question in turn, they may simply repeat an answer they have just heard from someone else, so invalidating the assessment. The guiding principle should be that each pupil in the group has as similar an assessment experience as possible; in other words, the task is as standardized as it can be made in these circumstances. The pupils must also be told that they will each be asked different things, or they may not listen to their question with sufficient care.

In a group context, a child who is slower than the rest (in both manipulating materials and responding to questions) can become embarrassed, or can slow down the activity to the detriment of the others. At the opposite extreme, an active or disruptive child may also have a negative effect. These kinds of problems can only be resolved by careful choice of group members and detailed preparation.

### The potential restrictiveness of the assessment

Almost by definition, this approach to assessment is very time-consuming and there is often pressure to keep the activities short and focused. This also helps pupil concentration on the activity and therefore the motivation to continue. However, the down side of this is that the domain that can be sampled in the assessment (be it knowledge or understanding ) is restricted and the generalizability of the assessment may therefore be limited in usefulness. There is no easy answer to this, except by increasing the number or the scope of the tasks which then in turn increases the time costs involved. As such this is not necessarily an efficient or wide-ranging form of assessment but one that can be justified in relation to particular pupils or particular purposes.

### Scoring the responses

In this kind of practically-based assessment, the pupil responses (spoken and behavioural) are scored by the teacher as they occur, usually on a mark sheet or check-list, which can potentially lead to unreliability in the assessment. The judgement is a 'snapshot' on the part of the scorer, and may be a misinterpretation of the pupil's intentions or be influenced by the preconceptions of the person scoring. It is a problem that should not be underestimated, and one where the only solution is the very careful planning and structuring of the activity, and the adequate training of the teachers/examiners. The use of video and agreement trials are appropriate for such training.

Summarizing these points, the following kinds of principles need to be employed by the task developers. The assessment activities and tasks should:

- interest, motivate and challenge the pupils, providing a sense of success and achievement;
- encourage the development of appropriate knowledge, skills and reasoning

in relation to the curriculum;

- incorporate a balance between open questions (which encourage children to pose their own questions and select from a range of possible answers) and more closed questions with pre-determined responses;
- involve materials which are stable and easy to handle and manage;
- provide guidance for the teachers which allows them to deploy standard assessment criteria but also to use professional judgement, so long as the validity and reliability of the assessment is not compromised.

## The written tests in the National Curriculum assessments

The assessment model outlined in *Figure 4.1* applies with equal force here, in relation to the written tests. The purpose and focus for the tests have to be decided and these decisions operationalized as questions in test booklets. These must then be implemented in the written mode (with all the constraints this brings) and then evidence gathered by administering the tests in agreed ways, marking them in relation to agreed standards and evaluating the marks gained on the range of questions in the test. Finally, the assessment judgement must be made (has the pupil attained a particular National Curriculum level?) and the results interpreted in their wider educational (and political) context.

Some of these points need to be examined further since they raise significant issues. In particular:

1. the changing meaning and implications of the criterion-referenced approach of the tests;

2. the relationship between formative and summative assessment in the testing programme;

3. the meaning and achievement of validity and reliability in the tests;

4. the 10-Level scoring scale and its implications.

Each of these will be dealt with in the subsequent sections.

### *The meaning and implications of criterion-referencing in the tests*

In earlier chapters (particularly *Chapter 2*) the following points were made about criterion-referencing. It was contrasted with norm-referenced approaches, while acknowledging that the distinction between them is not a 'pure' one: elements of both can, and do, occur in many kinds of assessment. For instance, in setting mastery levels within a criterion-referenced system, judgements must often be made to what is a reasonable expectation for performance – the norm. The point was also made that criterion-referencing is perceived as more attractive and appropriate in educational contexts, since it links directly to teaching and learning and has more educational value. For example, knowing that a pupil is in the top 20 per cent of their age cohort (as in norm-referencing) does not in any way indicate what they should be taught next or if there are gaps in their knowledge or understanding. We saw that there were attempts to introduce this approach into the GCSE examinations in the 1980s (Murphy, 1986) and that this persisted into the National Curriculum through the TGAT Report. In fact, it became one of the guiding principles of that document. The changes that have occurred since, most notably the Dearing review, have attempted to retain this, although this is open to some question.

As we saw in *Chapter 2*, criterion-referenced assessment had its origins in the USA, where there was and still is a tradition of extensive testing in the education system. It seems to hold the possibility of dealing with an individual's achievements, irrespective of the performance of others, which was and is seen as well suited to objectives-based teaching programmes (Glaser, 1963). In the American literature, many different terms are used, such as *domain-referenced, objectives-referenced, competency-based tests, mastery tests* and so on. In the British literature, the term *criterion-referenced* is applied to almost any approach that is not overtly norm-referenced.

The contrast with norm-referencing is worthy of further comment since the distinction is not by any means watertight. The major aim of norm-referencing is to distinguish between candidates, so the questions need to be devised so that they spread candidates out as far as possible in their scores on a test. A good question is one which some can answer very well, some in part and some not at all: the assessment is based on a normal distribution curve. Detailed mark schemes do not need to be made public on this kind of test, since the questions are largely there to act as a discriminator and feedback is not necessarily part of the picture, although it can be, of course. The cut-scores for the various grades or categories of outcome are agreed and implemented, but it is not part of the approach to try to learn *how* candidates gained their marks to obtain that grade. As Macintosh (1993) suggests, a grade 'C' in an 'O' Level exam was probably best described as not knowing 55 per cent of what you were asked on the day you were asked it! Such examinations do not, however, set out directly to create a given percentage of passes at the different grades; this is an indirect effect of creating a normal distribution of outcomes by the responses to the questions in the test.

On the other hand, criterion-referenced tests have a different purpose and nature. Their main characteristics are as follows (based on Macintosh, 1993, *op. cit.* ). The 'criteria' are publicly stated and known by teachers, candidates and the wider community. Similarly, the mastery scores, in other words, the conditions to be met in order to pass, are also usually clear and made public. However, the more 'criteria' there are, the more likely the assessments are to become fragmented and the matter of summarizing the scores becomes more problematic. The precise content of each question takes on a different significance, since they clearly have to address the 'criteria' in defensible ways and also serve as a means of providing educational feedback on the attainments of each candidate as well as the gaps in their knowledge and understanding. The aim is to devise questions which sample the domain effectively and address all aspects of it in terms of difficulty. In other words, there should be assessment of the easiest and hardest aspects of the domain, and points between. Of course, in this system, it is theoretically possible for all candidates to pass, since the approach is based on assessing the positive achievements of candidates, not creating a normal distribution of outcomes. Effective teaching and learning could, in principle, lead to 100 per cent success for all candidates.

Strictly speaking, criterion-referencing refers to the manner in which a score is interpreted, but in order to map out the parameters on which the score will be based, it is necessary to specify the relevant domains of knowledge, skills and so forth. (*domain definition*) and to set mastery criteria. When the purpose of a test is to estimate mastery of a domain, it is a domain-referenced test. Black and Dockrell (1984), working on diagnostic assessments with a large number of Scottish teachers, found it useful to distinguish between three different kinds of domain (single act, closed and open) and two types of domain definition (explicit and implicit domain definition). In the kinds of domain category, typically *single act* domains are limited and can be assessed by a single question or activity. For example, the domain 'ability to use scissors to cut paper' could be assessed in the single activity of cutting a piece of 80-gram paper. *Closed* domains are those which are well defined but include more than could be assessed in a single event. An example might be 'Recall the valency of each of the 40 common elements' in chemistry. Provided everyone agreed what these were, this could be defined as a closed domain, but no assessment could cover all of them: the domain must necessarily be sampled, on the assumption that this sample of responses can be used to estimate performance on the rest of the domain. *Open* domains, on the other hand, are those where there is effectively no limit to the number of elements in the domain. This is often signalled by such phrases as 'demonstrate understanding of' or similar broad statements. Black and Dockrell conclude that this kind of domain presents enormous difficulties in terms of sampling and mastery definition, but they represent a common (and in many ways appropriate) kind of educational objective. Paradoxically, they may be technically the most problematic, but they are often the most educationally valuable. Purists might argue that absolute precision in the criteria is vital for good assessment but, as this argument indicates, this is not necessarily a stance taken by all writers. Others (for example, Popham, 1987) have also suggested that broader specification rather than narrowly defined criteria may be the best way forward in educational contexts.

In the category of *type* of domain definition, *explicit domain definitions* are those in which the domain of interest is formally defined prior to the creation of the assessment tasks or questions and this is often the kind met in the assessment literature, based on stated criteria. Our earlier chemistry example can be used again here, since this total domain could be agreed and defined and assessments devised to sample this explicitly agreed topic. In *implicit domain definitions*, however, the 'domain' is generated by considering the kinds of assessment produced by teachers working with the domain and using these as the basis for agreeing a definition. An example of this might be the Statement of Attainment in English (Writing) that pupils should be able to *'produce, independently, pieces of writing using complete sentences, some of them demarcated with capital letters, full stops or question marks'*. This is a very open and ambiguous 'domain' which teachers had to address before the first national tests came along and helped to clarify the meaning and performance expectations associated with the requirement. In this situation, teachers were defining the meaning implicitly (often in moderation groups) before the domain became more formally defined for them via the first SATs.

There is, however, a further complication in the issue of defining, sampling and agreeing the standards of mastery of a domain, and that is the problem of *context*, a term frequently used but seldom defined with rigour in assessment research. The issue arises because it has been a fairly persistent finding that a pupil may give very different responses on two different occasions to what, on the surface, appear to be very similar tasks or questions, perhaps when different materials have been used. This could, of course, be due to motivational, affective or situational factors, but it could also be due to the fact that a response has been influenced by the precise 'context' in which the task or question was embedded. For example, a pupil may be able to spell a word in a spelling test but then mis-spell it when writing a story, or a pupil may be able to explain the process of condensation in relation to rainfall but not in the context of a question about water appearing on the inside surfaces of windows in houses on cold mornings. The problem is one of generalization: how knowledge which is relevant and appropriate in one situation becomes generalized to other situations where it is also applicable. If knowledge or understanding is not generalized, then the matter of defining and sampling domains for assessment purposes becomes very problematic indeed.

### *The National Curriculum and the 'criteria' which form the basis for the tests*

Perhaps the closest the National Curriculum assessments ever came to being fully criterion- referenced was in its earliest days, when the hundreds of State-ments of Attainment (SoA) provided the 'criteria' for the activities and written tests. As we saw in *Chapter 2*, these were originally arranged within the 10 levels in each Attainment Target, and award of a level was based on showing success and 'mastery' of a sufficient number of these at a particular level. However, it must not be forgotten that in the early days of assessing the National Curricu-lum, it was by no means clear whether the SoAs were to be interpreted as boundary definitions or as level descriptions, posing problems for both teach-ers and test developers alike. The vast amount of time and energy spent by teachers in recording attainment against each criterion/SoA proved impossi-ble, however, and hence the whole approach was changed. Faced with this massive range and breadth of curriculum, there have been those (for example, Murphy, 1994) who have suggested that a criterion-referenced approach to assessment is simply not possible.

In the first formal SATs at Key Stage 1 in 1991, the problems of criterion-referencing became obvious. In a sense, it is history, but it is nevertheless important in charting the evolution of the present situation with regard to test-ing. To give a flavour of some of the issues raised, the following points are important.

- As we have seen (pp. 38–39), the 1989 version of the curriculum for science contained 17 Attainment Targets and 393 SoAs over the 10 Levels. The first version of the mathematics curriculum comprised 14 Attainment Tar-gets and 296 SoAs across the 10 Levels. In the 1991 versions, these were reduced to four (Attainment Targets) in science and five in mathematics. The respective numbers of SoAs were 173 (science) and 117 (mathematics). Not only were there these vast number of 'criteria' to meet, but many of them were poorly specified as starting points for assessment. This problem was compounded by the fact that an SoA at a higher level might be phrased in terms of just being more than at an earlier level, so many became com-parative in their domain content, with few absolutes. Even with the reduced numbers of SoAs in later years, the task was not necessarily eased, because some of the reduction in the number of individual SoA was achieved by combining content, so making their use as starting points for assessment even more difficult.

- In terms of the content of the SoA (the assessment criteria), there was enor-mous variation in the breadth, specificity, not to mention ambiguity of the 'domains', making domain definition a very complex activity indeed. The following examples (all from the 1989 versions of the curriculum) show some of the very general and ambiguous statements that had to be assessed, though admittedly through activities rather than (at that time) pencil and paper tests.

| | |
|---|---|
| Science, Sc1, Level 5 | *'Pupils should identify and manipulate relevant independent and dependent variables, choosing appropriately between ranges, number and values'* |
| English, En3, Level 3a | *'Pupils should read aloud from familiar stories or poems fluently and with appropriate expression'* |
| Mathematics, Ma3, Level 1a | *'Pupils should add or subtract, using objects, where the numbers involved are no greater than 10'* |

Trying to pin down the meaning of phrases such as *'read aloud.......with appropriate expression'* for assessment purposes is no mean challenge: it is a classic example of an 'open' domain whose meaning gradually becomes defined by example, discussion and agreement (implicit domain definition). Given this kind of scope in some SoAs, it is interesting to speculate exactly what the 'domains' within the system were. Were they the complete SoAs, with all the potential sub-domains within them, or were the sub-domains the true domains to be sampled in the assessments? It is a question that was never formally answered, although from a test development point of view it was a crucial one.

These are all examples of the well-known problem of specifying assessment criteria. It is a tricky job, since a careful line has to be navigated between the extremes of vague and ambiguous criteria on the one hand and a proliferation of detailed but trivial objectives on the other. It also partly represents the inherent tension in the curriculum documents between providing teachers (not to mention test development agencies) with a degree of freedom and richness in both curriculum and assessment terms, yet being specific enough for valid and reliable assessments to be carried out. It is a tension that has never been resolved, either in national curriculum assessment or elsewhere: for instance, Wolf (1993) reports similar problems in relation to NVQ assessments. The end result of such proliferation and ambiguity were assessment outcomes at Key Stage 1 in 1991 (the first full assessments put in place) that were highly problematic in their dependability (Shorrocks *et al.*, 1992).

The changes to the curriculum that occurred in the Dearing review had considerable implications for the tests. As we saw in *Chapter 2*, SoAs were abolished in favour of more broadly specified Programmes of Study in each subject and for each Key Stage. There are now no clear 'criteria' within the system, only sections of the curriculum, with paragraphs and sub-paragraphs, as the following example from the current English curriculum (Key Stage 1) shows.

---

**Writing**

*2. Key Skills*

*a. Pupils should be taught to write with confidence, fluency and accuracy. They should be taught to differentiate between print and pictures, to understand the connections between speech and writing and to learn about the different purposes and functions of written language.Pupils should be introduced to the alphabetic nature of writing and be taught to discriminate between letters, learning to write their own name. Pupils' early experiments and independent attempts at communicating in writing, using letters and known words, should be encouraged.*

---

These 'domains' can, in principle, be sampled in a similar way to the former SoA, but a crucial difference is that no 'levels' are indicated within each Key Stage, a point that causes problems for test developers. The sections and paragraphs have to be interpreted in relation to the likely degree of difficulty of the concepts, knowledge or skills involved which then provides the basis for developing test questions. It is, however, a much more approximate procedure than previously, when SoAs were listed in levels. As we shall see in *Chapter 7*, this presents a particular problem at Key Stage 3, where the tests in mathematics and science are structured in overlapping tiers to cover the range of levels.

The revised curriculum introduced *Level Descriptions* into the National Curriculum assessment scene, and examples of this were outlined in *Chapter 2* (see p. 41). They are intended to be more general characterizations of what attainment should look like at each Level in each Attainment Target. The level descriptions contain many dimensions of attainment, brought together under the 'umbrella' of a level: in a sense they are attempts to impose some order on very diverse elements of attainment. But it is not clear exactly how they should be used or what 'best-fit' really means. If a particular pupil fits most of the description, should they be awarded the level, and what constitutes 'most' ? In a sense, it allows a pupil to be awarded, for instance, Level 3 without necessarily implying they are the same as every other 'Level 3' in the country (Sizmur and Sainsbury, 1996), although, of course, this has always been the case to some extent, even with SoA or mark-based approaches. Needless to say, this is not criterion-referencing in its true form but rather the use of general descriptions to allocate pupils to a level in quite a general way. It has yet to be seen how such a system will work for teacher assessments and it is not easy to estimate the dependability of the outcomes.

### Scoring and aggregating scores in a criterion-referenced system

The problem of domain ambiguity was (and is) also compounded by problems of defining mastery criteria for each Attainment Target (AT) and Level. It was evident from the responses of teachers in the 1991 evaluations of the Key Stage 1 tests that they were confused (despite training) about what constituted mastery and when an SoA could be deemed to have been 'attained'. For instance, in the teacher assessments in all three core subjects, a significant proportion of the participating teachers took mastery to mean displaying the relevant knowledge on one occasion only, while others required children to show evidence on several occasions. Some considered only 'typical' work from pupils, while others considered only highest achievement or 'best' work (Shorrocks *et al.*, ibid.).

A related problem was that of combining the results of the attainment of individual elements (criteria) into a single, meaningful score, bearing in mind that at each aggregation point potentially important information is lost. In the early versions of the National Curriculum, the situation was very complex. The core curriculum subjects, as we saw in *Chapter 2*, were structured into a complex hierarchy of Profile Components, Attainment Targets, Levels and Statements of Attainment. Rules of aggregation obviously needed to be set out for combining scores at these various points in the framework.

Given a variable number of SoAs at each Level and across subjects (varying from one SoA at a Level to more than 10), mastery criteria within the Level were needed as well as aggregation rules for then combining the scores from each AT into Profile Components and finally into a whole subject score. Looking back it seems amazing that a system of such complexity was allowed to develop, particularly as it had, in theory, to be applied not only in the SATs but also by teachers in their own record-keeping and assessments.

The solution reached in the early Key Stage 1 SATs was a combination of a minimal assignable grade plus a partial tolerance approach. In other words, where there were only one or two SoAs at a Level, they both had to be attained for the Level to be awarded (that is, the 'n-rule'). Where there were three or more SoAs at a Level, then the partial tolerance 'n-minus-1' rule applied, where one less than the total number was required for the awarding of the Level. The effect of this, noted afterwards (Shorrocks *et al.*, ibid. was that the attainment of a Level became increasingly more demanding as the number of SoAs increased beyond three, although this had been suggested as a potential problem even earlier.

The content domain for Levels where there were one or two SoAs was relatively small in relation to those where there were three or more. As the number of SoAs exceeded two, the application of the 'n-minus-1' rule became unfair in terms of comparative attainment. As the number of 'criteria' at a Level increased, not only were pupils required to perform successfully on a much greater range of content, they had to attain more in proportional terms. Also, the contents of the SoAs within a Level were often very different in the demands they made, so that the picture was even more complex.

The rules for combining scores across Attainment Targets (ATs) were also not easy. In the early days, when there were also Profile Components (PCs) there were PCs with several ATs within them, for example, in mathematics as we have already seen.

## MATHEMATICS

PC 1

Ma1 Ma2 Ma3 Ma4 Ma5 Ma6 Ma7 Ma8

PC 2

Ma9 Ma10 Ma11 Ma12 Ma13 Ma14

In this case, the level awarded was determined by the highest level attained or exceeded in not less than half the ATs. However, there were subjects where a PC contained only one AT, as in science, where the situation was as follows.

## SCIENCE

PC 1

Sc1

PC 2

Sc1 Sc2 Sc3 Sc4 Sc5 Sc6 Sc7 Sc8 Sc9 Sc10
Sc11 Sc12 Sc13 Sc14 Sc15 Sc16 Sc17

Where only one AT was included, the Level for that PC was determined by the score on that AT. As we have seen, when there were multiple Attainment Targets in a Profile Component, the requirements of the aggregation system were much less severe than when only one was involved. This raised the importance of PCs where there was only one AT. In science, for example, Sc1 was of considerably more importance than the remaining 16 ATs in terms of the contribution it made to the overall score, a fact that may or may not have been desirable in curriculum terms. Given the importance placed on the 'process' aspects of the curriculum at the time, this is perhaps not surprising.

There was yet a further complication in this early aggregation system. Given the large number of Attainment Targets in mathematics and science, it was clear that a Standard Assessment Task (SAT) could not cover all of them. Teachers had to provide a score in each AT for each pupil and, in the final aggregation, these Teacher Assessment scores were used to fill in the 'gaps' so the total subject score could be reached. However, for ATs where a SAT score was available, this was automatically entered as the definitive score, although with moderation procedures in place for cases of disagreement. In the first year of the SATs at Key Stage 1, the SAT outcomes were frequently higher than those awarded by the teachers (again evidence of teacher uncertainty about the criteria and mastery levels implied and the implicit defining of the assessment domain). The SAT therefore had the effect of raising the final scores in all three core subjects, although its precise effects varied from subject to subject. In the second year of full implementation (1992), teachers learned very rapidly, and the scores overall were higher (Shorrocks, 1995).

When Key Stage 3 assessments came on stream, using mark-based systems in written tests, different kinds of level-awarding problems were encountered, summarized by Schagen and Hutchison (1994). For instance, in the Key Stage 3 mathematics tests in 1992, each SoA was assessed through two different questions. The pupil needed to pass one of these two questions to be awarded the SoA, but they had to pass *all* SoAs at a level to be awarded that level. This was seen as rather a strict rule, so a 'rollback' procedure was introduced. Under this revised system, those who passed half or more of the SoA at a level could count SoAs passed at *higher* levels to increase their score at the lower level. This defied the basic principles of criterion-referencing, since the SoA at higher levels were unlikely to be directly related to SoA at lower levels, and therefore in what sense had the 'criteria' for a level been met? Also, an unintended consequence of the 'two questions per SoA' approach was that the assessments were dominated by the easier SoA and harder questions, in effect, contributed little to the level awarded. Thankfully, this was a system that did not survive long.

In 1993, two further aggregation methods were introduced, one in the Key Stage 2 first pilot tests and the other in Key Stage 3. At Key Stage 2, the tests were mark-based and the level awarded was based on the marks attained by the pupil. Threshold scores were decided, based largely upon the known number of marks available at each level and these 'cut-scores' decided which level was to be awarded. This proved a fairly clean system and one still essentially used today, since it has the advantage of simplicity for markers and teachers alike. The question still to be addressed is that of trying to ensure that the threshold scores represent reasonable approximations to patterns of attainment within the curriculum for most pupils.

By 1993, the Key Stage 3 tests used a completely different approach to the earlier 'rollback' extremes. Questions were linked directly to each level and separate scores were calculated for each level. The level could be awarded if the score achieved by a pupil equalled or was greater than the cut-score for that level. However, what this system did not address was the possibility of pupils gaining enough marks to pass at a higher level when they have failed to achieve enough marks to pass at lower levels.

It can be seen from these examples that the aggregation methods tried in the National Curriculum assessments have been varied and sometimes strange. The precise issues at each Key Stage will be discussed in later chapters, but the information presented here gives fuel to the arguments about the problems that exist in trying to amalgamate separate performances in a criterion-referenced system into a total score that reflects the whole of that performance.

## Formative and summative assessment

It was one of the major principles of the TGAT report that the new national assessments could be both formative and summative in purpose at the same time (see p. 34). Once the first assessments were implemented, the assertion that all these functions could be achieved via the same assessment system was questioned (Shorrocks *et al.*, 1992).

However, perhaps more explanation is needed here since it is important that justice is done in both theoretical and practical terms. Summative assessment has traditionally been seen as summarizing attainment at the end of a course or unit of work, while formative assessment provides feedback in teaching situations, helping the teacher (and pupil) to gain insight into what has been learnt and what has not been learnt so as to provide information about what needs to be taught next. In its many forms it should provide the bedrock for effective teaching. There are shades here of the Ausubel *et al.* (1978) principle that teachers must first find out what students know (and don't know) and plan/teach accordingly (see also Harlen, 1992).

Formative assessment can happen in a wide variety of ways in classrooms: by observing pupil behaviour, asking questions, appraising written work and so on. The aim is to use all this information to decide whether there is a mismatch or gap between what the pupil actually knows or understands and what the teacher or curriculum requires. There are also links here to the Vygotskian idea of the 'zone of proximal development', which he defines as the distance between what the child can do alone and what he or she can do with support from adults or competent peers (Siegler, 1998).

This is the most important distinction between formative and summative assessment: for formative functions, the assessment must be capable of yielding information that shows whether or not there is a gap between the actual and desired level of knowledge or understanding and suggest actions that could help to close that gap (Wiliam and Black, 1996). With this kind of definition, most kinds of assessment have the potential to serve summative purposes but they can only fulfil formative purposes if they have the potential for revealing gaps in knowledge or understanding. This usually requires questions that are detailed and focused, whether they take the form of formal test-like materials or classroom questioning strategies.

The question for the national tests is therefore not about whether a single assessment can serve both purposes but whether serving one purpose has negative consequences for the other. Wiliam and Black (ibid.) have argued that the difficulties in the National Curriculum arose because there was confusion from the beginning between eliciting assessment evidence and the interpretation of that evidence. They suggest that, in the early days, teachers used the listings of SoAs in formative ways, collecting evidence and interpreting it according to whether it seemed to indicate the beginnings of attainment of a particular 'statement', partial attainment to be confirmed later, or good evidence that attainment had been demonstrated. Later, however, this information had to become a summative judgement and so the processes of eliciting evidence and interpreting it became confused. This may indicate that the two kinds of function are, in principle, compatible but that unless the various aspects of the assessment process are distinguished (see the assessment model on p. 67) there may be problems.

Since the loss of the SoA from the curriculum in 1995 (the result of the Dearing review), some of these issues have changed. The formative and summative functions have to some extent been better distinguished; the tests and the outcomes derived from them are recognized as essentially summative in function, though with the possibility of deriving formative information from them. Teachers' own assessments are set alongside these test outcomes and also serve summative functions but based on different kinds of evidence and interpretation of that evidence. If there is discrepancy between the two kinds of 'summations', this should be explained to pupils and parents. Hopefully, teacher assessments will also continue to serve formative functions in the classroom in relation to planning and teaching.

## The validity and reliability of the tests

These two terms are inescapable in a discussion of assessment. They have already been mentioned earlier in this chapter in relation to the assessment tasks where it was pointed out that there were reliability problems with some of the early assessment activities. Validity and reliability are central to any discussion of assessment since all assessment needs to be fit for its purpose (validity) and to produce results that can be relied upon (reliability). The main question is the extent to which existing definitions of validity and reliability are appropriate in the National Curriculum assessments.

## Validity

Validity is conventionally defined (Jackson, 1997) as *what* a test measures and *how well* it does so. However, such a broad definition tells us little about how to set about defining it in more detail or estimating it. Different types of validity have been identified (well summarized in Wiliam, 1993). Among the most important are content validity (the extent to which the assessment is relevant to the content domain being addressed), predictive validity (the extent to which a test is capable of predicting future performance) and the extent to which the inferences being made in any assessment are warranted (more recent definitions of construct validity).

The assessment model outlined on p. 67 is helpful, since questions of validity enter into all aspects of the process. Validity is closely tied up with the purpose of the assessment, with agreeing the precise nature of what is to be assessed and decisions about how an assessment should be operationalized and implemented. Do the activities or questions that are devised address the agreed assessment purpose and domain? Will they engage the interest of pupils and motivate them to respond in relevant and 'revealing' ways? Is what is being assessed clear and direct or are extraneous factors acting as a barrier to the pupil revealing what they know or can do, for instance the language of the questions or the 'contexts' in which they are set? All these will influence the validity of the assessment enterprise. Is the evidence collected (Step 4 in the process) relevant and appropriate for its purpose and is the assessment judgement being made in the light of the agreed criteria and scales of performance/mastery? Finally, how are the results being interpreted and used, and what is their significance in the wider educational and political situation?

In order to meet validity requirements, the starting point must be an agreed purpose and focus for the assessment which are then manifested in a variety of appropriate questions or tasks. It is a truism that the validity of an assessment can be increased by extending the range of these questions/activities, but it is here that we run up against another vital consideration – the manageability of the package. A full and detailed assessment of any domain should be highly valid, but this is not possible in most cases, so realistic constraints have to be acknowledged. The National Curriculum tests, for example, are time-limited written tests which necessarily set limits on the nature of the validity that can be achieved (Fairbrother, 1993). Not all skills and knowledge can be assessed through this kind of test and the time limits set the boundaries for the content that can be covered: in other words the content validity of the tests comes into question.

Wiliam (1993 and 1994) has provided an interesting summary of more recent issues in validity. He suggests that notions of validity have widened over the years in three phases. Earlier definitions focused on validity as a property of an assessment, followed by a focus on validity as a property of the behaviours elicited by an assessment and ending most recently with an emphasis on validity as a property of the inferences made on the basis of the assessment. He makes the case that (in relation to the first two) it is important to consider not only whether a test measures what it is supposed to measure (face validity) but the extent to which it actually does so (content validity). In other words, it is not just about whether a test looks valid to those involved with it (pupils, teachers, the wider community and so on), but whether the responses elicited by it are in line with validity requirements. In terms of the National Curriculum assessments, it could be argued that the first extensive programmes of activity/task-based assessments at Key Stage 1 and in the pilots for Key Stage 3 (in 1991), although described as 'elaborate nonsense' for Key Stage 3 by the then Secretary of State for Education, Kenneth Clarke, were appreciated as valid assessments by many teachers. Political agendas, however, dictated a move to shorter, sharper written tests, a triumph of face validity and manageability over content validity.

The more recent emphasis on validity as a property of the inferences made on the basis of the assessment widens the responsibilities of the assessments, not only for the test developers but also for the users of the information derived from the tests. A good example of this wider kind of inference are the judgements made about schools on the basis of their performance in the 'league tables' at Key Stage 2. For better or for worse, parents may take important decisions about selecting a school for their child on the basis of these results which is indeed a case of going well beyond the domains being assessed in the tests. Many of these ideas were first suggested by Messick (1980).

The *uses* of assessment outcomes are, therefore, a significant consideration in the validation process. National Curriculum assessment is high-stakes assessment, where not only are individual pupils are being judged but also teachers, schools and in effect the whole schooling system. In these circumstances it is even more important to take this broader notion of validity and to recognize that there may be a significant tension between the evidence and consequences of testing.

It has already been suggested (p. 33) that testing always involves error and that what we are doing is making inferences about wider knowledge and skills based on sampling a comparatively small amount of the total possibilities. All assessment measures are subject to uncertainty, a fact that applies as much to measuring a piece of string as to measuring attainment. However, there are no unequivocal 'rulers' that can be used in measuring human attributes; it is even more inferential. This is the matter of reliability.

As with validity, the factors involved in estimating *reliability* are many. Unreliability can arise from the tests themselves, from pupil responses and from the marking and appraisal process that follows. In relation to the assessment instruments, be they tests, tasks or practical activities the questions may be poorly expressed, their meaning ambiguous or their assessment focus unclear. If the questions in a test vary from year to year, potentially more unreliability is introduced into the year-on-year scores and, in any case, pupils may interpret even the best-devised questions differently. The administration of the tests may also be poorly controlled. Pupils themselves are another source of introducing uncertainty into the assessment process. They may have knowledge and understanding in a particular topic, but they may use it differently on different occasions, in the light of their interpretation of a question; they may forget or simply be unwell or just have had a argument with someone. All these factors make responses unpredictable to some extent, even with the best-prepared candidate working on a well-constructed test.

Finally, the marking process may bring in further unreliability. Even with a totally clear and detailed mark scheme and trained markers, there will be inaccuracies in the marking, particularly with more open-ended questions or essays. In this type of question, there will always be an element of subjectivity which is, of course, a source of unreliability as we saw in relation to the marking of assessment tasks (pp. 70–71). Probably the most reliable form of question in written tests is multiple-choice, where a question is posed and a number of set responses provided. The candidates choose what they believe to be the correct one and tick the appropriate answer box. These are often so closed as assessment items that they can be machine-marked which is likely to increase reliability. However, reliability then potentially comes into conflict with validity: many kinds of knowledge, understanding and skills cannot be assessed effectively through this type of question (especially higher order evaluation and judgmental competencies). There has to be a trade-off between these two important dimensions of assessment. The reliability of a test or assessment task can also be increased by asking a number of questions on the same topic, so averaging out some of the factors mentioned in the last paragraph, but we then come up against the other problem of time and manageability. Balancing out these three requirements presents a major headache for test developers.

Just as the notion of validity demands some re-thinking in the context of the National Curriculum, so also does reliability. Traditional measures are usually expressed as *reliability coefficients* and can be achieved in several ways. Two or more 'parallel forms' of a test can be developed and the statistical agreement measured when the various forms are administered to pupils. Alternatively, the same group of pupils can be given the same test on two occasions (randomized in presentation) close in time, and the agreement between the two sets of scores calculated. In other versions, the two halves of a test can be treated as separate tests in statistical terms and correlated. All these techniques for estimating reliability are, however, based on the kinds of question response structures created in norm-referenced tests and do not transfer easily to criterion-referenced instruments.

Criterion-referenced tests (as classically conceived) are not designed to emphasize differences among individuals and so the range of scoring outcomes can be smaller. In fact, after an 'ideal' teaching programme and effective learning on the part of the pupils, it is theoretically possible for all candidates to obtain maximum scores. The more limited variability of criterion-referenced tests means that the traditional estimates of reliability outlined in the last paragraph are likely to generate misleading results. Of course, the fact that the National Curriculum tests cover several levels rather than just one criterion means that they will give a range of scores whose reliability can be measured in more traditional ways.

However, it may be more appropriate to use the term *dependability* (Brennan and Kane, 1977) for criterion-referenced tests so as not to create confusion. In National Curriculum assessment, the outcomes are expressed in terms of Levels for each subject. The main question therefore becomes one of how dependable are the outcomes in terms of accurately placing individuals in the appropriate 'category' (level). It is basically a matter of drawing accurate lines between 'masters' and 'non-masters' at each level, a situation shown in *Figure 4.2*), taking the example of probably the best known assessment of this kind, the driving test.

DOMAIN SCORE CLASSIFICATION

|  |  | 'Non-master' | 'Master' |
|---|---|---|---|
| TEST SCORE CLASSIFICATION | Fails test 'Non-master' | true-negative decision | false-negative decision |
|  | Passes test 'Master' | false-positive decision | true-positive decision |

**Figure 4.2**: Agreement between domain and test score mastery

The 'domain' score classification implies the 'true' skill situation which any test only ever samples. On the basis of this sampling (the test score classification) there are two kinds of correct decision (the 'true-positive' and 'true-negative' cells) and two kinds of incorrect decision (the 'false-positive' and 'false-negative'). Above all, this kind of test (the driving test in this example) must aim to maximize correct decisions and minimize incorrect ones. The test should be designed to achieve this, but it should be borne in mind that the two kinds of incorrect decisions have different consequences. From the point of view of road safety, false-positive decisions imply that incompetent drivers are being let onto the roads and false-negative decisions imply re-testing with all its resource implications. To minimize the false-positives, a stricter criterion could be applied, but this could increase the proportion of false-negatives.

By analogy, in the context of National Curriculum assessment, the aim must also be to minimize incorrect decisions and correctly assign pupils to Levels. However, as we have seen with the example of the driving test, the precise way in which the thresholds are drawn (the 'cut-scores' or dividing line between masters and non-masters) depends to some extent on the nature and purpose of the test. The driving test is vital in terms of road safety, so a strict mastery criterion is appropriate. In National Curriculum tests, there are also consequences, as the argument about validity emphasized. The aim should be to set thresholds that minimize incorrect placements, but consideration should be given to the implications of misplacements.

The testing programme represents high-stakes testing for schools and for individual pupils. The results may be used for selection (streaming, perhaps) or for grouping decisions within a class, both of which may influence the kinds of opportunities and learning experiences provided for the child as well as feelings of self-esteem and worth. These are not low stakes in relation to longer-term life chances.

The implications of the Dearing report (1993) for the test development agencies were also wide-ranging. In any case, at Key Stages 2 and 3, the use of pencil and paper tests, less recognizable content 'criteria' within the tests and a marks-based approach to scoring had already suggested a move away from direct criterion-referencing. From here on the term used in official circles was 'criterion-related assessment'. The message was that all questions in the various test papers were derived from the specification of the curriculum appropriate to each Key Stage, but that once generated and packaged into a test paper, the questions became vehicles for collecting a total score of marks which were not assigned to particular Attainment Targets or 'criteria'. Instead, threshold scores (cut-scores) were set, using a range of different kinds of judgements, which determined the level awarded on any test.

For example, in setting the Key Stage 2 mathematics tests in summer 1996 (addressing Levels 3–5), a total of five methods were used to determine where the scoring thresholds should be set for each level. These included the following:

• the application of a 'criterion-related algorithm', in which appropriate proportions of the number of marks attributed to each of the three Levels of questions were calculated. For example, if the test contained 27 'easy' questions (broadly speaking, Level 3), a two-thirds algorithm would mean that a pupil had to score 18 in order to be awarded Level 3;

- statistical equating with the scores of the previous year;

- Angoff procedures (Angoff, 1971).

A combination of information from these three sources was used to set the final thresholds. Of these three, the Angoff procedure is perhaps the least well known, but it is a technique used quite widely in the current setting of National Curriculum thresholds. A panel of expert judges (experienced Year 6 teachers of mathematics, for instance) considers each item in the tests and decides whether minimally competent pupils at Level 3, Level 4 and Level 5 would be able to answer the question correctly, bearing in mind the require-ments of the mark schemes. This is done independently and the scores recorded. At the next stage, the panel as a whole must agree on these decisions and it is a combination of the various probabilities generated by these judge-ments that can then be used to arrive at the decision about the appropriate cut-scores for Level 3, Level 4 and Level 5. As a technique, it is not without its weaknesses, but as part of a decision-making process it is potentially useful. It is being developed and extended in its usage in the context of the National Cur-riculum (D'Arcy, 1994b)

## Progression and the 10-Level (now 8-Level) scale

The main points made so far about the 10-Level scale were that the decision to create it was based on a judgement about both the age range to be covered (ages 5 to 16) and the likely extent of the curriculum. The diagram produced in the TGAT Report (see p. 36) indicated that the range of levels both achieved and assessed at each Key Stage would be likely to increase but that there would be 'expected' levels for pupils at each. There were clearly merits to a single 10-Level scale for all pupils, since it encouraged teachers to think in more differen-tiated ways about the attainments of pupils within a single class or group and it could potentially facilitate improved communication across the phases of schooling, from primary to secondary. These points now need further exami-nation.

The TGAT Committee was asked to consider the marking scale to be used in the national assessments, in keeping with a criterion-referenced approach to assessment and bearing in mind the wide age and attainment of the National Curriculum. The implication was that the scale should show what pupils should be expected to know and understand at various points in their school-ing. This would be a kind of benchmarking for each age group being assessed. However, the idea was not that simple. For example, a single set of perform-ance criteria for all 11-year-olds runs the risk of demotivating both the lower and higher attainers, since the benchmarks are likely to be too hard to achieve for the former and too easy for the latter. This suggested that multiple benchmarks were needed for each age group, but the question then becomes one of relating these to the various age points. The choice facing the committee was either to treat each Key Stage as independent or to create 'link' points across the age groups.

Having separate scales for each Key Stage (for example a grading system of A to E for all 7-, 11- and 14-year-olds) solves the problem of showing the range of attainments of the cohort in a fairly differentiated way but generates a problem of demonstrating progress across the age groups. An 'average' pupil may, quite appropriately, be awarded a 'C' grade at age 7 and then again at age 11, measured on the relevant age scales, but this may not feel like progress over four years for either pupil or parents. It may be showing a continued 'satisfactory' performance but doing so in a way that seems very static since the clock is re-set, as it were, at the beginning of each Key Stage. The solution was therefore to opt for a *common scale* across the Key Stages to address this problem of charting pupil progress in a direct way over the four Key Stages. But how many grades or categories should such a scale contain?

Experience of graded assessments in many subjects (see *Chapter 2*) suggested that perhaps 20 'levels' would be needed to span such a wide age and attainment range, but such advice was over-ruled. A 20-Level scale would allow more progress to be demonstrated each year but at the expense of having obviously different demands for each level. In some subjects, such fine-grained differentiation may be possible (for example in mathematics or modern languages) but in others it seems virtually impossible (for example in English or history) where distinguishing 20 levels of developing knowledge, skills and understanding could prove problematic. The decision was, therefore, to go for a 10-level scale for the National Curriculum although the precise designation and content of each level in each Attainment Target in each subject was left to the subject groups (see pp. 35–36). In some ways, the levels were specified in quite arbitrary ways in each subject, since they were clearly not based upon theoretical or formal developmental models of thinking, such as those of Piaget (Inhelder *et al.*, 1976).

The first years of test development in all three Key Stages necessarily focused on interpreting the meaning, range and content of each level in the assessed Attainment Targets, and it is clear that the tests themselves helped to clarify both the content (domains) and standards (mastery levels) implied in the Orders. Teachers were grappling with these problems for their own teacher assessment judgements too, and the test and task materials undoubtedly helped to consolidate such judgements, as did the official 'exemplification' materials produced by SCAA (see for example, SCAA, 1995a and b) and the many 'agreement trials' organized by Local Education Authorities. It is worth re-iterating the point that once such interpretations and standards for the 10

Levels were more widely agreed, the more reliable these teacher judgements became. It is also worth emphasizing that once such performance requirements are established and applied, the actual proportions of pupils attaining each level over time may vary. This is the implication of criterion-referenced assessment and the significance of government edicts that 'standards' (as manifested in these national assessment outcomes) must improve by the year 2002.

The original TGAT diagram suggested that roughly 80 per cent of each age cohort should fall within the required range of levels for each Key Stage, bearing in mind, however that this was a highly speculative projection. There have been arguments that the proportions should be less than this (Wiliam, 1992) but the reality has been rather different. At Key Stage 2, where national results are published and therefore the data are available, the percentage of 11-year-olds attaining below Level 3 in the tests in the three core subjects has been displayed in *Table 4.1*. The expected range of attainment levels for Key Stage 2 is Level 2 to Level 6. Data are not available for Level 2 separately, so the information in the table confounds the award of 'W' and Level 1 (outside the range) and Level 2 (within the range).

**Table 4.1:** The percentages of 11-year-old pupils awarded 'W', '1' or '2' in the national tests in English, mathematics and science in 1995, 1996 and 1997 (Source: QCA, 1998e)

| | Subjects | | |
|---|---|---|---|
| Years | English | Mathematics | Science |
| 1995 | 8% | 14% | 6% |
| 1996 | 7% | 8% | 6% |
| 1997 | 7% | 7% | 4% |

It is clear from *Table 4.1* that the national results in mathematics in 1995 were somewhat out of line with the others and that the rest have remained fairly constant over the three-year-period. This suggests that a similar-sized 'core' of pupils each year are not attaining at the level of the main test requirements, although we do not know what proportion of these scored Level 2 and were therefore technically within the expected range for the Key Stage.

Over the years, the 10-Level scale has come in for criticism from many quarters. Ironically, given the objections to implementing a 20-Level scale, some of the major complaints have been about the fairly gross categorizations that a 10-Level scale covering 11 years of schooling allows. Such comments have come from teachers working with pupils with special educational needs who point out that many of their lower-attaining pupils score consistently low levels over a number of years, an experience that is demotivating and does not recognize the progress they have made. Criticisms have also come from teachers that some of the levels have a very broad range of content (for example, Level 2 in the 'Reading' Attainment Target) and that children of very different capabilities can be awarded the same level – those who have just achieved it and those who almost attained the next level up. As Wiliam (1992) points out, however, these negative points are not necessarily the result of the 10-Level scale in itself, but rather the result of the particular specifications made by the subject working groups and not necessarily improved by later revisions of the curriculum.

The objective of the Dearing review was to provide a framework for assessing achievement which (Dearing, 1993, p.56):

- offers a clear statement of progression in each National Curriculum subject;

- encourages differentiation of work so that pupils of all abilities are fully stretched;

- provides an easily intelligible means of reporting pupil achievement to parents, teachers and pupils;

- is manageable in the classroom;

- helps to inform parents when deciding on a school for their child;

- helps teachers, parents, governors and society as a whole to assess the achievement of individual schools and the education system generally.

The review argued that there was a continued need for a framework common to all schools and to the assessment of pupil progress against common standards, to be achieved through streamlined national tests together with teacher assessment based on clear, shared judgements, and subject to moderation and audit.

The choice was between four main options for a marking scale (Dearing, 1993, p.58), namely:

1. retaining the 10-Level scale for all National Curriculum subjects except art, music and PE;

2. modifying the 10-Level scale in the light of experience;

3. abandoning the 10-Level scale and replacing it with end-of-Key Stage gradings;

4. using a modified 10-Level scale for subjects where there is most clearly a progressive build up of knowledge and skills, and using end-of-key stage gradings for the others.

The choice made was to retain the 10-level scale for most subjects, but to keep the problem under review. These arguments very much mirrored those discussed by the original TGAT Committee, including the significant point that the untried introduction of end-of-Key Stage gradings might generate its own crop of unforeseen problems. In effect, the risk was perceived as being too great.

Keeping the situation 'under review' has generated one significant change since 1993, brought about by an increasing emphasis on the fact that national testing focuses on pupils up to the age of 14 (the end of Key Stage 3) rather than 16. The 1995 revisions of the curriculum in the core subjects indicated that Levels 9 and 10 were to be considered as 'exceptional performance' for those aged 14+ and not formally awarded as Levels in the testing. In effect this created an 8-Level scale which became built into the testing programme in 1996. The scale remains, therefore, with its major principle of progression intact although it is still not clear how long this will continue. At the time of writing this book, the Qualifications and Curriculum Authority was still debating its future, raising it as a focus for discussion at the 1998 national Assessment Conferences.

## Summary

This chapter has presented some of the technical aspects of assessment related to national testing. Emphasis has been placed on the limitations of assessment as well as its advantages.

- Good assessment demands a clear purpose and focus. The assessment process has a number of phases and dimensions which are summarized in the form of a diagram. Being clear about these different aspects is crucial to understanding the nature of assessment and its implications.

- In the National Curriculum assessments, practically-based tasks and activities are used with younger and lower-attaining pupils, and their strengths and limitations are summarized. They have an important role to play in the system, provided that they are well constructed and used in agreed and standard ways.

- However, written tests now form the major part of the national testing programme at all three Key Stages, so it is the characteristics and problems of pencil-and-paper tests in a criterion-referenced/criterion-related system that need to be understood.

- The idea of criterion-referenced assessment, although very appropriate in education contexts, presents considerable problems of domain definition and domain sampling.

- The 'criteria' in the national tests have changed over time as the extent and form of the National Curriculum on which they are based, has changed. The original Statements of Attainment (SoA) presented problems for both teachers and test developers alike, but it is open to question whether the changes brought about by the Dearing review have necessarily improved the technical problems associated with the testing.

- Scoring and aggregation systems have also varied over the years and some of the approaches have been more appropriate and defensible than others.

- The possibility of combining formative and summative purposes in the testing has been questioned, perhaps because of a lack of theoretical clarity about the nature of the two.

- The validity of the tests is closely bound up with factors to do with the tests themselves, factors to do with the pupils and factors to do with administration and marking procedures. However, an important dimension of validity is the use to which the results are put and the consequences of using them.

- Estimating the reliability of criterion-referenced tests is not necessarily possible using traditional methods developed for use in norm-referenced testing. In the national tests, the main dependability issue is whether pupils have been correctly allocated to levels. This is a complex matter both for SoA-based systems and mark-based systems alike.

- The 10-Level scale was introduced for a variety of reasons. It has not been without its critics, but even the major 1995 review decided that changing it fundamentally would be too much of a risk. Moving to a system of assessment grades (A–E) at the end of each Key Stage would not fully solve the problems and might introduce further, unforeseen ones. In practice, since the Dearing review, the 10-Level scale has become an 8-Level scale.

# 5 The tests at Key Stage 1: the storm and the calm

This chapter, along with *Chapters 6 and 7*, will focus on each Key Stage in turn and try to show what has actually happened in the testing at these stages over time, indicating particular issues and problems which have occurred in each. Clearly, this material is extensive, so only some of the main points are addressed, and then only briefly. To some extent also, the analysis at each Key Stage will be used as a vehicle for addressing particular issues that have special significance for that phase but which apply to some extent to the others.

The test development process at Key Stage 1 began in 1989 (see diagram on p. 44), and the materials produced were intended to cover Levels 1, 2, 3 (also Level 4 from 1992 to 1994) in each core subject and to address most of the Attainment Targets. They were the first tests to be used nationally and there-fore raised many of the issues outlined in the last chapter in an overt and often controversial way, not least because they were being used with very young chil-dren. During these first years of national testing, the assessments were known as 'Standard Assessment Tasks', or SATs, although they are now referred to as *the national tests*.

Before we begin, it is perhaps worth pointing out that the tests for 7-year-olds envisaged in the TGAT Report (ibid.) were intended to have a screening function, identifying children in need of further help and those with excep-tional attainment (TGAT Report, para. 147). It was also expected that each child would carry out only three assessment activities as part of their 'ordinary school work' (para. 149), which should be appropriate to their skills and varied in presentation and response modes (para. 150). Most importantly, this was the first time anywhere in the world that a national assessment system had been put in place for such young pupils, and, moreover, one that was criterion-refer-enced to a detailed curriculum and carried out through classroom-based, practical activities. The specification to the test development agency had been that the assessments should reliably and validly assess the curriculum, using only normal classroom resources, and should be capable of being adminis-tered as part of the normal curriculum.

It is also the case that infant teachers were mostly inexperienced in such intensive assessment activity, although assessing children of 7 or younger was, and is, not a new activity in our educational system. In schools throughout the country children are assessed and tested informally by their teachers in spelling tests, 'review' pages in maths workbooks and by reading aloud. But another trend is also obvious, the use of standardized testing procedures by Local Education Authorities (LEAs) in various subjects. Caroline Gipps and her colleagues (1983b) carried out national surveys of the extent of such testing and found that 82 of the 104 LEAs had some kind of official testing programme for pupils of this age.

## The development work and piloting

In order to develop and trial as many assessment approaches as possible, the (then) School Examinations and Assessment Authority (SEAC) commissioned three groups to work on the first SATs. These 'consortia' were the National Foundation for Educational Research together with Bishop Grosseteste College, Lincoln (the NFER/BGC consortium); the Consortium for Assessment and Testing in Schools (CATS) including the University of London Institute of Education and the London and East Anglian Examining Board; and the Standard Tests and Assessments Implementation Research (STAIR) Consortium, including the Joint Matriculation and Examining Board and the Education Departments of the Universities of Manchester and Liverpool. A total of over six million pounds was allocated to these groups for the development work, but in practice the decision was taken in 1990 to proceed with only one of them, so not all this expenditure was deployed in the test development process.

The national piloting was held in 1990 and involved around 20,000 pupils in over 600 schools across 50 Local Education Authorities in England and Wales. The materials were also produced in Welsh for pupils for whom this was their home language. The experience was reported and evaluated by the consortia themselves (SEAC, 1991b, c and d) and finally by the Evaluation and Monitoring Unit of the School Examinations and Assessment Council (SEAC, 1992e) itself. In many ways, the findings foreshadowed those produced in the evaluations of the first national administration of the tests in 1991 – problems of teacher workload, impact on classroom teaching and management and questions about the reliability and validity of the results (Torrance, 1991) – which will be addressed in more detail later in this chapter. The outcome was that modifications to the specification were made for the full 1991 administration and only one of the three consortia, the NFER/BGC group, was retained to develop the 1991 materials.

## The first national tests in 1991

Notwithstanding the streamlining of the materials that occurred as the result of the 1990 pilot, the 1991 tests proved to be the source of a great deal of controversy and debate in professional circles and in the media. The full range of assessment activities which teachers had to carry out with each pupil is summarized in *Table 5.1* later. Many evaluations of the experience were published, ranging from individual teachers writing up their views (for example, Dutta, 1992) to the full national evaluation (Shorrocks *et al.*, 1992). The SAT agency itself also published its own evaluation (Whetton and Sainsbury, 1992). I will now look at the major points to emerge from all these sources, although many are based in the published national evaluation (Shorrocks *et al.*, 1992). Individual points will not be specifically referenced, however.

### Preparation and training of teachers

Some 20,000 Year 2 teachers, headteachers and assessment co-ordinators had to be trained both to deliver the SATs and to carry out their own teacher assessments. The Local Education Authorities were responsible for the training, moderation and support for the teachers, a task which different authorities tackled with varying degrees of effectiveness. The national approach was a 'cascade' model of training for the SATs in which each LEA sent a few key personnel to the national training conferences, who then 'cascaded' this training down through other LEA staff and finally to the teachers. The potential for 'Chinese Whispers' effects in this system was considerable. Most teachers received their one to two days of training, but support for carrying out their own teacher assessments was much more varied. All these points naturally have enormous implications for the validity and dependability of the first set of outcomes.

One form of experience that the teachers appreciated most was 'agreement trialling', as part of the moderation procedures. This involved teachers within schools and across clusters of schools meeting to discuss particular pieces of pupil work in order to reach agreement about the requirements for the awarding of the different 'levels'. These discussions were judged to be directly related to teacher needs and contributed in a positive way to their overall professional development. Later studies have also pointed up the value of agreement trialling, for example Clarke and Christie (1996).

### Teacher Assessment

In addition to delivering the SATs, teachers had to make their own Teacher Assessment judgements for each of the 32 Attainment Targets in the three core subjects (not including Welsh). They were supported in this by training from their LEAs and also by official documentation such as the three SEAC 'Guides to Assessment' (SEAC, 1990). However, the major issues in Teacher Assessment were undoubtedly the variable amounts of training received by Year 2 teachers and the inconsistency of interpretation of the meaning of the SoA. They were confused about the meaning of key terms, how much evidence they needed in order to be able to 'tick' an SoA as 'achieved' and whether the attainment had to be recent or could be carried forward from previous records, which in some cases were excellent but in others almost non-existent. Yet, as *Chapters 2 and 4* have emphasized, these points are crucial for valid and dependable assessment in a criterion-referenced system. One of the results in 1991 was that there was poor agreement between the scoring outcomes produced by Teacher Assessments and by the SATs (Shorrocks *et al.*, ibid.).

## The quality and delivery of the SATs

Responses to the SATs in 1991 were vociferous, both from the press, from schools and from teaching organizations. Most complaints focused on the time taken and the fact that teachers said they had learned little or nothing from the experience. With hindsight, this was not necessarily the case, but at the time teachers clearly felt threatened and overwhelmed by the demands being placed upon them, leaving them with a strong sense of becoming deskilled. Such feelings are not productive in encouraging professional development and thinking: claiming to have learned nothing from the 1991 experience was an effective way of defending against this threat to their sense of professionalism.

The SAT activities covered nine Attainment Targets in the three core subjects and were well rated by the teachers. They saw most of them as appropriate and challenging activities for 7-year-olds and the documentation that went with them was also judged clear and helpful. However, assessment through these (mostly) small-group activities was problematic: in many of them (for instance, the now infamous 'floating and sinking' activity in science, see p. 47) there was a fundamental tension between an activity that represented good infant classroom practice and the requirement to provide accurate and dependable assessment. All of this begged the question of what was meant by 'Standard' in the assessments. If this was to be taken as implying activities, procedures and performance requirements that were the same for all pupils, then the 1991 SAT fell considerably short of this.

## The impact of the SATs on school /classroom organization and functioning

Observational studies and teacher interviews all reveal that during the SAT administration period (half a term in 1991) school routines suffered considerably. Additional teaching support was diverted to Year 2 classrooms at the expense of other classes, and it was claimed that provision for children with special educational needs was affected negatively because of this. Teachers taught and grouped children differently during the SAT period, and the activities provided for the children in a class who were not the 'SAT group' for that session were less stimulating and challenging than normal. When teachers were focusing on administering the SAT activities with one small group at a time, they clearly could not effectively give their attention to the rest of the class. At the same time, the other pupils in the class needed to ask questions of the teacher from time to time, so potentially interrupting the flow of , and concentration on, the assessments.

The time taken to deliver the SATs was extensive and spread over half a term. In many cases, head teachers (for instance) supported the process by carrying out some of the assessments, often the individualized assessments of reading which were very time-consuming. The estimated times for each activity provided by the SAT agency (NFER) were fairly accurate, but the total time taken was much more because of the need to repeat each activity several times, with the different groups of pupils. The result was therefore a highly disrupted half term in most schools, with stressed teachers and fraught LEA staff. Even in schools that were well ahead in their assessment policy and practice and therefore, in principle, well prepared for the national assessments, they came as a considerable shock. The process was also not helped by the fact that many infant teachers were not necessarily tuned into the idea of assessment as an ongoing aspect of normal learning and teaching, seeing it instead as a 'bolt-on', additional requirement to their work, and an unwelcome one.

### *Pupils with special educational needs (SEN)*

Forthright comments about the SATs also came from teachers of pupils with special educational needs. As we saw in *Chapter 1*, this group of professionals had detected both positive and negative aspects to the introduction of a National Curriculum, but facing the reality of the first national tests with 7-year-olds, many of their comments became more focused. Even though pupils with statements of special educational need could be exempted by law from the first year of testing in 1991 (but not in 1992), many schools and teachers chose to include them in 1991 in order to explore the appropriateness of the assessments. Bartlett (1991) summarized some important points:

- Many teachers reported that the performance of some children surprised them, challenging their Teacher Assessments and causing them to re-think and re-evaluate. This change in expectation was positive.

- The fact that the assessments were activity-based worked in favour of these children with special needs, since they could respond orally and often surprised their teachers by the sophistication of their responses. In particular, some flexibility in delivering the activities was seen as helpful, provided the quality of the assessment was not compromised.

- However, teachers were critical of the fact that few fully worked examples were provided about exactly how certain of the activities could be adapted to meet the needs of SEN children, although this was in principle allowed under the regulations.

- The choice of entry and exit points for each child within the range of the assessment activities was also welcomed, so that pupils did not become stressed by being asked to complete activities beyond their competence.

- The time demands for teachers of children with special educational needs were even greater than for other, mainstream pupils, since many of the activities had to be administered on a one-to-one basis.

- Many of these teachers criticized the 10-Level model, arguing that the steps between the levels were too great for some of their pupils, and that many would probably not progress much beyond Level 1 in their school careers, despite having made real educational progress. There was a widespread suggestion that the requirements of Level 1 should become more detailed, so potentially allowing positive achievement to be recognized, even within a level.

The major problem seemed to be that of ensuring maximum access to the SATs, so that as many children as possible within the cohort could retain their entitlement to the curriculum. The aim, it was argued, should be to minimize the number of pupils exempted from the SATs ('disapplied'), except when their difficulties meant they could not undertake a particular activity (for example, exempting children whose physical problems prevented them from holding and using a pencil from the handwriting activity).

In fact, the 1991 national evaluation sample included pupils with statements (1 per cent of the total sample) and others defined by their teachers as having special educational needs (a further 11 per cent of the sample). It should be remembered that not all special educational needs involve learning difficulties and indeed some of these children attained the highest grade (Level 3) in the SATs. For example, there are children who have physical disabilities but who have average or above average mental capabilities. However, for most of the rest, the attainment of pupils with special educational needs was significantly lower than that of other pupils (Shorrocks *et al.*, ibid.).

## *Pupils with English as an additional language (EAL)*

A proportion of 7-year-olds taking the SATs in 1991 had only begun to use English on entering school at age four or five, often communicating in one or more other languages at home or in the community. Shan (1990) suggested that the guidance offered by SEAC (1990) was less than helpful in its advice about assessing emerging bilingual pupils. In a section on 'Exceptional cases', the advice was that bilingual children should receive the same amount of help and support in carrying out assessment tasks as they usually received in schools. The TGAT report had recommended that in such cases the assessments should be carried out in the pupil's first language, a principle endorsed by the government but without resources. It is clear, however, that bilingual pupils may learn concepts and gain understandings in one language or another, especially if the school encourages and supports the use of home languages in the classroom. If a concept has been learned in one language, it may not be helpful to assess it in another, so the question becomes one of accurately identifying the most appropriate channel of communication for pupils in particular contexts. Support in the first language may only be effective in some circumstances, and as far as the SATs were concerned those offering the support needed careful training in order to learn how to assess pupils validly and dependably in a first language.

In the earlier development work by the three consortia (SEAC, 1991b; c; d, ibid.) considerable thought had been given to this question. All three groups had procedures for evaluating items and activities for gender and ethnic bias, and all of them encouraged teachers and bilingual support staff to administer the SAT activities in the language that was most appropriate for their pupils. In the case of the STAIR Consortium, a set of materials was developed in Punjabi, but this idea was not pursued further when decisions were taken at a national level. The reasons for this lie in the fact that as there are so many first languages used in primary schools (over 160 nationally), the costs would have been prohibitive.

The main findings from these reported studies were that bilingual pupils responded well to the activities, and the oral/practical response modes allowed some of them to surprise their teachers by their level of performance. In so far as it occurred, this was a very positive outcome of the SAT experience. However, their overall scoring outcomes showed poorer performance than those of their English-speaking counterparts.

Gravelle (1990) argued that national testing might throw into focus some of the widening gulfs in education and society. Testing is never without its problems in multicultural and multilingual situations, as the earlier controversies about the measurement of intelligence testify (Richardson, 1991). Testing will always reflect the dominant culture and language in a society, and therefore different sub-cultural groups may perform less well in the outcomes. Notwith-standing all the efforts made to eliminate bias in the content and structure of the questions in the national tests, different groups perform differently, as we shall see later in this chapter. Given these important findings, what classroom influences and practices militate against ethnic minority and bilingual pupils? Gravelle (ibid.) suggested that among the most potent were: the lack of acknowledgement of ethnic minority pupils' rich history and experience; bilin-gualism and multilingualism not being perceived as an educational asset by predominantly white, monolingual teachers; little recognition of the learning that takes place out of school and in another language and culture; and the problems facing ethnic minority children when first encountering the culture, values and language of school. Her argument was that all teachers need to be conscious of their implicit expectations and evaluations of pupil responses and behaviours, and to be more open-minded about what constitutes success, given that all pupils should be interested by, and engaged with, the curriculum.

### The reporting of the results

Before the 1991 SAT period began, it was understood that this first national experience of the assessments should be 'unreported', implying that the results would not be published. As we shall see in the next chapter, this kind of report-ing needs careful contextualization of the information in order to interpret it in appropriate ways. However, in the winter following the first administration, the government in fact published a listing of performance on the SATs by Local Education Authority. Justifiably this caused outcry, not least because the LEAs had given rather varied messages to their schools about the signifi-cance of the assessments and in many cases had not submitted complete sets of results. In Bradford, for instance (Conway, 1992), teachers had been advised to carry out the assessments rigorously, even if they could not com-plete them all for every child. This gave rise to many partial scores which generated poor outcomes. Bradford performed poorly in these first 'league tables', partly because of the kind of pupils in many of its schools (very high proportions of bilingual, ethnic minority pupils) but also because of the advice they had given to schools. Amended versions of the results were pub-lished later, but this did little to mollify the sense of injustice felt by many LEA staff.

## The outcomes in 1991

Once the first national scores were available, at least from nationally represen-tative samples of pupils, it became possible to analyse whether particular groups of pupils performed differently from others in the scores they attained.

At Key Stage 1, with mainly three possible 'Levels' of outcome this might not seem significant, especially as particular activities or questions that appeared to favour one group over another would have been eliminated during trialling. In reality, however, there were many significant differences in the scores/levels between different groups which can be summarized as follows (Shorrocks *et al.*, ibid.). The findings reported here refer to the assessments in English, mathematics and science but not to the assessments of the Welsh language.

### Gender

- Girls' scores were significantly better than boys' scores in English. This applied to English subject scores as a whole and in each of the separate Attainment Targets. It also applied in the SAT scores and in Teacher Assessment scores.

- In mathematics, at whole subject level, there were no significant differences between boys' and girls' attainment. However, in some Attainment Targets (Ma2 and Ma5) girls scored significantly better than boys in Teacher Assessments, although this did not apply in the SAT scores.

- In science, at whole subject level, there were no significant differences between boys' and girls' scores, but girls outperformed boys in some Attainment Targets (Sc5, Sc13 and Sc16) in Teacher Assessment scores. The SAT confirmed this difference in attainment in Sc5.

It is interesting that these outcomes foreshadow some of the present findings on the higher achievements of girls in the education system.

### The performance of children with and without pre-school experience

When comparisons were made between the scores of 7-year-olds who had and had not had pre-school educational experience, the results showed that:

- children with pre-school educational experience performed significantly better than those without in English and mathematics (total subject scores);

- for Teacher Assessment and SAT assessment, scores on both 'Reading' and 'Writing' Attainment Targets were significantly better for children with pre-school education;

- in mathematics, for both Teacher Assessments and SAT scores there were no significant differences in outcomes in the Attainment Targets to do with

'Number', but there were differences in the 'process' Attainment Target, Ma1;

- in science, there were few significant differences in the scoring patterns of the two groups, except in one Attainment Target, Sc3 (Processes of Life).

### The performance of children from different ethnic backgrounds and the effect of home language

Using census categories of ethnicity (White, Black Caribbean, Indian/ Pakistani), analysis of the scores of the national sample showed that:

- whole subject scores, for both Teacher Assessments and the SATs in English, mathematics and science were significantly different for the ethnic groups;

- Pakistani children tended to attain lower levels in all three subjects than the other groups;

- Black Caribbean and Indian children tended to attain lower levels than White children in English and mathematics but not in science;

- whole subject scores and all Attainment Target scores, both in Teacher Assessment and in the SATs, showed significant differences in favour of children whose home language was English.

### The performance of children from different social backgrounds

Social background is not an easy variable to measure in such evaluation studies, since it either involves the collection of detailed (and potentially intrusive) family information, or relies on a problematic measure, such as the number of children in a school claiming free school meals. The free school meals measure is unreliable in a national sample, since the criteria for awarding them are locally determined and may therefore vary from region to region. The national evaluation (Shorrocks *et al.*, 1992) used postcodes as an index of social background, since this is now a well-established market research tool. The ACORN system was used, which yielded over 30 different categories of neighbourhoods which were then grouped into four broad categories, namely: *high status*; *high intermediate*; *low intermediate* and *low status*. Using these categorizations, the analysis showed that:

- at subject level, and for all individual Attainment Targets in both Teacher Assessment and the SAT scores, there was a declining pattern of attainment by neighbourhood status. Children from high status neighbourhoods scored significantly higher than those from lower social class areas.

This is one of the most pervasive findings of all: the social background of children, as designated by the neighbourhood in which they live, is one of the most significant influences on test scores.

### The performance of children of different ages

The cohort of children taking the tests in 1991 ranged in age from 6 years 9 months to 7 years 8 months. This is the result of the annualized intake policy that prevails in English and Welsh schools: the pupils in any one year group can have almost a year's difference in their ages, yet they are all assessed at the same point in time. The age cohort can therefore be divided into three age-sets, approximating to the three terms in the school year. When analysis of the scores was carried out in relation to these age categories, the results were that:

• for whole subject scores, and for all individual Attainment Targets, for both Teacher Assessments and SAT assessments, there were significant differences in the outcomes for the three age-sets.

However, this age effect may be the result of the length of time the child has spent in school. In England and Wales, schools have different intake policies at age 5. Some admit all children in the September of the year in which they are 5 and so, irrespective of birth date, all children will have three terms of schooling in their reception year in school. On the other hand, some schools stagger intakes so that the older children in the age-group begin in September, while the younger ones (the summer-born children) begin either in January or April. In this case, the youngest children may receive only one or two terms of schooling in their reception year in school.

This matter was investigated in the national evaluation sample (Shorrocks *et al.*, ibid., Daniels *et al.*, 1999) which contained children who had received seven, eight, or nine terms of schooling by the age of 7. In particular, it included a number of children who were summer-born (that is, the youngest in the age cohort) who, because of the regional location/intake policy of their school, had received either seven, eight or nine terms of schooling. Analysis showed that the number of terms of infant schooling did not have a significant effect on their scores in the assessments. It was their age position within the class that was of primary importance. This finding is of great significance, since it implies that we should look either to maturational factors or to processes going on in the classroom (such as teachers implicitly or explicitly having different expectations of, and giving different treatment to, younger and older pupils in the group) for an explanation of the effects of age on the scoring outcomes in the tests.

Essentially, all these findings are equal opportunities issues thrown up by the national testing, as they are by all assessment and monitoring. They give weight to the arguments made by Gipps (1992), who argues that equal opportunities issues in assessment rest on two questions: is there bias in the assessments themselves and are the comparisons fair? In other words, have all the pupils being tested had the same opportunities to learn? Wood (1987) referred to these as the opportunity to acquire talent and the opportunity to show this talent to good effect. The items in a test can be evaluated in terms of their *content* bias (does the content of a question favour one group over another, for instance girls or boys?) and in terms of their *statistical* functioning ( do the *scoring outcomes* appear to favour one group over another?). These should ideally be implemented during the early development and trialling of questions, so that biased questions can be eliminated. The matter of the scoring outcomes, however, presents more difficulties. The results reported earlier in this section show that gender, ethnicity/language, social background, age and the experience of pre-school education all influence the test results at Key Stage 1 – a finding that is repeated in much of the testing at the other Key Stages and in all other examinations where analyses have been carried out. This is an issue to which we will return in later chapters.

## The results of the 1991 experience

The outcry during and after the SATs in 1991 gave rise to a streamlining of the assessments for the subsequent year. This took the form of assessing only seven Attainment Targets in the SAT, distributing the SAT materials earlier, and allowing a longer time for the testing, dropping some of the more time-consuming group discussions and introducing more written testing. The time-consuming assessment of the 'process' Attainment Targets in mathematics and science was also eliminated, even though these were well regarded in educational terms. However, the assessments were increased, in that a spelling test was included for pupils at Levels 3 and 4, and a new Level (Level 4) was also added in the second year of testing (1992). The advent of the spelling test seems to have been the idea of the newly installed head of the School Examination and Assessment Council (SEAC), Lord Griffiths.

This process of streamlining and change has continued ever since, and the easiest way to summarize the changes is through tabulation. This is done in *Table 5.1* for the years from 1991 to 1998.

## The main points of change between 1991 and 1998

1. As we have seen, the tests were streamlined in 1992, in terms of their coverage and range and also in the time allowed to carry them out. By 1992 also, they had been extended to cover Level 4, in order to provide extension

**Table 5.1:** Summary of the structure of the assessments at Key Stage 1, 1991 to 1998

| Date | English | Welsh | Mathematics | Science |
|---|---|---|---|---|
| 1991 | **Test period/dates**<br>First half of Summer term<br>Approximately 17 hours per class *<br>**Levels covered**<br>1, 2 and 3<br>**Structure of tasks/tests**<br>Activities for each Attainment Target:<br>En2: reading aloud from a set book<br>En3: planning and writing a story<br>En4: spelling assessed via story<br>En5: handwriting assessed through story | **Test period/dates**<br>First half of Summer term<br>**Levels covered**<br>1, 2 and 3<br>**Structure of tasks/tests**<br>Activities for each Attainment Target<br>Tasks and activities to cover:<br>Cy1: group communication activities<br>Cy2: reading aloud from selected books<br>Cy3:/4 writing and handwriting assessed through story | **Test period/dates**<br>First half of Summer term<br>Approximately 8 hours per class*<br>**Levels covered**<br>1, 2 and 3<br>**Structure of tasks/tests**<br>Activities for each Attainment Target<br>Ma1: devising a game<br>Ma3: playing the game plus worksheet<br>Optional choice, one of the following:<br>Ma5: making number patterns with cubes<br>Ma8: shop activity, weighing, buying etc.<br>Ma10: sorting 2-D and 3-D shapes<br>Ma13: collecting information and representing it in a graph | **Test period/dates**<br>First half of Summer term<br>Approximately 9 hours per class*<br>**Levels covered**<br>1, 2 and 3<br>**Structure of tasks/tests**<br>Activities for each Attainment Target<br>Sc1: 'floating and sinking' objects in water<br>Optional choice, one of the following:<br>Sc3: naming parts of the body<br>Sc5: observing change and decay in materials<br>Sc6: sorting and comparing materials |
| 1992 | **Test period/dates**<br>Mid-point in Spring term to mid-point in Summer term<br>Approximately 22 hours per class *<br>**Levels covered**<br>1, 2, 3, and 4<br>**Structure of tasks/tests**<br>Activities for each Attainment Target<br>En2: reading aloud from a set book with A–E sub-gradings at Level 2<br>En3: planning and writing a story<br>En4: spelling assessed via story<br>En5: handwriting assessed through story | **Test period/dates**<br>Mid-point in Spring term to mid-point in Summer term<br>**Levels covered**<br>1, 2, 3, and 4<br>**Structure of tasks/tests**<br>Activities for each Attainment Target<br>Tasks and activities to cover:<br>Cy1: three group activities per pupil<br>Cy2: reading aloud from selected books<br>Cy3:/4: writing and handwriting assessed through story | **Test period/dates**<br>Mid-point in Spring term to mid-point in Summer term<br>Approximately 12 hours per class *<br>**Levels covered**<br>1, 2, 3, and 4<br>**Structure of tasks/tests**<br>Activities for each Attainment Target<br>Ma3: throwing a dice and adding and subtracting<br>Optional choice, one of the following:<br>Ma12: sorting objects into groups plus worksheet<br>Ma14: Number spinners (probability) plus worksheet | **Test period/dates**<br>Mid-point in Spring term to mid-point in Summer term<br>Approximately 7 hours per class *<br>**Levels covered**<br>1, 2, 3, and 4<br>**Structure of tasks/tests**<br>Activities for each Attainment Target<br>Optional choice, one of the following:<br>Sc6: sorting and comparing materials plus worksheet<br>Sc9: activity about the weather, using symbols |

*Estimated times based on individual activity timings for a class of 30 children

| | | | | |
|---|---|---|---|---|
| **1993** | **Test period/dates**<br>Mid-point of Spring term to one month before end of Summer term<br>Approximately 22 hours per class*<br>**Levels covered**<br>1, 2, 3 and 4<br>**Structure of tasks/tests**<br>Activities for each Attainment Target<br>En2: reading aloud from a set book with A-E sub-gradings at Level 2<br>En3: planning and writing a story<br>En4: spelling assessed via story<br>En5: handwriting assessed through story<br>Optional reading/spelling tests | **Test period/dates**<br>Mid-point of Spring term to one month before end of Summer term<br>**Levels covered**<br>1, 2, 3 and 4<br>**Structure of tasks/tests**<br>Activities for each Attainment Target<br>Tasks and activities to cover:<br>Cy1: two group activities per pupil<br>Cy2: reading aloud from selected books<br>Cy3/4: writing and handwriting assessed through story | **Test period/dates**<br>Mid-point of Spring term to one month before end of Summer term<br>Approximately 12 hours per class*<br>**Levels covered**<br>1, 2, 3 and 4<br>**Structure of tasks/tests**<br>Activities for each Attainment Target<br>**New Attainment Targets**<br>Ma2: (Number) number facts, 'Ring Game' and 'School Fair' activities with number and money<br>Ma3:(Algebra) repeating patterns, number patterns, and 'Number Machine' | **Test period/dates**<br>Mid-point of Spring term to one month before end of Summer term<br>Approximately 8 hours per class*<br>**Levels covered**<br>1, 2, 3 and 4<br>**Structure of tasks/tests**<br>**New Attainment targets**<br>Activities for each Attainment Target<br>Sc4: (Physical Processes)<br>Sunlight, electricity, magnets activities at the four levels |
| **1994** | **Test period/dates**<br>Mid-point of Spring term to one month before end of Summer term<br>**Levels covered**<br>1, 2, 3, and 4.<br>**Structure of tasks/tests**<br>Attainment Targets assessed through a mixture of activities and tests for the different Levels<br>En2: Reading Interview (Levels 1-2)<br>Reading Comprehension Test (Levels 3-4)<br>En3: writing activity (Levels 1-4)<br>En4: Spelling Test (Levels 2-4)<br>En5: assessed through passage of writing (Levels 1-4) | **Test period/dates**<br>Mid-point of Spring term to one month before end of Summer term<br>**Levels covered**<br>1, 2, 3, and 4<br>**Structure of tasks/tests**<br>Activities for each Attainment Target<br>Tasks and activities to cover:<br>Cy1: one group activity per pupil<br>Cy2: reading aloud from selected books<br>Cy3/4: writing and handwriting assessed through story, plus an optional spelling test | **Test period/dates**<br>Mid-point of Spring term to one month before end of Summer term<br>**Levels covered**<br>1, 2, 3, and 4<br>**Structure of tasks/tests**<br>Ma2; addition and subtraction activities, recipe ingredients (weights and temperature), visiting a Wildlife Park (fractions, decimals, percentages) (Levels 1-4)<br>Number Test (Levels 2-4) | **No compulsory standard task or test in science.** Teachers must make their statutory Teacher Assessments against the National Curriculum levels.<br>Optional materials to support Teacher Assessment provided for 1994. |

| Date | English | Welsh | Mathematics | Science |
|---|---|---|---|---|
| 1995 | **Test period/dates**<br>Mid-point of Spring term to two weeks before end of Summer term<br>Tests<br>**Levels covered**<br>1, 2 and 3. Level 4 covered by using Key Stage 2 tests in late May/early June.<br>**Structure of tasks/tests**<br>En2: Reading task (Levels 1-2)<br>Optional reading Comprehension test (Level 2)<br>Reading Comprehension Test (Level 3)<br>En3 and En5: writing task but without an assessment of re-drafting<br>En4: assessed through writing activity (Level 1)<br>Spelling Test (Levels 2-4) | **Test period/dates**<br>Mid-point of Spring term to two weeks before end of Summer term.<br>**Levels covered**<br>1, 2, 3, and 4<br>**Structure of tasks/tests**<br>Activities for each Attainment Target<br>Tasks and activities to cover:<br>**Cy1**: group response to a video<br>**Cy2**: reading aloud from selected books<br>**Cy3/4**: writing and handwriting assessed through several options: story, postcard, recording an experience.<br>Optional spelling test | **Test period/dates**<br>Mid-point of Spring term to two weeks before end of Summer term.<br>**Levels covered**<br>1, 2 and 3. Level 4 covered by using Key Stage 2 tests in late May/early June.<br>**Structure of tasks/tests**<br>Task for Level 1<br>Test for Mathematics (Levels 2 and 3)<br>Both these to cover **Ma3**: (Algebra), **Ma4**: Shape and Space as well as a major focus on **Ma2**: (Number) | **No statutory tasks or tests in science.** Optional assessment materials from 1993 could be used.<br>Teacher Assessments to be made according to agreed rules. |
| 1996 | **Test period/dates**<br>Task: assessment period from beginning January to one month before end of Summer term<br>Tests: during May, optional test approximately 40 minutes each<br>**Levels covered**<br>1, 2 and 3. Level 4 covered by using Key Stage 2 tests in late May/early June.<br>**Structure of tasks/tests**<br>**Based on revised National Curriculum**<br>**Reading:**<br>Task: Levels 1-2<br>Test: Optional Reading Comprehension test (Level 2)<br>Reading Comprehension test (Level 3)<br>**Writing:** writing task (Levels 1-3)<br>Spelling Test (Levels 2-3)<br>Supply cover funding available. | **Test period/dates**<br>Task: assessment period from beginning January to one month before end of Summer term<br>**Levels covered**<br>1, 2 ,3 and 4<br>**Structure of tasks/tests**<br>**Based on revised National Curriculum**<br>Activities for each Attainment Target<br>Tasks and activities to cover:<br>**Cy1**: group response to playing a board game<br>**Cy2**: Level 1: reading words on game board<br>Levels 2-4: reading aloud from selected books<br>**Cy3/4**: writing and handwriting assessed through several options linked to board game<br>Optional spelling test | **Test period/dates**<br>Task: assessment period from beginning January to one month before end of Summer term<br>Tests: during May, optional test approximately 45 minutes<br>**Levels covered**<br>1, 2 and 3. Level 4 covered by using Key Stage 2 tests in late May / early June<br>**Structure of tasks/tests**<br>**Based on revised National Curriculum**<br>Task: Level 1 activities<br>Test: Mathematics test (Levels 2-3)<br>Both these to cover **Ma3**: (Algebra), **Ma4**: (Shape and Space) well as a major focus on **Ma2**: (Number)<br>Supply cover funding available. | **No statutory tasks or tests in science.**<br>Teacher Assessments to be made according to the agreed rules.<br>Assessment at Level 4 possible but through Teacher Assessment. Key Stage 1 children not to be entered for Key Stage 2 tests in science. |

| | English (Reading) | English (Speaking/Listening) | Mathematics | Science |
|---|---|---|---|---|
| **1997** | **Test period/dates**<br>Task: assessment period from beginning January to one month before end of Summer term<br>Tests: during May, approximately 40 minutes and 30 minutes<br>**Levels covered**<br>1, 2 and 3. Level 4 covered by using Key Stage 2 tests in late May/early June.<br>**Levels covered**<br>Levels 1, 2 and 3<br>**Structure of tasks/tests**<br>**Reading:**<br>Task: Levels 1–2 activities<br>Test: Reading Comprehension Test (Level 2)<br>Reading Comprehension test (Level 3)<br>**Writing:** writing task (Levels 1–3)<br>Spelling Test (Levels 1–3)<br>Age standardized scores on tests.<br>Use of OMR sheets for recording results.<br>Supply cover funding available. | **Test period/dates**<br>Task: assessment period from beginning January to one month before end of Summer term<br>**Levels covered**<br>Levels 1, 2 and 3<br>**Structure of tasks/tests**<br>Activities for each Attainment Target<br>Tasks and activities to cover:<br>**Cy1:** group response to playing a (new) board game<br>**Cy2:** Level 1: reading words on game board<br>Levels 2–3: reading aloud from selected books<br>**Cy3/4:** writing and handwriting assessed through several options linked to board game<br>Optional spelling test | **Test period/dates**<br>Task: assessment period from beginning January to one month before end of Summer term<br>Tests: during May, optional test approximately 45 minutes<br>**Levels covered**<br>1, 2 and 3. Level 4 covered by using Key Stage 2 tests in late May/early June<br>**Structure of tasks/tests**<br>Task: Level 1 activities<br>Test: Mathematics test (Levels 2–3)<br>To cover **Ma3**: (Algebra), **Ma4**: (Shape and Space) and a major focus on **Ma2** (Number)<br>Use of OMR sheets for recording results.<br>Supply cover funding available. | **No statutory tasks or tests in science.**<br>Teacher Assessments to be made according to the agreed rules<br><br>Assessment at Level 4 possible but through Teacher Assessment. Key Stage 1 children not to be entered for Key Stage 2 tests in science.<br><br>Teacher Assessments done automatically through the use of OMR sheets.<br>Supply cover funding available. |
| **1998** | **Test period/dates**<br>Task: assessment period from beginning January to one month before end of Summer term<br>Tests: during May, approximately 40 minutes and 30 minutes<br>**Levels covered**<br>1, 2 and 3. Level 4 covered by using Key Stage 2 tests in late May/early June.<br>**Structure of tasks/tests**<br>**Reading:**<br>Task: Levels 1–2 activities<br>Test: Reading Comprehension Test (Level 2)<br>Reading Comprehension Test (Level 3)<br>**Writing:** writing task (Levels 1–3)<br>Spelling Test (Levels 1–3)<br>Age standardized scores on tests.<br>Use of OMR sheets for recording results.<br>Supply cover funding available. | **Test period/dates**<br>Task: assessment period from beginning January to one month before end of Summer term<br>**Levels covered**<br>1, 2 and 3<br>**Structure of tasks/tests**<br>Activities for each Attainment Target<br>Tasks and activities to cover:<br>**Cy1:** group response to a magazine<br>**Cy2:** Level 1: reading words in magazine<br>Levels 2–3: reading aloud from passage in magazine<br>**Cy3/4:** writing and handwriting assessed through several options linked to magazine<br>Optional spelling test | **Test period/dates**<br>Task: assessment period from beginning January to one month before end of Summer term<br>Tests: during May, approximately 40 minutes and 30 minutes<br>**Levels covered**<br>1, 2 and 3. Level 4 covered by using Key Stage 2 tests in late May/early June.<br>**Structure of tasks/tests**<br>Task: Level 1 activities<br>Test: Mathematics Test (Levels 2–3)<br>Age standardized scores<br>To cover **Ma3**: (Algebra), **Ma4**: (Shape and Space) and a major focus on **Ma2** (Number)<br>Use of OMR sheets for recording results.<br>Supply cover funding available. | **No statutory tasks or tests in science.**<br>Teacher Assessments to be made according to the agreed rules<br><br>Assessment at Level 4 possible but through Teacher Assessment. Key Stage 1 children not to be entered for Key Stage 2 tests in science<br><br>Teacher Assessments done automatically through the use of OMR sheets.<br>Supply cover funding available. |

activities for the higher attaining pupils, although this did not continue to be the case in Wales after 1996.

2. In fact, the situation has always been somewhat different in the assessment of the Welsh language as one of the core subjects. The most obvious point here is that the first Attainment Target (Oracy, Cy1) has always been assessed through a classroom-based task, unlike English. However, an even more significant difference is that the assessments in Welsh have never been marks-based. Pupil responses (both oral and written) are instead judged in relation to the National Curriculum levels, either through the Statements of Attainment (pre-1995) or against the Level Descriptions (post-1995) on a best-fit basis. This approach was adopted because of a fear that the use of marks would lead teachers away from looking in detail at the child's response and using more general criteria instead.

3. The general timing allocation continued from 1992 to 1995, with the test period running from the mid-point in the Spring term each year until just before the end of the summer term. From 1996 onwards, by which time the structure of the approach had changed, the task element of the assessments (Level 1) could be carried out between January and July with the written test elements occurring during May. This pattern continues.

4. In 1994, the decision was taken to restrict the testing to English, Welsh and mathematics: the statutory tests in science for this Key Stage were abandoned. After this, teachers still had to carry out Teacher Assessments in science, with support materials provided. Unlike English and mathematics (from 1995 onwards), the use of the Key Stage 2 tests to assess Level 4 was not encouraged: instead it had to be done through Teacher Assessment. It was thought that Key Stage 1 pupils would not have covered enough of the more specialized Key Stage 2 science curriculum for the use of the tests to be appropriate. In Welsh, the Key Stage tests were not used to assess Level 4 in any case.

5. As the curriculum became progressively modified over the years, with the number of Attainment Targets and their contents being reduced, the tests were able to address more of them, so putting a question mark on the precise role of Teacher Assessments in the core subjects, excluding science. The Dearing review (1993) clarified this by recommending that it should be reported to parents separately, with its particular qualities emphasized.

6. The move throughout this period has been away from practical, activity-based assessments towards pencil and paper tests, at least in English and mathematics. It is not the case for Welsh, however. This has no doubt improved the assessments in terms of their manageability and to some

extent their reliability, but at the expense of validity considerations. The move towards written tests has considerable implications for the performance of pupils with special educational needs and also for bilingual pupils. Level 1 continues to be addressed through tasks/activities, so this comment does not apply.

7. Hargreaves (1996) puts forward some interesting arguments about the new approach to testing (in mathematics) from 1995 onwards, when more formal tests became the order of the day. She suggests that there are question marks about the authenticity of these tests, since they are less likely to be an appropriate representation of the range of mathematical performance required by the curriculum. They give a better coverage of the range of content of the curriculum than did the previous tasks, but the pencil and paper format restricts the kinds of skills and strategies that can be assessed. There are special problems in assessing *Shape, space and measures* in test formats because of the need for practical handling of the shapes with pupils of this age. Even in the other aspects of the curriculum, however, there are problems devising simple questions that allow the assessment of such aspects of the mathematics curriculum as recognizing relationships, developing individualistic mental methods and solving problems through understanding and relating mathematics to purposeful contexts.

In addition to these changes, the wide-ranging review of testing (SCAA, 1996) recommended that age standardized scores should be provided for schools. This implies that a pupil's raw score becomes translated into a standardized score that takes account of their date of birth. In general terms, it has the effect of lowering the scores of the older pupils in the cohort and raising the scores of the younger ones. This was no doubt an attempt to interpret the scores in a more valid way, given the kinds of age-effects presented in the previous sections.

This review recommended the introduction of external marking for the tests at Key Stages 2 and 3, but not at Key Stage 1. This was justified on the grounds of the smaller scale of the testing at Key Stage 1. However, in acknowledgement of the time needed to administer the tests and tasks with 7-year-olds, limited supply cover (costs to cover staff time) was allowed to support the work. It was also recommended that the rigour of the audit of the Key Stage 1 assessments (carried out by LEA staff) should be improved.

In 1996, NFER were commissioned to carry out a formal evaluation of the Key Stage 1 assessments (Sizmur and Burley, 1997) and their conclusions were that the assessment system overall was functioning 'reasonably satisfactorily' (p. 115). There was still some resistance among teachers to the idea of testing 7-year-olds, but they commented that the workload involved was now more appropriate, helped by the externally funded supply cover. They also reported that the balance and pattern of the tasks/written tests was appropriate, although they did not feel the use of the Key Stage 2 tests was appropriate, even with the higher-attaining pupils at this age. From 1997, the Reading Comprehension test was made statutory, as part of the increased drive towards more formalized testing, even of 7-year-olds. This was not well received by teachers, and it seemed to pose a threat to the manageability of the testing programme as a whole. Also, the 1995 curriculum review, introducing as it did the use of Level Descriptions for teacher assessment, were the source of some apprehension and deemed to be in need of monitoring for the first few years of their use.

The evaluation also suggested that there was still a 'degree of inconsistency in teachers' administration' of the tasks and tests, particularly the Level 3 Reading Test' (p. 117). They found wide variation in the conditions in which the pupils took the tests and there were differences in the amount and nature of the support offered by teachers and the speed with which pupils had their queries answered. The recommendation was that the test procedures should be further clarified, with clearer guidance about what kind of support could be offered. Surprisingly, even after several years of experience of the Key Stage 1 assessments, the evaluation concluded that there was still some insecurity and variation in the way teacher assessments were carried out and good practice was still in need of wider dissemination. Finally, it was pointed out that more use could be made of the outcomes of the assessments, in terms of the planning of teaching and monitoring of the curriculum.

It is interesting to note that, in general, later evaluations and comments have been kinder to the Key Stage 1 assessments: we have come some way from the strident newspaper headlines and criticism that emerged in the early years. In fact it is now the Key Stage where most assessment expertise seems to lie, teachers having carried out the work since 1991.

### The results of the testing: performance data

How well have pupils done on the tests since 1991 and what percentages of the age group have been awarded the three/four possible levels? National performance information has been published at Key Stage 1 since 1994 and this is presented in *Table 5.2*. It is based on official figures from the Qualifications and Curriculum Authority (QCA, 1998f) and does not include the outcomes in Welsh. *Table 5.2* separates out the *Reading* and *Writing* elements of English for both the tests and tasks and Teacher Assessment. However, Teacher Assessment information is not provided for mathematics in any of these years because, in the official documentation, they are given for each of the four aspects of the mathematics curriculum separately rather than for the subject as a whole. The only other comment that needs to be made concerns the data for

**Table 5.2:** The percentage of pupils attaining Levels 1–4 in English and mathematics in the national testing at Key Stage 1, 1994 to 1997

| Year | Subject | Assessment | W* | 1 | 2 | 3 | 4+ |
|------|---------|-----------|-----|-----|-----|-----|-----|
| | | | | | *Percentage of pupils at each level* | | |
| 1994 | English | | | | | | |
| | *Reading* | Tests/Tasks | 1 | 18 | 51 | 29 | 0 |
| | | TA** | 1 | 19 | 53 | 27 | 0 |
| | *Writing* | Tests/Tasks | 1 | 31 | 54 | 13 | 0 |
| | | TA | 1 | 29 | 57 | 13 | 0 |
| | Mathematics | Tests/Tasks | 2 | 16 | 59 | 22 | 0 |
| 1995 | English | | | | | | |
| | *Reading* | Tests/Tasks | 1 | 20 | 45 | 33 | 0 |
| | | TA | 1 | 20 | 50 | 29 | 0 |
| | *Writing* | Tests/Tasks | 1 | 18 | 65 | 15 | 0 |
| | | TA | 1 | 21 | 63 | 14 | 0 |
| | Mathematics | Tests/Tasks | 2 | 18 | 59 | 19 | 0 |
| 1996 | English | | | | | | |
| | *Reading* | Tests/Tasks | 3 | 18 | 45 | 33 | 0 |
| | | TA | 3 | 18 | 50 | 29 | 0 |
| | *Writing* | Tests/Tasks | 5 | 15 | 65 | 15 | 0 |
| | | TA | 5 | 18 | 63 | 14 | 0 |
| | Mathematics | Tests/Tasks | 3 | 15 | 63 | 19 | 0 |
| 1997 | English | | | | | | |
| | *Reading* | Tasks | 3 | 16 | 54 | | 0 |
| | | Tests | | | 49 | 26 | 0 |
| | | TA | 3 | 17 | 54 | 26 | 0 |
| | *Writing* | Tasks | 5 | 13 | 74 | 6 | 0 |
| | | Tests | | | 47 | 14 | 0 |
| | | TA | 5 | 17 | 68 | 10 | 0 |
| | Mathematics | Tests/Tasks | 3 | 14 | 63 | 20 | 0 |

\*  W=those pupils still working towards Level 1
\*\*  Teacher Assessment

1997. As *Table 5.1* showed, this was the year when the divide between assessment through tasks and tests was reported separately.

*Table 5.2* tells some interesting stories about the performance of our 7-year-olds over this time period. Since 1994, there has been a small increase in the numbers of pupils awarded 'W', implying that they have not yet demonstrated attainment of the Level 1 curriculum requirements. What is also interesting is that the outcomes for *Writing* are consistently lower than those for *Reading*. This finding does not seem to be in line with current government policies of focusing on the improvement of reading skills in our schools. However, given the information in this table, it is not easy to talk about more general trends in attainment over time for this Key Stage. This is largely because of the introduction of a more formal testing regime since 1997, which makes direct comparison across the years almost impossible. Even between 1994 and 1997, when the assessments were more comparable, there seem to be few clear trends in either English or mathematics.

## Subject comments on pupil performance in the assessments

### English

This *Standards Report* for Key Stage 1 (QCA, 1998f) indicated that in *Reading*, the task-based assessments for Level 1, the involvement of discussion about selected books was well liked by teachers. At Levels 2 and 3, however, there was the suggestion that pupils needed more experience of making inferences beyond the literal meaning of the text and drawing conclusions from across texts as a whole. In *Writing*, the major criticism was that pupils too often chose to write narrative, rather than show experience of other forms which they seemed to have little idea how to structure and organize. Their stories often contained dialogue, but this was seldom used to develop the plot or characters in a positive way and most sentence co-ordination was through the use of 'and' and 'but'. The assessment of *Spelling* revealed that pupils were relying too much on the sounds of words and not enough on their visual pattern and that consonant doubling was a problem for many.

### Mathematics

Detailed consideration of the mathematical performance of pupils at Key Stage 1 showed that children's counting strategies were well established with smaller numbers but still in need of consolidation with larger numbers. In *Number*, only the higher attaining 7-year-olds showed real understanding of the 'equals' sign and subtraction, multiplication and division operations were a weakness with all but the highest attainers. In *Shape, space and measures*, pupils could recognize simple geometric properties of two-dimensional shapes and in *Handling data*, they could interpret simple information in a table but not make more difficult comparisons. In general, questions involving two-step reasoning were badly done, suggesting a need for more experience of deciding upon the mathematics involved in a problem and then carrying it out.

## Summary

Key Stage 1 was the first to be assessed within the National Curriculum, and it represents one of the first attempts anywhere in the world to implement a classroom-based, criterion-referenced assessment system with such young pupils. The TGAT report had suggested an activity-based approach to assessment for 7-year-olds, but the scope of the curriculum in the core subjects meant that the SATs could address only a small part of this specification, leaving the matter of the assessment of the rest rather problematic. Teacher Assessment was the first solution to be tried, but the scale of the curriculum made this a daunting and unacceptable answer. Political considerations also precluded having Teacher Assessment (even well-moderated assessments) as the major monitoring device for the new curriculum. This was no doubt part of the beginning of the questioning of the first versions of the National Curriculum. The main points made in this chapter are as follows.

- The first SATs had been extensively and expensively developed and piloted and important lessons were learned. However, the pilots involved only small numbers of schools and teachers, so the vast majority of schools in England and Wales were almost totally unprepared for the scale and intensity of the first assessments.

- The 1991 SAT administrations caused controversy because of the massive demands made upon teachers and pupils and the disruption they caused in schools. The quality of the outcomes was also to some extent suspect. Consultation conferences were held on a national scale after the experience, and changes were made to the assessments for 1992.

- The 1991 administration had originally been intended to be unreported and was in fact referred to in the early days as the 'First Unreported Run' (FUR). There was therefore some consternation when the government decided to publish a 'league table' of performance, listed by LEA. It was clear that different LEAs had interpreted the significance of the 1991 run in very different ways, and therefore there was a sense of injustice at the unexpected publication of the results.

- Analysis of the scoring outcomes in relation to different groups of pupils showed that the kinds of influences that affect all assessment outcomes were at work in the national testing too, despite considerable efforts to make the assessment activities as fair as possible. The scores were influenced by such factors as gender, ethnicity and pre-school experience and, most particularly, by age and social background. This raises important equal opportunities questions about the tests.

- However, one of these significant influences, the age of the child, was not found to be a direct result of the length of time the child had been in school. In 1996, age-standardized scores were introduced at Key Stage 1 in order to support schools in interpreting the scoring in a more valid and equitable way.

- From 1991 to 1996, a changing curriculum and a changing emphasis about the purpose and nature of the assessments led to an approach based very much more on pencil and paper tests, a move that undoubtedly improves manageability for the teachers but which may have less validity in educational terms for pupils of this age.

- In 1996, the major national review of testing revealed that the Key Stage 1 assessments were mostly satisfactory but that, even after many years of implementation, there were still question marks about the dependability of the outcomes.

- The published national results of the assessments show that pupils do better at reading than at writing but that it is not really possible to detect any trends over time in terms of improvements or deterioration. The nature of the testing has changed so such comparisons cannot be made.

# 6 The tests at Key Stage 2: high profile testing

The test development process at Key Stage 2 began in 1991 (for English) and 1992 (for mathematics and science), with the first pilot tests being used nationally in 1994. By this time, many of the main educational and political issues had been confronted and to some extent ruled upon, at Key Stages 1 and 3 by the powers that be. For instance, the idea of small group, practically-based assessment activities for most of the age cohort had been firmly quelled at Key Stage 3 (Daugherty, 1995), and even with 7-year-olds at Key Stage 1 the move was increasingly towards pencil and paper tests (see *Table 5.1*). At Key Stage 2, therefore, there was little question about the kind of assessment to be put in place: pencil and paper tests were the requirement for the majority of the age group, but with some wider assessment scope for the lower attainers.

As with Key Stage 1, the idea of formal testing with this age group is not new. A few decades earlier, the 11-plus exam was in widespread use in England and, even today, selection at age 11 using this kind of testing is prevalent in some parts of the country. Similarly, schools and LEAs often use published tests of reading and mathematics attainment to screen and monitor performance in the Key Stage 2 years (7- to 11-year-olds). As we have noted before, however, what was new about the national tests was the fact that they were curriculum-based, criterion-referenced assessments, developed in relation to a detailed curriculum specification.

This curriculum (see *Chapter 1*) was, and still is, broad and demanding, a fact which poses problems for primary/middle schools, where the organization of teaching is often class-teacher based, with little scope for specialist teaching (Alexander *et al.*, 1992). This implies that most of the complex and extensive curriculum has to be delivered by the class teacher, albeit with specialist support from subject co-ordinators in schools and LEA staff. It has been recognized that this is not necessarily appropriate and that it requires high levels of knowledge across many subjects on the part of class teachers. It is often cited as one of the main causes of some of the perceived underachievement in the Key Stage 2 years (Richards, 1993).

At the risk of oversimplification, it is important to ask the global question of whether there are general cognitive characteristics of 11-year-olds that may have an influence not only upon the kinds of ideas and concepts they can deal with in curriculum content terms but also upon the kinds of assessment questions and presentational modes they can handle. In curriculum content terms, it could be argued that such developmental constraints should be built into the curriculum specifications themselves, with the requirements of the different levels reflecting and embodying what is known about children's developing cognitive skills and understandings. To some extent this is the case, but the progression through the 10 Levels in most subjects and Attainment Targets is not intended to represent a psychological/developmental model of understanding and skills, nor would such a model be possible given the present state of our knowledge about children's development. In any case, this does not address the matter of assessment as opposed to curriculum constraints.

Research findings on the kinds of understandings, concepts and skills children of this age possess are, to say the least, mixed. In the last two decades, there has been a move away from the formalized 'stages of development' approach to children's thinking, exemplified most clearly in the work of Piaget (1954; 1970), in the light of research findings which seem to indicate that his theory underestimates the capabilities of young children and overemphasizes the rationality of adult thinking (Siegler, 1998). Also, in many ways the Piagetian framework may have acted as a constraining force in setting limited and inappropriate expectations in the minds of child educators (Donaldson, 1987). More open-minded, information-processing and cognitive skills approaches have yielded more productive insights about the detail of children's developing capacities, focusing as they often do on particular aspects of development such as memory, perception, cognitive strategies and reasoning.

This research has been well summarized by Meadows (1993). The main findings are that from birth to, say, the end of the primary school years, children's cognitive skills and understandings are progressing in many ways. Memory (the bedrock of all learning in psychological terms) is becoming more organized, strategic and focused, as are meta memory insights (knowing about the problems of remembering and understanding one's own memory strategies), and knowledge about how to remember and relate items of knowledge to each other (Schneider and Pressley, 1989). Reasoning capacities are increasing and fast developing literacy skills are opening up wider learning possibilities. By the end of the primary years, reading is becoming more skilled, and strategic and writing abilities are increasing, with a gradual move towards being able to structure text and argument and use writing not just in the 'knowledge-telling' way exhibited by young children but rather in more sophisticated, 'knowledge-transforming' ways (Scardamalia and Bereiter, 1986). These are the general patterns that seem to be evident, but, of course, the literature also points to the very great individual variation that exists among children in these kinds of developments.

In relation to the tests, these general and individual pupil characteristics pose interesting challenges. Basic literacy skills can be assumed for the vast majority of the age group, making pencil and paper tests a reasonable possibility, but many pupils of this age will not be able to handle abstract ideas nor sustain a line of thinking through a problem for an extended time. What also characterizes this age group is the very great range of skills, understandings and attainments within any group, a factor that poses particular problems for the assessment process.

## Range of attainments

One of the first problems that had to be addressed in the testing at Key Stage 2 was precisely this range of attainments. The TGAT projection (see p. 36) suggested that by the end of the Key Stage, attainment could span five or six levels, with an average attainment of Level 4. The majority of the cohort should therefore attain Levels 3, 4 or 5, but provision had to be made for measuring attainment and progress outside this range, at Levels 1, 2 and 6. How should the tests be organized to cover all these levels and what are the constraints and issues? Are pencil and paper tests the best medium for testing all these levels?

### *Possible models*

This is in part the issue of 'tiering', which will be discussed further in the next chapter in relation to Key Stage 3, but since the problem also arises at Key Stage 2, I will mention it here. Given that at Key Stage 2 there are six levels to be covered in the assessments, what are the available ways of doing this? Some of the possibilities ('models' A H) are set out in diagrammatic form in *Figure 6.1*. This shows some of the possible ways in which the tests could be structured or packaged in order to assess the six levels.

In evaluating these possibilities, four factors have to be considered, namely:

- the appropriateness of what each pupil is faced with by way of a task or test;

- the appropriateness of the presentation and response modes at the various levels of attainment;

- manageability in the classroom;

- the need for teachers to make significant 'entry' and 'exit' decisions for each pupil.

**Levels**                                          **Possible models**

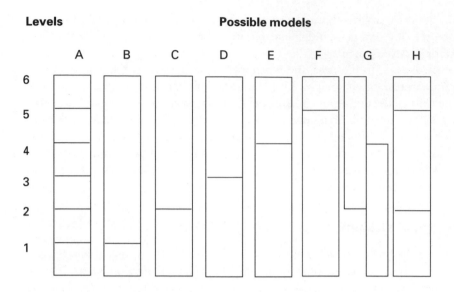

**Figure 6.1**: Some possible test structures ('packages' of Levels within tests) for Levels 1–6 at Key Stage 2.

Applying these to the various models in *Figure 6.1*:

**Model A** shows a situation where each level would be assessed through a level-specific assessment, which could take the form of either a written test or an assessment task/activity. In this situation, the teacher would decide the most appropriate level or levels for each child and would administer the tests accordingly. This approach relies heavily on teacher judgements, which may under- or over-estimate the abilities of some pupils, a very important factor when trying to ensure that each pupil can achieve to their maximum capacity in the testing. Such a model also potentially presents enormous organizational problems in the classroom, since different tests or tasks would have to be administered to different groups, with some pupils perhaps needing to complete more than one test.

**Models B, C, D, E and F** potentially solve some of these problems, but introduce others. All of them show versions of tests or tasks that cover more than one level of attainment, which certainly eases the classroom manageability issue and reduces the number of entry decisions for the teacher. However, addressing multiple levels within a test may cause problems for the pupils. In Model B, for instance, imagine a child who is capable of dealing with questions or activities at Level 2 or 3, but who is also faced at the end of the test with questions that are intended for Level 6. The effect could well be daunting and put them off completely, with fatigue perhaps also posing a problem, given the number of questions to answer. On the other hand, given the 'patchiness' of many children's knowledge, they may well be able to deal with some of the harder questions, which would indeed enable them to show their maximum competence. By the same token, it could be argued that asking a high-attaining pupil to do questions at levels very far below their competence is a waste of testing time and may in fact detract from their performance at the higher levels, since they may be disconcerted by very easy questions and try to read more complexity into them than is intended. These problems are somewhat less in Models C, D and E, where fewer levels are covered in each test package.

Of course, the packaging of the tests in any of these ways also has to be seen in relation to presentation and response modes. Mixing practical assessment tasks with pencil and paper testing seems awkward, especially for classroom organization, so this also imposes constraints. However, the problem in most of these models is that they package the tests in non-overlapping ways, so that the teacher faces difficult decisions for borderline pupils. For example, in Model D, which test should pupils attaining at Level 3 take, the Levels 1–3 test (which may underestimate their possible attainment) or the Levels 3–6 test (which may be very daunting for them)? This particular issue is addressed in Model G.

**Model G** shows overlapping tiers in the test structure; in this case, one test package covering Levels 1 to 4 and another covering Levels 3 to 6. This may solve the problem we have just encountered with Model D since pupils attaining at Level 3 could be entered for a test (the Levels 1– 4 test) which would allow them to show their capabilities at the lower levels but then potentially go beyond to Level 4, if appropriate. In many ways this form of test structure has advantages, providing sustained yet appropriate experiences for most pupils. However, this structure does present some manageability problems since more than one test would need to be administered in most classrooms to cater for the range of attainment, and it does not solve completely the entry decisions for the teacher.

A similar model was trialled in the Key Stage 2 mathematics tests in the early days of development (1993), using a Levels 2–4 test alongside a Levels 3–5 test. Evaluation of the trial, however, revealed an unexpected problem. The Levels 2–4 test was preferred by most Year 6 teachers and they therefore chose it disproportionately to the Levels 3–5 test. If repeated nationally, this could have the effect of potentially lowering attainment overall, since some pupils who could perhaps have attempted the Level 5 questions were denied the opportunity to do so (Shorrocks *et al.*, 1993).

**Model H** shows the kind of structure in fact adopted for most of the Key Stage 2 tests. Bearing in mind many of the points discussed in relation to the other models, it was judged that three attainment levels were probably the maximum that could be addressed in one test, and that for Key Stage 2 these would be Levels 3– 5. The levels outside this range were to be assessed separately, indicating performance well beyond the expected (Level 6, an 'extension' test) or below the expected (Levels 1–2) which, may need to be assessed through activity-based modes more appropriate to these levels of attainment.

In the case of the English assessments, decisions about tiering were difficult and controversial. The Level 3 requirements indicated that pupils should not necessarily be expected to be able to read in a sustained manner, a competence that was only expected at the higher levels. There were therefore good arguments for tiering the papers in a different way, but this was not allowed. Conversely, in the writing test, there may have been good grounds for giving all pupils the same starting-point for their writing and letting the level be judged by the marking later. This is differentiation by outcome, but again it was not allowed.

### Criterion-referencing in the Key Stage 2 tests

When the core subject Key Stage 2 tests were initially developed, the 1991 versions of the curriculum still prevailed which meant that the test questions were based on the Statements of Attainment at each level. As we discussed in *Chapter 4*, however, criterion-referencing was not fully applied in most of the testing. The questions, once developed and based on the 'criteria' in the curriculum, became a vehicle for collecting marks, but these marks were not counted up according to the 'criteria' at each level. Instead, the levels were awarded in the light of 'threshold' scores for each level, irrespective of where the marks had been achieved in the test. This was a version of criterion-referencing, but rather an indirect one.

The changes to the curriculum in 1995 brought about even more changes in the Key Stage 2 assessments. The revised curriculum divided the Programmes of Study according to Key Stages, and hence Levels 1 and 6 were no longer represented in the specification for Key Stage 2. Also, the Programme was not 'levelled' so it was no longer clear what each level should address by way of the detail of the curriculum in any of the assessed core subjects. The implications were that the individual questions in the tests had to be based loosely on the different 'paragraphs' of the curriculum and judgements taken about the appropriate level of difficulty. Attainment levels were still awarded on the basis of marks gained overall in each test, judged in relation to required threshold marks.

To summarize, *Table 6.1* shows the structure of the tests and tasks each year in the core subjects.

**Significant points about the structure and content of the tests, 1994 to 1998**

1. From the first Key Stage 2 pilots in 1994, there had been established an overall structure of assessment tasks at Levels 1 and 2, written tests at the 'main' Levels 3–5 and an 'extension' test to cover Level 6. One exception to this was English in the first years of the assessments, when the written tests covered Levels 3–6, a range that was used because of the nature of the subject, where separating off Level 6 attainment was judged inappropriate. However, from 1996 onwards, largely as a result of the national evaluations of the testing, English was brought into line with the other subjects and separate Level 6 tests were produced.

2. As at Key Stage 1, the assessment of the Welsh language as a core subject in Wales has also had its own character at Key Stage 2. *Oracy* (Cy1) has always been assessed through a classroom task at all levels (though tiered), and the activities have ranged from group discussions of a magazine to discussion of a video. *Reading* (Cy2) has also been assessed partly through an oral task but also through a formal reading test, much as in English. However this has not been mark-based: instead, the Statements of Attainment and later Level Descriptions were used to award a Level for each pupil. The three Attainment Targets were then weighted in the ratio 40:30:30 for *Oracy, Reading* and *Writing*. All evaluations (SCAA, 1995a; 1997a) have suggested that the content of the assessments in Welsh was appropriate and that the materials were of a high quality, often enjoyed by the pupils even though done under test conditions. Teachers in Wales have expressed satisfaction with the overall approach, including the Level 1 and 2 tasks.

3. This notion of weighting the Attainment Targets also applies to English, where marks have been scaled (in various ratios over the years as the pattern of testing has changed) and weighted.

4. Again, virtually from the beginning of the development process, it was judged appropriate to assess Levels 1 and 2 in a different way, through practical assessment activities delivered in either a small-group context or on a one-to-one basis. The pros and cons of this approach to assessment were discussed earlier in *Chapter 4*. Until 1997 these assessments were statutory, but from then on they became optional, with teacher assessment being used instead at these levels. Teachers were advised to use previous assessment activities and materials to support their judgements. It is also worth emphasizing that the Level 1 and 2 assessment approach and materials had always been very well received by teachers, as revealed in most of

**Table 6.1:** The structure of the tests and tasks at Key Stage 2, 1994 to 1998

| Year | English | Welsh | Mathematics | Science |
|---|---|---|---|---|
| 1994 | **Test period/dates/ timings**<br>May<br>**Levels covered**<br>Levels 1–6<br>**Structure of the tasks / tests**<br>**En2: Reading**<br>Task: Levels 1–2 Reading aloud<br>Tests: Levels 3–6 Reading Comprehension Test<br>**En3 / 4 /: Writing** (not En5)<br>Tests:Writing Test (Levels 1–6)<br>Spelling Tests (Levels 1–2 and Levels 3–6)<br>Reading Test: 65 minutes and 60 marks<br>Writing Test: not timed and 24 marks<br>Spelling Test: 10 minutes and 20 marks | **Test period/dates**<br>May (Task dates January– May)<br>**Levels covered**<br>Levels 1–6<br>**Structure of tasks/tests**<br>**Cy1:** A combined oracy and response to reading task (Cy2), Levels 1–2 and 3–6. Silent reading and group discussion.<br>**Cy2:** Reading test, Levels 3–5<br>Reading test, Level 6<br>**Cy3:** Creative writing task, Levels 1–6 (Spelling assessed as part of this)<br>Transactional writing task, Levels 1–3 and 4–6<br>Reading test: 45 minutes<br>Creative writing: untimed<br>Transactional writing: 45 minutes | **Test period/dates**<br>May<br>**Levels covered**<br>Levels 1–6<br>**Structure of tasks/tests**<br>Task: Levels 1–2, practical activities<br>Tests: Paper A (Levels 3–5)<br>Paper B (Levels 3–5)<br>Paper C (Level 6)<br>Papers A and B together: 75 minutes and 120 marks (including 'quick response' questions in Paper A).<br>Paper C: 45 minutes and 35 marks.<br>Tasks and tests cover **Ma2, Ma3, Ma4** and **Ma5.** | **Test period/dates**<br>May<br>**Levels covered**<br>Levels 1–6<br>**Structure of tasks/tests**<br>Task: Levels 1–2, practical activities<br>Tests: Paper A (Levels 3–5)<br>Paper B (Levels 3–5)<br>Paper C (Level 6)<br>Papers A and B together: 70 minutes and 90 marks.<br>Paper C: 45 minutes and 45 marks.<br>Paper C designed for those who have worked on the Key Stage 3 Programme of Study.<br>Tasks and tests cover **Sc2, Sc3** and **Sc4.** |
| 1995 | **Test period/dates**<br>May<br>**Levels covered**<br>Levels 1–6<br>**Structure of tasks/tests**<br>**En2: Reading**<br>Task: Levels 1–2 Reading aloud<br>Tests: Levels 3–6 Reading Comprehension Test<br>**En3:Writing**<br>Tests: Writing Test (Levels 1–6)<br>Spelling Tests (Levels 1–2 and Levels 3–6)<br>Reading Test: 60 minutes and 63 marks<br>Writing Test: 60 minutes and 24 marks<br>Spelling Test: 15 minutes and 20 marks<br>Handwriting: 3 marks | **Test period/dates**<br>May (Task dates January– May)<br>**Levels covered**<br>Levels 1–6<br>**Structure of tasks/tests**<br>**Cy1:** A combined oracy and response to reading task (Cy2), Levels 1–2 and 3–6. Silent reading and group discussion.<br>**Cy2:** Reading test, Levels 1–6<br>**Cy3:** Creative writing task, Levels 1–6 (Spelling assessed as part of this)<br>Reading test: 60 minutes<br>Creative writing: untimed but controlled conditions. | **Test period/dates**<br>May<br>**Levels covered**<br>Levels 1–6<br>**Structure of tasks/tests**<br>Task: Level 1. practical activities<br>Level 2, practical activities<br>Tests: Test A (Levels 3–5)<br>Test B (Levels 3–5)<br>Test C (Level 6)<br>Task timings: 30 minutes each level.<br>Tests A and B together: 70 minutes and 80 marks, with some calculator and some non-calculator questions included.<br>Test C: 30 minutes and 30 marks.<br>Tasks and tests cover **Ma2, Ma3, Ma4** and **Ma5.** | **Test period/dates**<br>May<br>**Levels covered**<br>Levels 1–6<br>**Structure of tasks/tests**<br>Task: Levels 1–2, practical activities<br>Tests: Test A (Levels 3–5)<br>Test B (Levels 3–5)<br>Test C (Level 6 )<br>Task timing; 30 minutes each level.<br>Test A and B together: 70 minutes and 70 marks.<br>Test C: 30 minutes and 30 marks.<br>Test C designed for those who have worked on the Key Stage 3 Programme of Study.<br>Tasks and tests cover **Sc2, Sc3** and **Sc4.** |

| | | | | |
|---|---|---|---|---|
| **1996** | **Test period/dates**<br>May: specific dates<br>**Levels covered**<br>Levels 1–6<br>**Structure of tasks/tests**<br>**Based on revised National Curriculum**<br>**En2: Reading**<br>Task: Levels 1–2 Reading aloud<br>Tests: Levels 3–5 Reading<br>Level 6 Reading Test + Writing<br>Comprehension Test<br>**En3: Writing**<br>Task: Levels 1–2, Writing and spelling<br>Tests: Writing Test (Levels1–2 and 3–5)<br>Spelling Tests (Levels 1–2 and Levels 3–6)<br>Reading Test: 60 minutes and 50 marks<br>Writing Test: 60 minutes and 35 marks<br>Extension Test: 60 minutes and 42 marks<br>Spelling Test: 10 minutes and 10 marks<br>Handwriting: 5 marks | **Test period/dates**<br>May: specific dates (Tasks, January–May)<br>**Levels covered**<br>Levels 1–6<br>**Structure of tasks/tests**<br>**Based on revised National Curriculum**<br>Cy1: A combined oracy and response to reading task (Cy2), Levels 1–2 and 3–6. Silent reading and group discussion.<br>Cy2: Reading test, Levels 3–6<br>Cy3: Transactional writing task, Levels 1–6. Spelling assessed as part of the activity.<br><br>Reading test: 60 minutes<br>Transactional writing untimed but controlled conditions | **Test period/dates**<br>May: specific dates<br>**Levels covered**<br>Levels 1–6<br>**Structure of tasks/tests**<br>**Based on revised National Curriculum**<br>Task: Level 1, practical activities<br>Level 2, practical activities with optional workbooks<br>Tests: Test A (Levels 3–5)<br>Test B (Levels 3–5)<br>Test C (Level 6)<br>Task timings: 30 minutes each level.<br>Tests A and B together: 90 minutes and 80 marks, Test A to be done without a calculator, Test B calculator allowed.<br>Test C: 30 minutes and 30 marks, based on Key Stage 3 Programme of Study. Tasks and tests cover **Ma2, Ma3,** and **Ma4** in 2:1:1 ratio | **Test period/dates**<br>May: specific dates<br>**Levels covered**<br>Levels 1–6<br>**Structure of tasks/tests**<br>**Based on revised National Curriculum**<br>Task: Levels 1–2, practical activities with optional workbooks for Level 2.<br>Tests: Test A (Levels 3–5)<br>Test B (Levels 3–5)<br>Test C (Level 6)<br>Task timing:30 minutes each level.<br>Test A and B together:70 minutes and 89 marks<br>Test C: 30 minutes and 30 marks.<br>Test C designed for those who have worked on the Key Stage 3 Programme of Study.<br>Tasks and tests cover **Sc2, Sc3** and **Sc4.** |
| **1997** | **Test period/dates**<br>May: specific dates<br>**Levels covered**<br>Levels 3–6, Level 1–2 tasks optional, assessed through Teacher Assessment and use of previous materials<br>**Structure of tests**<br>**En2: Reading**<br>Tests: Levels 3–5 Reading<br>Comprehension Test<br>Level 6 Reading Test + Writing<br>**En3 Writing**<br>Tests: Writing Test (Levels 1–5)<br>Spelling Test (Levels 3–5)<br>Reading Test: 45 minutes and 50 marks<br>Writing Test: 60 minutes and 35 marks<br>Extension Test: 60 minutes and 42 marks<br>Spelling Test: 10 minutes and 20 marks<br>Handwriting: 5 marks | **Test period/dates**<br>May: specific dates (Tasks, January–May)<br>**Levels covered**<br>Levels 1–6<br>**Structure of tests**<br>Cy1: A combined oracy and response to reading task (Cy2), Levels 1–2 and 3–6. Silent reading and group discussion.<br>Cy2: Reading test, Levels 3-6<br>Cy3: Creative writing task, Levels 1–6. Spelling assessed as part of the activity.<br>Reading test: 60 minutes<br>Creative writing untimed but controlled conditions | **Test period/dates**<br>May: specific dates<br>**Levels covered**<br>Levels 3–6, Level 1–2 tasks optional, assessed through Teacher Assessment and use of previous materials<br>**Structure of tests**<br>Tests: Test A (Levels 3–5)<br>Test B (Levels 3–5)<br>Test C (Level 6)<br>Tests A and B together: 90 minutes and 80 marks, Test A to be done without a calculator, Test B calculator allowed.<br>Test C: 30 minutes and 30 marks based on Key Stage 3 Programme of Study.<br>Tests cover **Ma2, Ma3** and **Ma4** in 2:1:1 ratio<br>Optional Mental Arithmetic Test | **Test period/dates**<br>May: specific dates<br>**Levels covered**<br>Levels 3–6, Level 1-2 tasks optional, assessed through Teacher Assessment and use of previous materials<br>**Structure of tests**<br>Tests: Test A (Levels 3–5)<br>Test B (Levels 3–5)<br>Test C (Level 6 )<br>Test A and B together 70 minutes and 80 marks.<br>Test C: 30 minutes and 30 marks.<br>Test C designed for those who have worked on the Key Stage 3 Programme of Study.<br>Tests cover **Sc2, Sc3** and **Sc4.** |

| Year | English | Welsh | Mathematics | Science |
|---|---|---|---|---|
| 1998 | **Test period/dates**<br>May: specific dates<br>**Levels covered**<br>Levels 3–6<br>**Structure of tests**<br>**En2: Reading**<br>Tests: Levels 3–5 Reading Comprehension Test<br>Level 6 Reading Test + Writing<br>**En3 / 4 / 5: Writing**<br>Tests: Writing Test (Levels 1–5)<br>Spelling Test (Levels 3–5)<br>Reading Test: 60 minutes and 50 marks<br>Writing Test: 60 minutes and 35 marks<br>Extension Test: 60 minutes and 42 marks<br>Spelling Test: 10 minutes and 10 marks<br>Handwriting: 5 marks | **Test period/dates**<br>May: specific dates (Tasks January–May)<br>**Levels covered**<br>Levels 1–6<br>**Structure of tests**<br>**Cy1:** A combined oracy and response to reading task (Cy2), Levels 1–2 and 3–6. Silent reading and group discussion.<br>**Cy2:** Reading test, Levels 3–6<br>**Cy3:** Creative and Transactional writing tasks, Levels 1–6. Spelling assessed as part of the activity.<br><br>Reading test: 60 minutes<br>Transactional writing: untimed but controlled conditions | **Test period/dates**<br>May: specific dates<br>**Levels covered**<br>Levels 3–6<br>**Structure of tests**<br>Tests: Test A (Levels 3–5)<br>Test B (Levels 3–5)<br>Mental Mathematics Test (Levels 3–5)<br>Test C (Level 6)<br>Tests A and B together: 90 minutes and 80 marks, Test A to be done without a calculator, Test B calculator allowed.<br>Mental Mathematics Test: 20 minutes and 20 marks (tape-recorded)<br>Test C: 30 minutes and 30 marks based on Key Stage 3 Programme of Study.<br>Tests cover **Ma2, Ma3** and **Ma4** | **Test period/dates**<br>May: specific dates<br>**Levels covered**<br>Levels 3–6<br>**Structure of tests**<br>Tests: Test A (Levels 3–5)<br>Test B (Levels 3–5)<br>Test C (Level 6)<br>Test A and B together: 70 minutes and 80 marks.<br>Test C: 30 minutes and 30 marks.<br>Test C designed for those who have worked on the Key Stage 3 Programme of Study.<br>Tests cover **Sc2, Sc3** and **Sc4** |

the published evaluations (see for example, SCAA, 1995a; 1997a). In all subjects, they were thought to be sound assessment activities and the exemplification of good classroom practice for these lower-attaining pupils.

5. In 1997, a test of mental arithmetic was introduced into the mathematics testing profile as a pilot, and this became statutory in 1998. This will be discussed in more detail later in this chapter.

6. Examples of test items in English were given in *Chapter 3* and it should be reiterated that En1 (*Speaking and listening*) has never been included in the testing. *Reading* was, and is, assessed through a written test based on the reading of a specially prepared reading booklet containing narrative passages as well as information text, all on a related theme. The questions testing this reading are of many kinds, some involving literal recall from the text and others requiring more complex judgements and inferences to be made. *Writing* is assessed by having pupils prepare and write either a story or a piece of non-narrative text which is then assessed via a structured mark scheme that assesses three dimensions of writing: *Purpose and organization; Style*; and *Grammar and punctuation. Spelling* is assessed through the reading aloud of a short passage (again on the related theme) from which certain words have been omitted. The pupils listen as the teacher reads it aloud and they write the missing words into the gaps in their version of the passage. Finally, handwriting is judged against set criteria and graded accordingly. All the published evaluations indicate that this approach to the testing of English was well received, both by teachers and other education professionals. In 1995 the reading booklet was thought to be too long so this was shortened in subsequent years. The only other complaint has been that the time given to produce the piece of writing was too short for some pupils.

7. The mathematics tests have retained the same format over the years, namely tasks at Level 1 and 2, and two parallel tests to cover the main Levels 3–5, together with an extension test. The mathematics assessments do not formally cover the process Attainment Target, *'Using and Applying'*. The tasks and tests have been judged to have an appropriate content (SCAA, 1995a; 1997a) throughout this period, although teachers and mathematics educators have pointed to some 'rogue' questions each year that have been unclear in their purpose or their relationship to the Programme of Study. Questions have also been raised about the extent to which two fairly short tests can address the wide range of the mathematics curriculum, notwithstanding the omission of one of the Attainment Targets. Critics have also mentioned the complexity of some of the mathe-

matical language used in the tests (Close *et al.*, 1997), a point that will be dealt with later in this chapter.

The use of calculators in the tests has been somewhat controversial, involving as it does a significant area of dispute between those who might be termed traditionalists and others within the mathematics education fraternity. To this point in time the use of a calculator has been retained for one of the two test papers, although it is not clear how much longer this situation will continue. It should also be emphasized that for some parts of each test the distinction is irrelevant, since a calculator cannot be used for some questions, say in geometric drawing or co-ordinates. However, the remaining questions on the paper for which a calculator is allowed are developed with this in mind: they can be answered without a calculator, but can be tackled much more efficiently and rapidly with the support of a calculator, which therefore penalizes pupils who have not been taught to use a calculator in a functional and strategic way.

8. The assessment of science has also followed the basic structure of tasks for Level 1 and 2, two parallel tests for Levels 3–5 and an extension test for Level 6. As in the other subjects, the range of types of question and content in science is varied, but once again, none of the assessments cover the process Attainment Target in science, *Experimental and investigative science*. The overall content of the tests has been judged appropriate in the national evaluations (SCAA, 1995b; 1997a) although, as in mathematics, teachers have pointed to one or two questions each year that seem inappropriate to the Programme of Study. Overall though, the tests have been judged in a positive way, although again the scientific language used in some of the questions has been commented upon (Close *et al.*, 1997). The science tests have also been judged to be rather easier than the tests in the other subjects.

9. In all subjects, the issue of the appropriateness of having an extension test covering Level 6 has been questioned (SCAA, 1995b; 1997a), especially after the 1993 revisions to the curriculum which removed this level from the programme of Study at Key Stage 2. The assumption is that pupils being entered for the extension tests will have studied the relevant Key Stage 3 Programme of Study. The result is that only a limited number of pupils nationally are entered for the extension tests and only a very small percentage each year are awarded the level. For instance, in 1997 the published data show that less than 1 per cent of the cohort gained Level 6 in each of these subjects. It should be added that assessment at Level 6 no longer exists statutorily in Wales.

10. In more technical terms, the internal consistency of the tests (as measured by Cronbach's Alpha) has proved satisfactory in all subjects. However, in English ('*Writing*'), reliability is not amenable to being estimated in this way. Marker consistency is a better measure and this achieves high and acceptable coefficients.

11. The Level 1 and 2 tasks have proved consistently popular with teachers. However, it is interesting to study the national results for these levels, in the light of the TGAT expectations. The number of pupils attaining Levels 1 and 2 at Key Stage 2 is currently a sizeable group: the national test outcomes show it to be about 7 per cent of the cohort (very broadly speaking and averaged across the test results), at least as far as English, mathematics and science are concerned. This represents about 42,000 11 year olds nationally, a figure that is in line with recent news that approximately 50,000 pupils leave school at the age of 16 with no formal qualifications at all.

## Specific issues in the Key Stage 2 testing

### *Accessibility*

At all Key Stages, it is important that as many pupils as possible have access to the tests and that no unnecessary hurdles are placed in the way. Each year, QCA (formerly SCAA) publish advice on 'special arrangements' for pupils who may have particular difficulties in reading or responding to the test papers. Each year, the tests at Key Stage 2 (and at the other Key Stages) are provided in modified large-print or braille versions for pupils with visual impairments and special arrangements can be made for pupils with statements of special educational need who are shown on the SEN Register at Stage 4 of the SEN Code of Practice. Pupils at Stage 3 of the process may also be entitled to special arrangements to be made for them if their learning difficulty or disability significantly affects access to the tests (QCA, 1997). 'Special arrangements' can also be applied for pupils who cannot work at the tests for the period of time required because of emotional or behavioural difficulties and for pupils for whom English is an additional language.

All these arrangements are part of implementing a notion of entitlement, but care needs to be taken that they are not over-used or misused. Within a single LEA, the pattern of take-up of the special arrangements can be very diverse, with schools that seem on the surface to have similar kinds of pupils making very different judgements about whether or not the special provisions are necessary. If this happens (and there is some informal evidence that it does) then the outcomes may be distorted for those pupils whose schools and teachers choose to implement them. This is particularly the case where teachers read the questions aloud for large groups of pupils.

In 1998, however, particular problems of access were encountered with the introduction of the statutory test of mental arithmetic at Key Stages 2 and 3. Trialling of these tests in 1996 and 1997 had revealed that the fairest way of administering this test nationally was by means of tape recordings, this being the only way of ensuring accurate reading and timing of the questions in a standardized way. In terms of access, the test posed challenges. Pupils with visual impairments required modified large-print or braille versions of the answer sheets while pupils with severe hearing impairments needed the questions to be signed to them, using either British Sign Language or sign-supported English. The results of these special arrangements in 1998 have yet to be evaluated.

However, there is another, wider aspect of accessibility concerned with ensuring that the test booklets themselves or the questions within them do not present unnecessary barriers to pupils demonstrating their capabilities. This is clearly related to test validity, which has already been discussed in *Chapter 4*. The instructions for completing the tests must be clear and the format of the questions should support effective performance. At Key Stage 2, there has been some criticism of the tests on these dimensions. Close *et al.* (1997) argued (admittedly on the basis of a very small sample of pupil responses) that both the language and layout of the tests (in English, mathematics and science) were problematic in some cases. They suggested, for instance, that there were too many questions in both the mathematics and science tests that used subject-specific vocabulary, and that in all subjects there were examples of unclear or ambiguous general wording. The first of these points is a difficult one since the National Curriculum requires that pupils become familiar with the appropriate technical vocabulary in each subject. It therefore seems vital that this is assessed in the tests. To suggest (Close *et al.*, *ibid.*) that marks should be awarded separately for knowing the concept and knowing the vocabulary seems to be somewhat misplaced. The issue of unclear wording is, however, a different matter; it is important that points like this are investigated and researched further.

A further aspect of accessibility, especially in relation to the mathematics and science tests, is that of *context*, a topic that has attracted attention in assessment circles over the years. The National Curriculum in these subjects requires that pupils should, for example, *'use their knowledge and understanding of science to explain and interpret a range of familiar phenomena'* (p. 7) so the issue cannot be ducked, either in teaching or assessment terms. The case has already been made in mathematics (Boaler, 1994) that it is important to locate mathematical thinking in meaningful, 'real-world' contexts, so the assessment issue is one of what this does to the nature and difficulty of the questions, and how this affects performance (Nickson, 1996). The APU studies found that it was unpredictable in its effects, precisely because it is not known how individual pupils react to particular contexts. We do know that 'transfer' (using a skill or applying understanding in a different situation to the original setting of learning) is a highly complex process and that it is closely tied up with exactly how information about the original learning experience is represented within memory and the perceived similarity in the mind of the pupil between the original learning context and any new one. This clearly makes any simple statements about the effects of context both unlikely and unwise. As Pollitt *et al.* (1985) argue, we need to understand the sources of difficulty in questions and take a judgement about the 'contextual' balance across a whole test.

### Performance data from the Key Stage 2 tests

What do the tests at Key Stage 2 show us about how pupils have been performing over time? National performance data have been published by SCAA/QCA since 1995, both for the tests and for Teacher Assessment. *Table 6.2.* shows the percentage of pupils attaining Levels 1–6 in these two forms of assessment.

In very broad terms, the information in *Table 6.2* shows that at Key Stage 2, Teacher Assessment scores have shown some tendency to be higher than the test scores and that this was especially the case in 1995, when the assessment system was still being established. It is much less the case in 1997. What is also clear is that, over the three years, the scores have shown improvement in that fewer pupils attain Level 3 and more attain Levels 4 and 5. (Discussion of how the mark thresholds are set each year and the year-on-year statistical equating that takes place was given in *Chapter 4*.)

However, not much information is available for Key Stage 2 about performance in relation to many important pupil characteristics such as birthdate or ethnicity so it is not really possible to follow through the kinds of information discussed for the Key Stage 1 results. Such data that have been published (QCA, 1998a) show that girls outperform boys in English, but that in mathematics and science, the situation is less clear-cut. This information is given in *Table 6.3*.

Each year, the SCAA/QCA publish the results of investigations of the kinds of errors pupils make in the tests and the strengths and weaknesses these reveal in relation to the curriculum (SCAA, 1995d; 1996; QCA, 1998e). The aim seems to be to provide feedback to schools (and also to LEA staff) in a situation where teachers no longer mark the tests and therefore are less likely to be able to use the results to evaluate their teaching and plan the work for the coming

**Table 6.2:** The percentage of pupils attaining Levels 1–6 in English, mathematics and science in the national testing, 1995 to 1997

| Year | Subject | Assessment | Percentage of pupils at each level | | | | |
|------|---------|------------|------|-----|-----|-----|-----|
| | | | B3* | 3 | 4 | 5 | 6+ |
| **1995** | *English* | Tests | 8 | 39 | 41 | 7 | <1 |
| | | TA*** | 9 | 33 | 43 | 13 | 0 |
| | *Mathematics* | Tests | 14 | 37 | 32 | 12 | <1 |
| | | TA | 10 | 35 | 41 | 13 | 0 |
| | *Science* | Tests | 6 | 19 | 48 | 22 | <1 |
| | | TA | 7 | 29 | 50 | 14 | 0 |
| **1996** | *English* | Tests | 7 | 30 | 45 | 12 | <1(1020) |
| | | TA | 9 | 30 | 45 | 15 | 0 |
| | *Mathematics* | Tests | 8 | 34 | 40 | 14 | <1(435) |
| | | TA | 8 | 31 | 44 | 16 | 0 |
| | *Science* | Tests | 6 | 28 | 48 | 14 | <1(120) |
| | | TA | 7 | 28 | 50 | 15 | 0 |
| **1997** | *English* | Tests | 7 | 26 | 47 | 16 | <1(493) |
| | | TA | 8 | 28 | 46 | 17 | 0 |
| | *Mathematics* | Tests | 7 | 28 | 44 | 18 | <1(763) |
| | | TA | 7 | 29 | 46 | 18 | 0 |
| | *Science* | Tests | 4 | 23 | 50 | 18 | <1(385) |
| | | TA | 5 | 25 | 51 | 18 | 0 |

\*   B3 (Below Level 3) represents children who are working at a level below that assessed by the tests, i.e. those at Levels 1 and 2 and those still working towards Level 1.

\*\*  No figures are published for Teacher Assessment numbers at Level 6, hence the recording of '0'. The numbers in brackets in each subject for 1996 and 1997 are the actual numbers of pupils awarded Level 6, from a total age cohort of approximately 620,000 pupils.

\*\*\* Teacher Assessment

year. The latest results (QCA, 1998e) show that in English pupils show significantly weaker performance in writing than in reading, a pattern that we also saw at Key Stage 1. The main weaknesses in writing seem to be in the structure and organization of the text and in the consistent use of appropriate punctuation, while in reading it was reported that pupils need to learn to read the text more closely, and to focus more upon different types of text and the author's purposes.

**Table 6.3:** The percentage of boys and girls attaining each level

| Subject | Gender | Percentage attaining each level | | | | |
|---------|--------|-----|-----|-----|-----|-----|
| | | B3 | 3 | 4 | 5 | 6 |
| English | Boys | 13 | 30 | 45 | 12 | <1 |
| | Girls | 8 | 23 | 49 | 20 | <1 |
| Mathematics | Boys | 10 | 27 | 43 | 19 | <1 |
| | Girls | 10 | 29 | 44 | 17 | <1 |
| Science | Boys | 8 | 23 | 49 | 19 | <1 |
| | Girls | 7 | 24 | 51 | 18 | <1 |

In mathematics, one of the main reported findings was that pupils at Key Stage 2 should be encouraged to use more efficient methods and strategies in their calculations, and that there were still areas of weakness in multiplication, percentages, decimals and accurate mathematical drawing. The need to be familiar with appropriate mathematical vocabulary was also stressed. In relation to the science tests, the report suggested that pupils needed experience of a wider range of investigative and experimental work and that more emphasis needed to be given to explaining scientific ideas, using appropriate scientific vocabulary. Areas of weakness were pointed out as magnetism, forces and a deeper understanding of life processes, and the need to explore all scientific ideas in a range of contexts so as to consolidate learning.

### The external marking of the tests at Key Stage 2

The curriculum review of 1993 suggested that the tests at Key Stages 2 and 3 should not be marked by the teachers themselves (unlike Key Stage 1) but that they should be marked externally, a recommendation that was formally announced in summer 1994. There were pros and cons to this decision: it undoubtedly reduced the workload for teachers and it could perhaps ensure more standardized marking, but it also removed the potentially formative aspects of the national testing, since teachers were no longer able to monitor their pupils' performance in as much detail and use this information to gain feedback about their teaching.

The evaluation of the first year of marking (SCAA, 1995c) indicated an efficient approach to the task by the External Marking Agency in recruiting markers (mostly teachers and head teachers, retired or in post), organizing the training and meeting the extremely tight deadline for completion, a period of some five weeks. During this period, each marker had to mark ten scripts according to the detailed mark scheme (also augmented during the training), have them scrutinized for accuracy and then mark the remainder of their 300–400 scripts. The marking 'cascade' was hierarchical, in that there was a complex system of chief markers, deputy chief markers, senior markers and team leaders. The marking enterprise at Key Stages 2 and 3 cost 19.1 million pounds in 1995, the majority of which consisted of the fees paid to the markers themselves, and the overall conclusion of the evaluation agency (Price Waterhouse) was that it was generally well conducted and represented value for money. However, more recent studies have raised further questions about this (Close *et al.*, 1997).

From the point of view of the markers themselves, the experience was viewed as hard work and time-consuming (McCallum, 1995b). Their motives for marking had been largely monetary, but this study showed that many had also wanted to 'keep their finger on the pulse' (p. 15) and compare the work of pupils in a range of schools. There was a fair amount of marker drop-out in the first year which meant that other markers had to take on extra loads at short notice. Many markers in this sample said they were conscious of their responsibilities and the importance of the work and worked very conscientiously at it. In the first year, the general response seemed to be that the marking of the mathematics and science papers was acceptable, although the marking of the English papers was judged less appropriate. In fact, in 1995 the English results were lower than those in mathematics and science (see *Table 6.1*), an outcome that was not well received by schools (see the *Times Educational Supplement*, 30.6.95) and which is not easy to account for. McCallum suggests that primary teachers may have felt confident that they understood pupil abilities in English quite thoroughly, but when faced with detailed criteria and mark schemes (the schools were all supplied with copies of the mark schemes) their judgements were called into question.

### Publication of the results of the Key Stage 2 tests

In 1988, the TGAT Report had anticipated the question of the reporting of the assessment results at a national level and had advised that any reporting should:

> include a general report for the area, prepared by the local authority, to indicate the nature of socio-economic and other influences which are known to affect schools. This report should give a general indication of the known effects of such influences.
>
> (Recommendation 31)

Given the 'monitoring' function of the assessment system, this anticipation proved well grounded since in 1996 the DfEE published the results, by school and LEA, of the Key Stage 2 national tests. This produced outcry from schools and from the teachers' professional organizations (for example, NUT, 1996), not least because commitments had been made that results would not be published in 1996. An 'about-turn' had happened early in 1996, no doubt at ministerial / DfEE level.

The case against the publication of raw results was made on several grounds (NUT, 1996; Murphy, 1996). The essence of the argument was that:

- raw scores for a school took no account of school intake factors and the kind of catchment area it served;

- the Key Stage 2 tests were not sufficiently established and reliable to provide a valid basis for such comparisons;

- the administration of the tests was not sufficiently monitored and the accuracy of the results not sufficiently established;

- particular groups of pupils were particularly disadvantaged by the test, for example pupils for whom English was an additional language;

- no assessment system is sufficiently free of limitations to be used for comparisons across subjects, across years or across schools;


The issue of 'league tables' was also proving controversial at other points in the education system too, mostly in relation to GCSE results. Here, many counter arguments had also being raised (Birnbaum, 1993; Weinstock, 1996) and for similar kinds of reasons. The drive towards publication was clearly part of the government move to consumerism in educational policy, parental rights to have information about schools at all levels in the system and the general drive towards raising standards of performance in schools.

These are issues and arguments to which we shall return in *Chapter 8*, but in relation to the publication of the test results at Key Stage 2 the counter arguments were and are well founded. Presenting the raw results of the testing in this comparative way does severe injustice to schools with certain kinds of pupil intakes, namely those in socially deprived areas with disadvantaged pupils. To try to overcome this, measures have been devised which allow these factors to be taken into account and to show the results in terms of the 'value' added by a school to the 'raw material' it begins with. Several measures have been devised and, in fact, a national 'Value Added' project has been put in place, seeking to exploit the best of these and to deliver more appropriate school performance tables (SCAA, 1997c). This seems like a step forward, provided that the technique selected is the most appropriate. There are indications that the proposed national measure may have its weaknesses in terms of the social background measure it uses, in this case the number of pupils in a school claiming free school meals. Other studies (Shorrocks-Taylor and Daniels, in press) have shown that this may not be a robust enough indication, and that other measures of social background (in this case postcodes) may be more effective at a national level. What does emerge from all such studies is that the social background of the pupils in a school has a major effect on the test results and on progress made between Key Stage 1 and Key Stage 2.

## Summary

The Key Stage 2 tests were the last to come on-stream and their development was therefore influenced by experiences at the other Key Stages. One of the earliest ideological struggles was the decision as to whether the approach to testing should be more like that of Key Stage 1 or Key Stage 3. The 'written test' argument won the day, for both political and manageability reasons. It came on-stream last because it is the longest Key Stage of all (four years) and therefore took four years to reach the point where the curriculum had been fully implemented and could be assessed. This very length is now perceived as something of a problem, so that optional Year 4 and Year 5 tests and assessment materials have now been introduced to bridge the gap. The introduction of the National Numeracy and Literacy Projects and the initiatives that have sprung from them also figure at this Key Stage, albeit with rather different agendas.

- The pattern of testing, with tasks for Levels 1 and 2 and written tests for Levels 3–5 and for Level 6, was established almost from the beginning, although there has been some experimentation along the way with different 'tiering' and response modes.

- The testing at this Key Stage is extremely high profile: the 'junior' years of education are perceived to be the weak link in the system and test results are published in a very up-front kind of way, school by school. This places enormous pressure both on the test development process and on schools.

- The capabilities of 11-year-olds are enormously varied and testing needs to accommodate this fact, both in terms of content and assessment approaches.

- The use of assessment tasks for lower-attaining pupils has been well received. It is an approach seen as appropriate, but it is not without its problems too. These Level 1 and 2 tasks are now non-statutory, a decision which conveys some unfortunate messages.

- The tests have gradually 'bedded down' and are now apparently accepted by schools and teachers. Some aspects could even be said to embody good practice both in curriculum and assessment terms and they appear to have acted as a source of clarification about the requirements of the curriculum and an important vehicle for conveying important curriculum messages.

- The position of the extension tests is still somewhat problematic, not least because they are based on the Key Stage 3 Programmes of Study. Political imperatives seem to dictate that they remain, providing scope for very high-attaining pupils to show what they can do and to have these achievements recognized. This is part of the wider agenda of raising standards.

- The issue of the accessibility of the tests is an important one, given an entitlement curriculum. Pupils should be able to demonstrate what they know and can do in as direct a way as possible, with few barriers preventing this. The special arrangements for test-taking try to ensure this, but it is important to monitor that these are not applied inappropriately, so potentially distorting the outcomes for some pupils.

- Issues are still being raised about the validity of some aspects of the tests, in particular the formats and language used, and the relevance of the contexts used in some papers. These are important matters that warrant further research.

- The published performance data show rising attainment at a national level between 1995 and 1997. There is differential performance between boys and girls in English and there are still some questions about the outcomes for pupils from the ethnic minorities, pupils for whom English is an additional language and pupils from more deprived backgrounds.

- The external marking of the tests at Key Stage 2 and 3 was a response to outcry and complaint from teachers about time and workload. It is a large-scale and costly enterprise each year although formal evaluations have judged it to be value for money. There are, however, some questions being raised about the accuracy of the marking, especially in English, and these need further investigation.

- The publication of results is not a popular enterprise with schools, since raw data are used and therefore the rank orderings show predictable links to the kinds of catchment areas in which they are located. Value-added measures are being considered and developed, but these are also not without their problems.

# 7 The tests at Key Stage 3: controversy and change

It is in some ways logical to have arranged these three 'Key Stage' chapters (*Chapters 5, 6* and *7*) in their chronological sequence: this makes it clear that the demands and nature of the assessments are, to some extent, different for the different age groups. However, this is not the sequence in which the test development process took place, as we saw in *Chapters 2* and *3*, so in discussing the testing at Key Stage 3, we now have to go back in time to the point when the Key Stage 3 development process was beginning in 1989, alongside the developments for Key Stage 1.

It also means that by the time we come to this final Key Stage, many of the major issues have already been addressed. Much of what has been said about Key Stages 1 and 2 applies here too: issues of pencil and paper tests or tasks; the structuring of the tests; the sampling of the curriculum; accessibility for as many pupils as possible; scoring and aggregation problems; and matters of marking and the publication of results. Similarly, assessment at all three Key Stages was radically affected by the Dearing review in 1993.

The aim of this chapter therefore will be to add discussions about matters which have special significance at Key Stage 3. Of course, parallel information about Key Stage 3 test structures and content and performance data will also be included.

Before doing so, however, some discussion is needed about the particular characteristics of 14-year-olds that can influence the nature of the assessment. By the age of 14, most pupils will have experienced three years of secondary education, although some may have been through a three-tier system (still prevailing in some areas) of first school, middle school and then high school. In this case they may only have been in a full secondary education context for one year, even though most middle schools provide specialist subject teaching for their older pupils (Enright, 1993; Gorwood, 1994). Most secondary schools in England and Wales are larger than primary schools and can offer a wider range of subject specialist teaching, each subject with its own approach, vocabulary and so on. Also, size and curriculum considerations often dictate some form of attainment grouping in secondary schools, either in the form of banding, setting or full streaming (Simon, 1993).

By the age of 14, most pupils will have been exposed to different ways of working, demands, concepts, skills and vocabularies in the different subjects and may well spend much of their time in fairly homogenous, attainment-based groups. The additional years of experience from the age of 11 will also have seen many of them move towards dealing with more difficult and abstract ideas and the requirement to develop an activity or line of thinking over a longer period of time. All these considerations suggest that the national assessments for most pupils at Key Stage 3 can contain longer sections of material, requiring detailed and sustained thinking and the use of more abstract concepts and contexts of application. It should also be the case that it becomes even more appropriate to invoke specialist terms and vocabularies in the assessments and to require longer 'outputs' from pupils. These are some of the general considerations that inform the test development process for this Key Stage.

However, it must not be forgotten that there are still significant numbers of pupils with special educational needs in secondary schools and, in fact, a very wide span of attainment in all age groups. This poses even greater challenges to test developers than at the earlier Key Stages if the notion of an entitlement curriculum and the assessment that goes with it are taken seriously. The scope for Key Stage 3 assessments is therefore in some ways wider than at the other Key Stages but also in some ways more challenging.

## The development of the Key Stage 3 assessments

As we have seen, the development process for the Key Stage 3 assessments began (in some subjects, at least) at more or less the same time as the assessments at Key Stage 1. However, in the early stages it was the aim to assess seven subjects in the national testing at Key Stage 3, namely English, Welsh (in Wales), mathematics, science, technology, history, geography and modern languages. Accordingly, it was proposed that test development groups be set up first for mathematics and science (1989), English, Welsh and technology (1990), history and geography (1991) and modern languages (1992). Unlike Key Stage 1, and perhaps for obvious reasons, the early contracts at Key Stage 3 were awarded to separate agencies for each subject, so that by 1990 seven groups were at work, one for mathematics, science and Welsh, and two each for English and technology. Subject-specific test development agencies undoubtedly had, and have, strength in terms of in-depth subject knowledge, but the downside of this situation was that there was little coherence in the approaches adopted and highly subject-specific philosophies were allowed to prevail. At Key Stage 1, coherence was achieved by having one agency develop the assessments in all three subjects to be tested and by the time Key Stage 2 came on stream, lessons had been learnt. Much effort was therefore put into maintaining consistency of approach even though different agencies were at work in the different subjects.

At Key Stage 3, the development work in mathematics and science (the first contracts to be awarded) therefore began in the same way as at Key Stage 1, with close adherence to the TGAT principles of wide-ranging assessment activities and a variety of presentation and response modes. Matters such as whether the SAT activities should be detailed and content-specific or should give only broad principles for the teacher and allow these to be applied to a content area chosen by the teacher were also under active consideration. Similar technical issues were also faced, notably the problems of sampling a very wide curriculum, ambiguous Statements of Attainment as the starting points for the assessments and the major problem of aggregating the scores (see *Chapter 4*). More were of course added at Key Stage 3, since 10 Levels of attainment potentially had to be addressed in each subject. However, the Key Stage 1 assessments were piloted and used earlier (Key Stage 1 lasts for two years and Key Stage 3 lasts for three), so the controversy surrounding the 1990 Key Stage 1 pilot undoubtedly had its effects on the Key Stage 3 development process. A significant change of ministerial responsibility also occurred at this time, when John MacGregor was replaced as Secretary of State for Education by Kenneth Clarke.

The result of these influences was a sudden change of direction in the test development process at all Key Stages but particularly at Key Stage 3. The crunch came when the pilot materials for 1991 were shown to the new Secretary of State and he rejected the activity-based assessment tasks as 'elaborate nonsense' (Clarke, 1991a). Policy became rewritten and from then on the notion of a SAT (Standard Assessment Task) was replaced by the phrase 'written terminal examinations' (Clarke, 1991) to be taken under controlled conditions at one particular time in the year. This edict covered all the designated 7/8 subjects to be assessed, except for Welsh and technology, where more wide-ranging assessment approaches were still allowed. As Daugherty (1995) suggests, this radical change was a watershed for the testing at Key Stage 3. The result was that the specifications for the tests had to be rewritten almost overnight and new materials developed at enormous speed, a requirement not necessarily designed to produce high-quality tests. As at Key Stage 1, validity aspects had been over-ridden in favour of putative reliability and manageability considerations. It should be pointed out, however, that when the 1991 pilot took place, using the 'old-style', activity-based materials, manageability was not seen as a problem by teachers, who seemed to appreciate the quality and flexibility of many of the materials (see for example Barnes, 1993).

The new specification required the tests to assess all Attainment Targets (the new versions of the mathematics and science curricula were now in play) except for the 'process' ones which were to be assessed instead through teacher assessment. New contracts were awarded in English, mathematics and science, and these groups were commissioned to produce the new tests for piloting in June 1992. These new demands, of course, had major implications for the nature of the assessment theory to be applied. The requirement to produce fairly short, sharp tests in these subjects posed even greater technical problems of curriculum sampling, demonstrating capability on each Statement of Attainment, the range and organization of the test papers, the marking and aggregating of the final scores and the overall reliability of the outcomes. There was no time to research these vital matters; instead, the development agencies had to think on their feet and come up with the best solutions they could.

## The English testing

Perhaps predictably, testing in English at Key Stage 3 became the arena for major controversy, a battleground for warring philosophies of what the discipline itself was about and how it should be assessed. As Barnes (1993) argues, teachers of English in secondary schools were probably some of the most sceptical in relation to the whole idea of testing but were somewhat reassured by what they saw of the first task materials produced in 1990 and 1991. These had been developed by two groups, ELMAG (a consortium based at the then Polytechnic of East London) and the CATS group, based in the London Institute of Education. The evaluation reports produced about these first trials showed that they seemed to work well and that they fitted appropriately into the work in most classrooms.

However, the change in political climate towards short, sharp testing revived the apprehension, compounded by yet a further change in agency, this time to the NEA (the Northern Examinations Association). Problems were encountered in producing short tests of writing, but these were small in comparison to the problems of testing reading in this way. Should this be assessed via the traditional 'passage of comprehension' type approach, or through reading the pupil had done before, implying agreed booklists? Both these have major limitations, voiced loudly in the English-teaching community, and with yet a further change in policy in 1992 the situation became even more fraught.

In 1993, another new Secretary of State for Education, this time John Patten, announced that the 1994 tests would be rigorous and would include tests of reading, comprehension, writing and a 'Shakespeare' paper. Yet another contract was awarded to a different test development agency (the University of Cambridge Local Examination Syndicate) who proposed a more traditional approach to testing. This was the fourth agency in three years to try to tackle the job and when a proposed booklist was leaked, furore followed. However, the factor that caused most problems for teachers was the fact that the tests to be used in 1993 in the national pilot had not been trialled and pre-tested properly and they were therefore technically suspect, a claim that was probably valid in the light of the very short development time.

In retrospect, it is possible to see the broadly-based cauldron of discontent that was brewing about the 1993 tests, even though at the time it seemed that it was the massive controversy about English testing that appeared to dominate. As Daugherty (1995) points out, there was discontent on many fronts: Key Stage 1 teachers had been informed about the extension of the testing to other subjects; there was general apprehension about the move towards written tests at all Key Stages; and the publication of the GCSE results and A Level results in 1992 had caused outcry, as had the publication of the Key Stage 1 results. A massive rift seemed to be opening between the government and its advisors and the education community as a whole.

The 1993 boycott of the tests, driven largely by the teacher unions and pro-fessional organizations precipitated a major crisis that could not be ignored. The two largest teaching unions, The National Union of Teachers (NUT) and the National Association of Schoolmasters/Union of Women Teachers (NAS/UWT), took up the protest on the grounds of the poor quality of the English tests and the issue of workloads. Balloting showed considerable sup-port for a boycott of the tests, a move that in Scotland had resulted in the authorities there backing down. The only climb down that occurred in Eng-land and Wales was the announcement that the government would not publish the results of the 1993 tests in English and technology, the least trialled and developed of the subject tests then on stream. The stand-off culminated in the High Court, with the local Council in Wandsworth taking action against the NAS/UWT about the proposed boycott. The Union won the case, a judge-ment that was then upheld by the Appeal Court. The final crisis point came in March 1993, when the arguments against testing reached a crescendo, from both left and right, and the Secretary of State accepted the need for a full review, to be carried out by Sir Ron Dearing.

### The Dearing review: implications for Key Stage 3

Developments at Key Stage 3 had clearly been instrumental in bringing about a review of both the curriculum and its testing, and we have already seen some of the changes the review put in place (see *Chapter 2*). More cynical commenta-tors might argue that teachers at Key Stage 1 had been struggling with the almost unworkable system since 1990, but it was only when the more powerful secondary teachers and their professional organizations came on board that the complaints were listened to. Nevertheless, the result was a streamlined cur-riculum and more manageable tests for all, together with the reaffirmation, in principle at least, of the role of teacher assessment alongside the test results.

For Key Stage 3, the outcomes of the review were significant. As at the other Key Stages, teacher assessment was still a statutory requirement, but based on much reduced requirements for record keeping. In the testing, the 10-Level scale was initially retained, only to be, in effect, transformed into an 8-Level scale by the time of the 1995 revised curriculum. Announcements by John Patten just before the review was set up had also decreed that only the core subjects would be assessed at Key Stage 3, and that the tests would be shorter and sharper. They would be externally marked to ease the workload issue for teachers, and the results at Key Stage 3 would not be published on a school-by-school, 'league tables' basis.

These were clearly enormous changes, derived either from ministerial response to the threat of the boycott or from the Dearing review, and these are reflected in the structure of the tests after 1994 and 1995. *Table 7.1* shows the development of the Key Stage 3 tests from 1994 to 1998, but, in line with the present, post-Dearing changes, only the core subjects are included.

## Specific issues in the Key Stage 3 testing

In the introduction to this chapter, it was made clear that the aim was not to repeat points made about the assessments at the earlier Key Stages but rather to take these as given and focus instead on matters that have special significance for this Key Stage. However, before doing this it is important to comment on the assessments in the Welsh language as a core subject in Wales as for the other Key Stages in *Chapters 5 and 6*. As at those Key Stages, the approach to the assessment of Welsh is also distinctive at Key Stage 3. Again, *Oracy* (Cy1) is assessed at all levels through a classroom-based task, the content of which has varied over the years. *Reading* (Cy2) has also been partly assessed through this task. However, *Reading* and *Writing* (Cy3) are also assessed through formal tests which are timed and administered under controlled examination conditions (as in the other subjects). As at Key Stages 1 and 2, these tests are not mark-based but are instead scored according to the Statements of Attainment (pre-1995) or the Level Descriptions (post-1995). It should also perhaps be mentioned that the assessments in Welsh, perhaps because of their rather different emphasis, do not appear to have attracted the same controversy as the English tests.

The following additional points now need discussion in relation to the structure and content of the tests at Key Stage 3 and the quality of the outcomes.

## *Tiering*

This topic has already been discussed in detail in *Chapter 6*. However, as *Table 7.1* shows, the tiering structures at Key Stage 3 in the core subjects are very different from each other and the reasoning behind this needs to be considered. *Figure 7.1* shows the general structure of the tests in these subjects, with the consideration that Levels 9 and 10 have been seen differently since 1995.

What is clear from *Figure 7.1* is that the general structure, once fairly formally established, has changed little since, although some variations have been tried. It is interesting to ask why the structures should be so different in the core subjects. Undoubtedly, a large part of the answer lies in the difference in the content of the curriculum in each subject and the different approaches adopted in response to this by the test development agencies in each subject. In English, notwithstanding all the agencies who have worked with the tests since the early days, there is no doubt a perception that the National Curriculum presents a fairly holistic view of the knowledge, concepts and skills required so that the idea of tiering the test papers would be unnecessary and inappropriate. Similar arguments could be made for Welsh, except that different patterns of quite complex tiering have been tried for the various dimensions of the assessments. This could explain the straightforward test structures which have prevailed most recently in these subjects. The mathematics and science curricula, on the other hand, cover a very wide range of fairly diverse knowledge, skills and concepts which have to be addressed in rather different ways. The response is at its most complex in the mathematics tasks and tests, with no less than four overlapping sets of main test papers. This certainly addresses the problem of the range of the curriculum and the offering of choice of entry points to teachers but only at the expense of enormous difficulties in test construction.

The idea of any kind of tiering at all in the national tests is considered problematic by some. The arguments are those rehearsed in the last chapter, since the question of tiering also cropped up for Key Stage 2. It is all too easy for pupils to be entered for a 'tier' of the tests that either does not allow them to show what they can do, or that de-motivates them. Entry decisions become crucial. However, given the 10 Levels (now 8) to be addressed by the tests and tasks at Key Stage 3, it is not easy to see how else the problem could be solved, especially with the range and complexity of the curricula. A single test approach could only really work if the nature of the curriculum content allowed test questions to be set that were amenable to differentiation by outcome; in other words, a task that was general enough for all pupils to be able to work with it and have the quality of the outcomes assessed against the criteria for all relevant levels so that any answer could be located at its appropriate point on the scale and the level awarded accordingly. Such a task may be possible for, say, the *Writing* Attainment target in English or Welsh, or perhaps for the 'process' ATs in mathematics and science, but for the rest it seems unlikely to work. To construct a single test that contained materials relevant to each of the levels would mean that only a small part of it could be completed by most pupils, a very inefficient and uninformative approach to assessment.

Wiliam (1995) investigated this tiering issue by taking the results of 1000 pupils who had taken the Key Stage 3 tests in English in 1994 and whose level of performance was known. Using a computer to model the effects of pupils taking a lengthy untiered test with a low reliability resulted in many of them being awarded incorrect levels. In fact, of the 1000 pupils, only 452 would have got their correct level and the majority would have been awarded one level above or below their true (that is, attained) level. He also calculated that had they been given tiered test papers only a very small number would have been mis-classified. The conclusion of the research was that tiering leads to more consistent awarding of levels, given that teacher judgements about the best tier for each pupil are fairly accurate.

### Accessibility

As with the other Key Stages, accessibility issues are also important at Key Stage 3, where the same kinds of special arrangements prevail in order to support all pupils, including those with physical disabilities, learning difficulties and emotional and behavioural problems. Clearly, in extreme cases, some of these pupils may have to be disapplied from part or all of the testing, but the aim is to keep this number to a minimum. So, as at Key Stages 1 and 2, modified large-print versions of the tests are available, as are braille versions. Children for whom English is a second language can also receive language support for the tests if this is part of their usual classroom routine. In the case of the mental arithmetic tests which became statutory at Key Stage 3 in 1998, provision was made for the questions to be signed via British Sign Language or Sign Supported English to pupils with hearing impairments.

The topics, content and language of the tests and tasks is also of great importance in ensuring maximum accessibility for pupils. The most recent formal evaluation of these aspects of the tests, at least in English, mathematics and science, came from the University of Exeter, who published their findings in 1997 (SCAA, 1997b). The subjects are dealt with separately in the report, and that is how they will be presented here, although all three subjects' test papers were found acceptable in these aspects. In English, the evaluation considered that the vocabulary used on Paper 1 was straightforward and clearly expressed and the format of the questions was an improvement from 1995. On Paper 2 (the Shakespeare paper), however, the vocabulary was broader and more difficult. The set passages for reading varied in their readability levels

**Table 7.1:** Summary of the structure of the assessments at Key Stage 3, 1994 to 1998

| Year | English | Welsh | Mathematics | Science |
|---|---|---|---|---|
| 1994 | **Test period/dates**<br>May, 2 hours 45 minutes in main tier<br>**Levels covered**<br>Levels 1–10<br>**Structure of tasks/tests**<br>Tasks: Levels 1–3, reading and writing<br>Test: Levels 4–7 (Papers 1 and 2)<br>Extension Test: Levels 8–10<br>Tasks untimed<br>Tests: Paper 1, 60 marks and 1 hour 30 minutes, full test conditions<br>Paper 2, 40 marks and 1 hour 15 minutes, full test conditions<br>Extension Test: 1 hour and 35 marks, full test conditions<br>Paper 1 : covers **En2, En3, En4** and **En5**<br>Paper 2 : Shakespeare Paper | **Test period/dates**<br>May, 1 hour 45 minutes plus oral tasks<br>**Levels covered**<br>Levels 1–10<br>**Structure of tasks/tests**<br>**Cy1:** Oracy task, Levels 1–3, 4–6, 7–10<br>**Cy2:** Oral response to reading task, Levels 1–2, 3–4, 5–6, 7–10.<br>Written tests, Levels 1–3, 2–5, 4–7, 6–10.<br>**Cy 3:** Writing tests, Levels 1–3, 2–5, 4–7, 6–10.<br>Reading tests: 45 minutes (plus 15 minutes reading time in higher tiers)<br>Writing tests: 60 minutes<br>Full test conditions | **Test period/dates**<br>May, 2 hours of tests at each tier<br>**Levels covered**<br>Levels 1–10<br>**Structure of tasks/tests**<br>Tasks: Levels 1–2, practical activities<br>Tests: four 'tiers', choice with teacher<br>Levels 3–5 (Papers 1 and 2)<br>Levels 4–6 (Papers 1 and 2)<br>Levels 5–7 )Papers 1 and 2)<br>Levels 6–8 (Papers 1 and 2)<br>Extension Test: Levels 9–10 (1 Paper)<br>Tasks untimed<br>Test tiers: two Papers (2 hours) and 120 marks, full test conditions<br>Extension Test: 1 hour 30 minutes and 80 marks, full test conditions<br>Tasks and tests cover **Ma2, Ma3, Ma4** and **Ma5**<br>Some calculator questions in tests | **Test period/dates**<br>May, 2 hours of tests at each tier<br>**Levels covered**<br>Levels 1–10<br>**Structure of tasks/tests**<br>Tasks: Levels 1–2, practical activities<br>Tests: two 'tiers', choice with teacher<br>Levels 3–6<br>Levels 5–7<br>Extension Test: Levels 8–10<br>Task untimed<br>Test tiers: two Papers (2 hours) and 180 or 150 marks (tiers), full test conditions<br>Extension Test: 1 hour 30 minutes and 120 marks, full test conditions<br>Tasks and tests cover **Sc2, Sc3** and **Sc4** |
| 1995 | **Test period/dates**<br>May, 2 hours 60 minutes in main tier<br>**Levels covered**<br>Levels 1–10<br>**Structure of tasks/tests**<br>Tasks: Levels 1–3, reading and writing<br>Test: Levels 4–7 (Papers 1 and 2)<br>Extension Test: Levels 8–10<br>Tasks untimed<br>Tests: Paper 1, 60 marks and 1 hour 30 minutes, full test conditions<br>Paper 2, 40 marks and 1 hour 15 minutes, full test conditions<br>Extension Test: 1 hour 15 mins and 35 marks, full test conditions<br>Paper 1 : covers **En2, En3, En4** and **En5.**<br>Paper 2 : Shakespeare Paper | **Test period/dates**<br>May, 1 hour 45 minutes plus oral tasks<br>**Levels covered**<br>Levels 1–10<br>**Structure of tasks/tests**<br>**Cy1:** Oracy task, Levels 1–3, 2–5, 4–7, 6–10<br>**Cy2:** Oral response to reading task, Levels 1–3, 2–5, 4–7, 6–10<br>Written tests: Levels 1–3, 2–5, 4–7, 6–10<br>**Cy 3:** Writing tests, Levels 1–3, 2–5, 4–7, 6–10<br>Reading tests: 45 minutes (plus 15 minutes reading time in higher tiers)<br>Writing tests: 60 minutes.<br>Full test conditions | **Test period/dates**<br>May, 2 hours of tests at each tier<br>**Levels covered**<br>Levels 1–10<br>**Structure of tasks/tests**<br>Tasks: Levels 1–2, practical activities<br>Tests: four 'tiers', choice with teacher<br>Levels 3–5 (Papers 1 and 2)<br>Levels 4–6 (Papers 1 and 2)<br>Levels 5–7) Papers 1 and 2)<br>Levels 6–8 (Papers 1 and 2)<br>Extension Test: Levels 9–10 (1 Paper)<br>Tasks untimed<br>Test tiers: two Papers (2 hours) and 120 marks, full test conditions<br>Extension Test: 1 hour 30 minutes and 80 marks, full test conditions<br>Tasks and tests cover **Ma2, Ma3, Ma4** and **Ma5**<br>Some calculator questions in test | **Test period/dates**<br>May, 2 hours of tests at each tier<br>**Levels covered**<br>Levels 1–10<br>**Structure of tasks/tests**<br>Tasks: Levels 1–2, practical activities<br>Tests: two 'tiers', choice with teacher<br>Levels 3–6<br>Levels 5–7<br>Extension Test: Levels 8–10<br>Task untimed (suggest 1 hour 30 minutes)<br>Test tiers: two Papers (2 hours) and 180 or 150 marks (tiers), full test conditions<br>Extension Test: 1 hour 30 minutes and 120 marks, full test conditions<br>Tasks and tests cover **Sc2, Sc3** and **Sc4** |

| | English | Welsh | Mathematics | Science |
|---|---|---|---|---|
| **1996** | **Test period/dates**<br>May, 3 hours in main tier<br>**Levels covered**<br>Levels 1–7<br>**Structure of tasks/tests**<br>**Revised national Curriculum**<br>Tasks: Levels 1–3, reading and writing<br>Tests: Levels 4–7 (Papers 1 and 2)<br>Exceptional performance (EP) test<br>Tasks untimed<br>Tests: Paper 1, 61 marks and 1 hour 45 minutes, full test conditions<br>Paper 2, 38 marks and 1 hour 15 minutes, full test conditions<br>Extension Test: 1 hour 30 minutes and 36 marks, full test conditions<br>Paper 1; covers **En2 and En3**<br>Paper 2: Shakespeare Paper | **Test period/dates**<br>May, 2 hours plus oral tasks<br>**Levels covered**<br>Levels 1–7<br>**Structure of tasks/tests**<br>**Cy1**: Oracy task, Levels 1–3, 2–5, 4–7, 6–Exceptional Performance (EP) test)<br>**Cy2**: Oral response to reading task, Levels 1–2, 3–4, 5–6, 7–EP<br>Written tests, Levels 3–6, 5–EF<br>**Cy 3**: Writing tests, Levels 3–EP<br>Reading tests: 60 minutes<br>Writing tests: 60 minutes<br>Full test conditions | **Test period/dates**<br>May, 2 hours of tests at each tier<br>**Levels covered**<br>Levels 1–8<br>**Structure of tasks/tests**<br>**Revised national Curriculum**<br>Tasks: Levels 1–2, practical activities<br>Tests: four 'tiers', choice with teacher<br>Levels 3–5 (Papers 1 and 2)<br>Levels 4–6 (Papers 1 and 2)<br>Levels 5–7 (Papers 1 and 2)<br>Levels 6–8 (Papers 1 and 2)<br>Exceptional Performance (EP) test<br>Tasks untimed<br>Test tiers: two Papers (2 hours) and 120 marks, full test conditions<br>Extension Test: 1 hour and 42 marks, full test conditions<br>Tasks and tests cover **Ma2, Ma3 and Ma4** in the ratio 2:1:1<br>Some calculator questions in tests | **Test period/dates**<br>May, 2 hours of tests at each tier<br>**Levels covered**<br>Levels 1–7<br>**Structure of tasks/tests**<br>**Revised national Curriculum**<br>Tasks: Levels 1–2, practical activities<br>Tests: two 'tiers', choice with teacher<br>Levels 3–6<br>Levels 5–7<br>Exceptional Performance (EP) test<br>Task untimed (suggest 1 hour 30 minutes)<br>Test tiers: two Papers (2 hours) and 180 or 150 marks (tiers), full test conditions<br>Extension Test: 1 hour and 60 marks, full test conditions<br>Tasks and tests cover **Sc2, Sc3 and Sc4** |
| **1997** | **Test period/dates**<br>May, 3 hours in main tier<br>**Levels covered**<br>Levels 1–7<br>**Structure of tasks/tests**<br>Tasks: Levels 1–3, reading and writing<br>Test: Levels 4–7 (Papers 1 and 2)<br>**Pilot** for 'Grammar, punctuation and spelling' Test<br>Exceptional performance (EP) test<br>Tasks untimed<br>Tests: Paper 1, 61 marks and 1 hour 45minutes, full test conditions<br>Paper 2, 38 marks and 1 hour 15 minutes, full test conditions<br>Extension Test: 1 hour 30 minutes and 36 marks, full test conditions<br>Paper 1: covers **En2 and En3**<br>Paper 2:- Shakespeare Paper (revised) | **Test period/dates**<br>May, 2 hours 30 minutes plus oral tasks<br>**Levels covered**<br>Levels 1–7<br>**Structure of tasks/tests**<br>**Cy1**: Oracy task, Levels 1–2, 3–4, 5–6, 7–EP<br>Exceptional performance (EP) test<br>**Cy2**: Oral response to reading task, Levels 1–2, 3–4, 5–6, 7–EP<br>Written tests: Levels 3–6, 5–EP<br>**Cy 3**: Writing tests, Levels 3–EP<br>Reading tests: 60 minutes<br>Writing tests: 90 minutes<br>Full test conditions | **Test period/dates**<br>May, 2 hours of tests at each tier<br>**Levels covered**<br>Levels 1–8<br>**Structure of tasks/tests**<br>Tasks: Levels 1–2, practical activities<br>Tests: four 'tiers', choice with teacher<br>Levels 3–5 (Papers 1 and 2)<br>Levels 4–6 (Papers 1 and 2)<br>Levels 5–7 (Papers 1 and 2)<br>Levels 6–8 (Papers 1 and 2)<br>Exceptional performance (EP) test<br>Tasks untimed<br>Test tiers: two Papers (2 hours) and 120 marks, one calculator and one non-calculator Paper<br>Tier 4–6, 122 marks<br>Extension Test: 1 hour and 42 marks, full test conditions<br>Tasks and tests cover **Ma2, Ma3 and Ma4** in the ratio 2:1:1<br>**Pilot** for Mental Arithmetic Test | **Test period/dates**<br>May, 2 hours of tests at each tier<br>**Levels covered**<br>Levels 1–7<br>**Structure of tasks/tests**<br>Tasks: Levels 1–2, practical activities<br>Tests: two 'tiers', choice with teacher<br>Levels 3–6<br>Levels 5–7<br>Exceptional performance (EP) test<br>Task untimed (suggest 1 hour 30 minutes)<br>Test tiers: two Papers (2 hours) and 180 or 150 marks (tiers), full test conditions<br>Extension Test: 1 hour and 60 marks, full test conditions<br>Tasks and tests cover **Sc2, Sc3 and Sc4** |

| Year | English | Welsh | Mathematics | Science |
|---|---|---|---|---|
| 1998 | **Test period/dates**<br>May, 3 hours in main tier<br>**Levels covered**<br>Levels 1–7<br>**Structure of tasks/tests**<br>Tasks: Levels 1–3, reading and writing<br>Test: Levels 4–7 (Papers 1 and 2)<br>Exceptional performance (EP) test<br>'Grammar, punctuation and spelling' Test<br>Tasks untimed<br>Tests: Paper 1, 61 marks and 1 hour 45 minutes, full test conditions<br>Paper 2, 38 marks and 1 hour 15 minutes, full test conditions<br>Extension Test: 1 hour 30 minutes and 36 marks, full test conditions<br>Grammar Test:<br>Paper 1: covers **En2 and En3**<br>Paper 2: Shakespeare Paper (revised) | **Test period/dates**<br>May, 2 hours 30 minutes plus oral tasks<br>**Levels covered**<br>Levels 1–7<br>**Structure of tasks/tests**<br>**Cy1**: Oracy task, Levels 1–2, 3–4, 5–6, 7–EP (Extension Paper)<br>**Cy2**: Oral response to reading task, Levels 1–2, 3–4, 5–6, 7–EP<br>Exceptional performance (EP) test<br>Written tests: Levels 3–6, 5–EP<br>**Cy 3**: Writing tests, Levels 3–EP<br>Reading tests: 60 minutes<br>Writing tests: 90 minutes<br>Full test conditions | **Test period/dates**<br>May, 2 hours of tests at each tier<br>**Levels covered**<br>Levels 1–8<br>**Structure of tasks/tests**<br>Tasks: Levels 1–2, practical activities<br>Tests: four 'tiers', choice with teacher<br>  Levels 3–5 (Papers 1 and 2)<br>  Levels 4–6 (Papers 1 and 2)<br>  Levels 5–7 (Papers 1 and 2)<br>  Levels 6–8 (Papers 1 and 2)<br>Exceptional performance (EP) test<br>Mental Arithmetic Tests (tiered): Levels 3–5 and 4–7<br>Tasks untimed<br>Test tiers: two Papers (2 hours) and 120 marks, one calculator and one non-calculator Paper<br>Tier 4–6, 122 marks<br>Extension Test: 1 hour 30 minutes and 42 marks, full test conditions<br>Mental Arithmetic Tests, 20 minutes<br>Tasks and tests cover **Ma1, Ma2, Ma3 and Ma4** in the ratio 1:2:1:1 | **Test period/dates**<br>May, 2 hours of tests at each tier<br>**Levels covered**<br>Levels 1–7<br>**Structure of tasks/tests**<br>Tasks: Levels 1–2, practical activities<br>Tests: two 'tiers', choice with teacher<br>  Levels 3–6<br>  Levels 5–7<br>Exceptional performance (EP) test Task untimed (suggest 1 hour 30 minutes)<br>Test tiers: two Papers (2 hours) and 180 or 150 marks (tiers), full test conditions<br>Extension Test: 1 hour and 60 marks, full test conditions<br>Tasks and tests cover **Sc2, Sc3 and Sc4** |

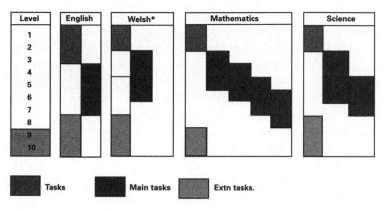

Key to Figure 7.1:

Welsh *    The tiering system in Wales has changed considerably over the years. and differs for
oral and written activities. This diagram represents the situation in the written tests.

**Figure 7.1:** The structure of the tests in the core subjects at Key Stage 3

and some had unacceptable ambiguities of wording. The questions were not judged to show any gender bias in terms of the topics and questions chosen.

The format of the test papers in mathematics was criticized for potentially not focusing pupil attention on where responses should be written, even though the questions themselves were deemed well structured and set out in small, logical steps. The size of some of the print was thought to be too large for 14-year-olds. There was no evidence of gender or ethnic bias in the questions, although other studies have pointed out some of the problems in the contexts chosen (Cooper, 1993). In science, the layout of the test papers was judged good, with clear and well-labelled diagrams. However, it was thought that the differences in layout in the science and mathematics tests may have caused confusion for pupils. In terms of the language used and the contexts chosen in the science questions, the judgement of the evaluators was that this did not cause a barrier to pupils being able to answer the questions.

### External marking

Once again, the findings reported here come from the University of Exeter evaluation of the 1992 and 1996 testing (SCAA, 1997b). This information was, however, based on responses to teacher questionnaires rather than on any detailed quantitative study or large-scale re-marking. In English, the 1995 evaluation voiced considerable concern about the quality of the marking. The recommendations were that better training should be provided for markers, clearer mark schemes produced and more streamlined administrative procedures put in place. They also recommended the annotation of scripts so that teachers could see why marking decisions had been made when the scripts were returned. Most of these points were taken up by SCAA, and the 1996 marking was judged to be much better. In terms of the accuracy of marking, this was thought to be poor in English in 1995, but by 1996 this too had improved, with fewer teachers in the evaluation sample judging accuracy to be low (only 16 per cent as opposed to 51 per cent in 1995).

In the mathematics tests, judgements of the marking in 1995 had been that it was good (unlike English), and this was reinforced in 1996. Teachers commented on the time it saved and the more 'objective' view it gave them of their pupils' performance. There was generally less controversy about the marking of the mathematics papers, although some teachers still complained about the lack of marks given for the 'method' used in calculation, even if the answer was incorrect. In 1996 accuracy was judged to be higher than in 1995 by the evaluators, although no detailed figures were provided. In the science papers too, the marking and accuracy were generally judged positively by teachers in both 1995 and 1996. The 'saving time' argument was again made, as was the idea of a more 'objective' measure. Other studies that have addressed this matter of the quality of the external marking (for example, Close, Furlong and Swain, 1996) found a similar pattern of response, with most problems being found in the English test papers.

### The validity and reliability of the results

We have already seen that it was questions about the reliability of the English tests in 1993 that helped to trigger the major review of the curriculum in that year. At the other Key Stages too, some doubts have been expressed about the reliability of the test outcomes, but often for different reasons. As we saw at Key Stage 1, the dependability of the results was brought into question in the early evaluations of the assessments, mostly because of the inherent problems of assessment through relatively open-ended activities when teachers are not fully aware of all the requirements (see *Chapter 5*). Reliability has also been discussed in relation to mark-based systems in the newer versions of the tests and problems of aggregating scores and setting thresholds (see *Chapter 4*).

At Key Stage 3, however, not only have some of the scoring systems been questioned (see *Chapter 4*), but major queries have been raised about the validity of some, if not all the tests. The general point made is that, given such wide-ranging curricula in the core subjects, it is difficult to imagine that a two-hour test can be a valid and reliable reflection of a pupil's capabilities. Iven (1992) complained about 'testamania' by the government and questioned whether short, sharp tests were up to the task. In particular, he worried whether the Key Stage 3 tests (in 1992, of course) adequately paved the way for GCSE testing two years later. Others too have taken up the cry, for instance Gill (1994) who carried out detailed analyses of performance in the mathematics and science tests at Key Stage 3 and found fairly high correlations not only between performance on different aspects of the tests within each curriculum area but also high correlations between test results in the two subjects. He concluded that this was a sign of the poor validity in the tests, arguing that the short pencil and paper tests were not discriminating between performances in the different areas. The underlying capacity which the tests seemed to be measuring was the ability to cope with a series of short, sharp questions in a limited time frame. This may be an important point to make about the tests or, alternatively, it could indicate some kind of general underlying capacity that feeds into all performance. At present we seem to have no way of distinguishing these matters, but what is clear is that some educationists feel the tests are invalid because of their very 'short, sharp' nature.

### The effects of the testing on schools

Over the years, concerns have also been expressed, at all Key Stages, that testing may begin to predominate in the minds of teachers, so that the assessment 'tail' begins to wag the 'curriculum' dog. This is a topic to which we shall return in the next chapter, but several studies at Key Stage 3 have investigated the issue and are therefore worth a brief mention here.

Close, Furlong and Swain (1996) carried out an investigation (supported by the National Union of Teachers) to evaluate the impact of the tests on the curriculum, teaching and learning in schools, as perceived by headteachers. Four hundred secondary schools were sampled, with a 50 per cent response rate, and the findings suggested considerable variability in school responses to the testing. In particular, they varied in whether they had provided additional funding for the subjects being tested, the extent to which they made use of the test results in Year 7 grouping decisions, how far they provided extra support for the Year 9 classes around the testing period, and how the school prepared the pupils for the tests. As such, this study did not provide clear answers to questions about the impact of the testing on school organization and functioning.

Fairbrother, Dillon and Gill (1995) asked rather different but related questions about how schools use information from the tests in the context of science teaching. The teachers involved saw the test results as part of the range of information available to them but often modelled their own informal testing on the national tests, saying that they had helped to clarify the meaning of some aspects of the curriculum. They were not teaching *to* the tests as such, but clearly wanted to teach in ways that would help their pupils to do well in the tests since they represented a very public show of the school's achievements.

Ferriman, Lock and Soares (1994) found that the National Curriculum had changed teacher perceptions of, and approaches to, their own assessments, even though many were not using the results to good effect in their planning and teaching. What all these studies seem to indicate is that the tests have clearly had some impact in secondary schools, but that this is varied and depends upon a range of variables and issues within each school situation.

## Performance data from the Key Stage 3 tests

As at the other Key Stages, national performance data have been published by SCAA/QCA since 1994 for Key Stage 3, for the tests and for Teacher Assessment in English, mathematics and science. *Table 7.2* shows the percentage of pupils attaining Levels 1–10 in these two forms of assessment and is based on data published by SCAA/QCA (QCA, 1998b, c and d).

### Subject comments

Before discussing individual subjects, an important caveat must be entered here. Many of the lines in *Table 7.2* do not add up to 100, even taking into account possible rounding effects. This is explained in the QCA documentation (QCA, ibid.) by the fact that pupils who were absent or disapplied from the testing are not shown. The following comments must therefore be seen in this light.

### English

The information in *Table 7.2* appears to show a small decline in the percentage of pupils attaining Level 7 for both the tests and Teacher Assessment. It also seems to be the case that fewer pupils attained Level 5 or higher in English (the supposed 'standard' for the age group) than in mathematics and science. However, the line totals (less than 100) are problematic in some cases and we do not know at which levels any absence or disapplication would have their effects. It is therefore not really possible to draw firm conclusions about trends over time.

Detailed analysis of performance in English (QCA, 1998b) showed that there were considerable disparities between the 'reading' and 'writing' aspect of performance on Paper 1; pupils who achieved Level 7 as their overall level often barely scored this level on the writing component. In other words, as at Key Stages 1 and 2, it is the writing scores that pull overall English scores down. In relation to spelling, there were approximately 2.3 spelling errors in 100 words of writing. Certain aspects of punctuation also caused problems, most notably the use of commas, although the use of capital letters and full

**Table 7.2:** The percentage of pupils attaining Levels 1–10 in English, mathematics and science in the national testing at Key Stage 3, 1994 to 1997

| Year | Subject | Assessment | Percentage of pupils at each level | | | | | | |
|------|---------|------------|------|------|------|------|------|------|------|
| | | | B4* | 4 | 5 | 6 | 7 | 8 | 9/10 E/P** |
| 1994 | *English* | Test | 14 | 23 | 27 | 22 | 8 | 1 | 0 |
| | | TA*** | 15 | 21 | 26 | 23 | 12 | 2 | 0 |
| | *Mathematics* | Tests | 15 | 19 | 22 | 26 | 10 | 2 | 0 |
| | | TA | 15 | 20 | 24 | 25 | 13 | 3 | 0 |
| | *Science* | Tests | 12 | 19 | 28 | 27 | 9 | 0 | 0 |
| | | TA | 14 | 22 | 30 | 26 | 9 | 0 | 0 |
| 1995 | *English* | Test | 11 | 28 | 35 | 16 | 3 | 1 | 0 |
| | | TA | 14 | 23 | 30 | 22 | 9 | 1 | 0 |
| | *Mathematics* | Tests | 14 | 21 | 24 | 23 | 9 | 1 | 0 |
| | | TA | 14 | 23 | 27 | 23 | 10 | 1 | 0 |
| | *Science* | Tests | 12 | 24 | 31 | 18 | 7 | 0 | 0 |
| | | TA | 13 | 26 | 31 | 21 | 7 | 0 | 0 |
| 1996 | *English* | Tests | 12 | 23 | 31 | 18 | 7 | 1 | 0 |
| | | TA | 15 | 24 | 30 | 21 | 9 | 1 | 0 |
| | *Mathematics* | Tests | 13 | 23 | 23 | 22 | 10 | 1 | 0 |
| | | TA | 14 | 24 | 27 | 23 | 11 | 2 | 0 |
| | *Science* | Tests | 11 | 26 | 35 | 17 | 4 | 0 | 0 |
| | | TA | 13 | 26 | 32 | 21 | 7 | 0 | 0 |
| 1997 | *English* | Tests | 12 | 27 | 34 | 17 | 5 | 1 | 0 |
| | | TA | 15 | 25 | 32 | 20 | 7 | 1 | 0 |
| | *Mathematics* | Tests | 12 | 22 | 23 | 25 | 11 | 1 | 0 |
| | | TA | 13 | 23 | 27 | 24 | 11 | 2 | 0 |
| | *Science* | Tests | 10 | 24 | 31 | 22 | 7 | 0 | 0 |
| | | TA | 12 | 26 | 32 | 22 | 7 | 0 | 0 |

\*  B4 (Below Level 4) represents pupils who are working at Levels 1, 2 and 3 and those still working towards Level 1
\*\*  Levels assessed by the Extension Paper
\*\*\*  Teacher Assessment

stops, as well as speech marks was quite well established. The main criticism made of Paper 2 (Shakespeare) was the difference in demand in the tasks associated with the choice between three plays. The overall conclusion for both papers was that pupils had worked hard on the plays and had organized their answers in much better ways in 1997 than in previous years. They also showed the capacity to back up their points with close reference to the text.

## Mathematics

The information in *Table 7.2* appears to show that, in mathematics, the percentage of pupils attaining Level 5 or higher was fairly stable over this four-year period, although with some small fluctuations. The figures were similar to those in science but higher than for English. However, the problem of the line totals again applies, so these comments must be taken with caution.

In terms of performance in different areas of the curriculum, the analysis of the national sample of scripts showed that pupils, especially those attaining Levels 3, 4 and 5, found the questions on *Shape, space and measures* and *Handling data* more straightforward than those in *Algebra* and some aspects of *Number*. Pupils attaining the higher levels (6, 7 and 8) could successfully calculate percentages, interpret complex graphs and work with geometric concepts such as finding angles and drawing nets of shapes. However, performance was generally poor on drawing involving the use of geometric instruments, and pupils were still not performing well on written descriptions or explanations of mathematical ideas. There was a general feeling in this analysis of performance on the tests that schools still needed to emphasize test-taking techniques such as reading questions carefully, deciding what the question involved and checking answers afterwards.

## Science

The information in *Table 7.2* showed that there had been some fluctuation in the percentage of pupils scoring Level 5 or above in science but with some evidence of a slightly rising trend from 1995 onwards. However, the proportion attaining Level 6 and above fell over this time period. Again, the issue of line totals not always adding up to 100 means that these comments must be highly tentative.

Analysis of performance on each question in the different curriculum areas showed that, in general, pupils were better able to apply their knowledge in different contexts and to recognize the difference between description and explanation. There was also evidence that they could provide effective extended responses to questions, even though labelling of diagrams was sometimes careless. In terms of *Life Processes and Living Things*, questions on cell structure, human reproduction and parts of the flower were answered better than in previous years. They showed good understanding of information about states of matter, the properties of materials and acids and alkalis in *Materials and their Properties*, and also sound knowledge of electrical circuits, magnetism and how sounds travel in *Physical Processes*.

## Performance in relation to particular pupils' background characteristics

The information to be used in these sections on pupil background characteristics (gender and first/additional language performance) comes mainly from the University of Exeter's evaluation report. It refers to 1996 (although there is also some referencing back to 1995) and comes from the evaluation sample of pupils, intended to be a nationally representative one. However, insufficient detail is provided in the report for each individual subject to be able to verify this. The information covers English, mathematics and science – Welsh was not included in this evaluation. The results are reported by the separate subjects under each heading since the way the information was presented in the report precludes combining information across subjects.

### *Gender*

ENGLISH

**Table 7.3:** The percentages of boys and girls attaining each level in English in 1996

| Subject | Gender | Percentage attaining each Level | | | | | | |
|---------|--------|---|---|---|---|---|---|---|
| | | N | 3 | 4 | 5 | 6 | 7 | 8 |
| English | Girls | 2.3 | 6.5 | 23.3 | 36.4 | 22.2 | 8.4 | 1.0 |
| | Boys | 3.4 | 14.4 | 29.1 | 31.0 | 16.8 | 4.4 | 1.0 |

Table 7.3 indicates very clearly that girls outperformed boys in English: larger numbers of boys scored at the lower levels and fewer at the higher ones. This is repeated in 1997 (QCA, 1998) where in the tests, 66 per cent of girls achieved Level 5 or above but only 46 per cent of boys nationally. As at the other Key Stages, where similar kinds of patterns are found, there is little evidence why this should be the case or if particular aspects of the curriculum or particular skills are the cause.

MATHEMATICS

The information for mathematics is given in Table 7.4 .

**Table 7.4:** The percentages of boys and girls attaining each Level in mathematics in 1996

| Subject | Gender | Percentage attaining each Level | | | | | | | |
|---|---|---|---|---|---|---|---|---|---|
| | | N | 2 | 3 | 4 | 5 | 6 | 7 | 8 |
| Mathematics | Girls | 2.6 | 1.1 | 13.4 | 23.2 | 25.4 | 24.7 | 8.8 | 0.7 |
| | Boys | 1.5 | 1.0 | 11.0 | 22.8 | 25.4 | 23.4 | 13.3 | 1.6 |

Here, the picture is rather different from that in English. The evaluation suggests that in mathematics, the subject with the most complex tiering system (see *Figure 7.1*), a slightly higher percentage of girls than boys were entered for tier 4–6 but a slightly higher percentage of boys were entered for tier 6–8 (QCA, 1998). This suggests that there are a number of very competent mathematicians among the boys in the cohort, but we do not know how far teacher expectations may be a factor. In relation to performance, boys generally (in 1996) gained rather more of the higher levels and girls rather more of the lower, but at the middle levels (4, 5 and 6) the attainments were very close. The information given for 1997 (QCA, 1998), indicates that there was little difference in the percentage of boys and girls being awarded Level 5 or above nationally, but no further detail is provided.

SCIENCE

*Table 7.5* gives the details of the science outcomes in 1996.

**Table 7.5:** The percentages of boys and girls attaining each Level in science in 1996

| Subject | Gender | Percentage attaining each Level | | | | | | |
|---|---|---|---|---|---|---|---|---|
| | | N | 2 | 3 | 4 | 5 | 6 | 7 |
| Science | Girls | 0.3 | 1.2 | 11.2 | 25.9 | 44.4 | 15.0 | 2.1 |
| | Boys | 0 | 1.3 | 8.9 | 26.2 | 36.9 | 19.9 | 6.9 |

*Table 7.5* shows that the award of levels in science generally favours boys, with fewer of them scoring at the lower levels and more at the higher levels. However, in the central Levels 4 and 5, the picture is not clear. As with the mathe-

matics outcomes, there is the intervening issue of the tiering of the papers and the entry decisions made by teachers. In science, more boys seemed to be entered for the tier 5–7 tests and more girls for the tier 3–6 tests. Again, we do not have enough information to go beyond this, except to say the teacher expectations may once again be playing a part. The national results published in 1998 (QCA, 1998) show that in 1997 in science, the proportion of both boys and girls attaining Level 5 and above is approximately the same, while more boys than girls attain Levels 6, 7 and 8.

### Pupils with English as an additional language

The 1996 evaluation (QCA, 1997) provided analysis of the performance of pupils for whom English was either a first or an additional language (EAL pupils). This information is given on a subject-by-subject basis in the next three sections, but the report makes it clear that not all schools may have designated 'EAL' pupils in the same way.

ENGLISH

**Table 7.6**: The percentages of EAL pupils and non-EAL pupils attaining each Level in English in 1996

| Subject | Pupils | Percentage attaining each Level | | | | | |
|---------|--------|----|----|----|----|----|----|
| | | N | 3 | 4 | 5 | 6 | 7 |
| English | EAL pupils | 8.1 | 15.1 | 37.6 | 21.5 | 15.6 | 2.2 |
| | Non-EAL pupils | 2.7 | 10.2 | 25.1 | 34.6 | 19.8 | 7.8 |

The overall picture, even by the age of 14, is that EAL pupils did not perform as well as pupils with English as their first language, a fact that mirrors the findings at the other Key Stage too. These EAL pupils were more likely to stick closely to the text in their answers to the questions and to quote extensively, although weaknesses in spelling and punctuation were common to all pupils. In writing, their active vocabulary seemed more limited than their non-EAL counterparts.

MATHEMATICS

**Table 7.7:** The mean scores of EAL pupils and non-EAL pupils on each tier and paper of the tests in mathematics in 1996

| | | Mean scores for the KS3 test papers at each tier and paper in mathematics for EAL pupils and non-EAL pupils | | | | | | | |
|---|---|---|---|---|---|---|---|---|---|
| | | Tier 3–5 | | Tier 4–6 | | Tier 5–7 | | Tier 6–8 | |
| | | P1 | P2 | P1 | P2 | P1 | P2 | P1 | P2 |
| **Subject** | **Pupils** | **N** | **2** | **3** | **4** | **5** | **6** | **7** | **8** |
| Mathematics | EAL pupils | 24.3 | 24.3 | 24.3 | 24.3 | 24.3 | 24.3 | 24.3 | 24.3 |
| | Non-EAL pupils | 32.5 | 32.5 | 32.5 | 32.5 | 32.5 | 32.5 | 32.5 | 32.5 |

Bearing in mind the problems of designation referred to earlier, EAL pupils performed less well than the non-EAL pupils in general, but closer analysis shows that the situation may be a little more complex and diverse, not least because more EAL pupils were entered for the lower tier papers (tiers 3–5 and 4–6) than for the higher tiers. Again, this may be masking true performance to some extent, but we have no further evidence on this point. Much more research is needed at all Key Stages.

SCIENCE

**Table 7.8:** The mean scores of EAL pupils and non-EAL pupils on the relevant tier and paper of the tests in science in 1996

| | | Mean scores for the KS3 test papers for each tier in science for EAL pupils and non-EAL pupils | | | |
|---|---|---|---|---|---|
| | | Tier 3–6 | | Tier 5–7 | |
| | | P1 | P2 | P2 | P2 |
| **Subject** | **Pupils** | **N** | **2** | **3** | **4** |
| Science | EAL pupils | 39.0 | 39.1 | 40.3 | 33.7 |
| | Non-EAL pupils | 46.0 | 44.5 | 43.9 | 30.4 |

In the evaluation sample on which this information is based, EAL pupils were entered for the tier 3–6 tests (10 per cent) and the tier 5–7 tests (6 per cent). Again, few further details are provided in the main report, except to suggest that a complex set of factors may be at work, with different entry judgements by teachers and some diversity in the range of performance.

### The effects of term of birth

The evaluation report (QCA, 1997) suggests that the birthdate effect was investigated but that, in this sample at least, the differences in scores related to term of birth were small. This seems a strange finding since both earlier (Key Stage 1) and later, in external examinations at ages 16 and 18, there is evidence of birthdate effects on performance. However, the evaluation team do suggest that more research may be necessary.

## Summary

- The development of the assessments at Key Stage 3 began at approximately the same time, at least in some subjects, as at Key Stage 1. The brief was therefore the same, in that the early assessments were very much in line with the TGAT principles of wide-ranging and varied assessment activities, eventually to cover seven (eight in Wales) subjects.

- By the age of 14, it is expected that almost the full range of the 10-Level scale (now an 8-Level scale) needs to be covered in the testing, a range that poses very considerable challenges for the test developers.

- By Year 9, most pupils will have experienced three years of secondary education, with much more subject specialist teaching than earlier and a more complex curriculum. This implies that there are more possibilities open to the test developers in terms of the kinds of questions that can be written for the tests.

- The early development process was affected by the response to the Key Stage 1 tests in 1990 and 1991. The result was a sudden change of direction in the nature of the testing at Key Stage 3, when it became clear that the government required written examinations, time-limited and taken at a fixed date in the year.

- The testing in English caused problems from the beginning. It became an arena for major controversy between the English teaching community and the government, the result of very differing views of what English was about and how it should be assessed.

- This, along with other problems and outcries from teachers and their professional organizations, proved to be the catalyst for the major review of the curriculum in 1993.The Dearing review and the other changes announced by the government at the same time meant that after 1994 only the core subjects would be tested at Key Stage 3 and the results would not be published on a school-by-school basis.

- The structure of the Key Stage 3 tests was set at this time and has changed little since. However, the structure of the tests (in relation to 'tiering) is very different in the four subjects.

- National figures are, however, published and these are available from 1994 onwards. The outcomes during this period have varied in the core subjects.

- In English, the same trend is detectable as at the other Key Stages: the writing scores lower the overall levels of attainment.

- The mathematics results nationally show a fairly steady pattern over this period, but with somewhat poor performance in the areas of geometric drawing and giving mathematical descriptions and explanations.

- In science, fluctuations in the national outcomes at each level are evident over this four-year period. There is, however, increasing evidence of pupils being able to apply scientific ideas in a range of contexts.

- The outcomes in relation to gender (available only for 1995 and 1996 and even then not for Welsh) show that girls outperform boys in English but that the situation in mathematics and science is more varied. In both mathematics and science, the 'tier' entry decisions made by teachers may influence the outcomes.

- The overall picture for pupils who have English as an additional language (EAL) is that they do not in general do as well as pupils who have English as their first language, but once again in mathematics and science teacher decisions about which tier a pupil should be entered for may influence the outcomes.

# 8 Some conclusions: purposes, ideals and realities

We have seen the imperatives that gave rise to the whole idea of a National Curriculum and its assessment system, and charted the course of developments in the testing at the three Key Stages that are the focus of this book. We have also explored the nature of the tests themselves and the technical issues that surround them. The time has now come to attempt to draw these strands together and consider the broader picture in order to reach some kind of conclusion about the experience of the last ten years.

## The 'why?', 'what?', 'when?' and 'how?' of the National Curriculum

The origins of the National Curriculum were both educational and political, responding in part to a situation of great diversity of curriculum and organization within schools, especially primary schools, but also to the emotive perception that 'standards' in our schools were falling. This summary can be extended by answering four basic questions – the 'why?', 'what?', 'when?' and 'how?' of the National Curriculum and its testing, viewed with the benefit of experience and hindsight.

From the vantage point of the present day, the answer to the 'why' question seems clear. Political agendas dictated a need for greater accountability in schools, greater transparency about what was going on in them and greater responsiveness to change. The purposes of the National Curriculum, at least those purposes officially stated, were for greater uniformity and coherence of experience for pupils, clearer progression between the different phases of the school system and increased clarity of information for parents and the community. For rather different reasons, these aims were espoused by very diverse groups: educational reformers and professionals and the political right alike.

As to the 'what?' question, the curriculum itself as it finally emerged in 1988 was fairly traditional in conception, in that it was based around conventional subjects. The subject working groups who were responsible for the content of the curriculum were briefed to outline the major dimensions within the discipline and to indicate in detail what these should contain. The breadth and detail of the curricula that emerged in each subject werein many ways impressive, but problematic when taken in total, as we have seen.

However, the curriculum embodied a very radical edge – the integral assessment system. Assessment was not, of course, an unknown experience in England and Wales, not even in primary schools, but until this point it had always been administered through the examination boards (for example, GCSE, A Levels), through Local Education Authorities (monitoring of reading progress, the 11-plus tests, for example) or schools offering entrance exams. In 1988, for the first time it was being required by legislation that this should be carried out at a national level and on a scale never before experienced in the UK. The TGAT group, briefed to provide the blueprint for the whole assessment system, brought together educationists, researchers, teachers and administrators in a coalition with the aim of producing proposals sufficiently enlightened in assessment terms to convince other education professionals that all was well, but at the same time to convince the political right that radical changes were to be brought about which would improve the quality of what was going on in schools. It was a difficult tightrope to walk and the considerable achievement of the group was that they appeared to succeed, at least in the early days (Black, 1998a). This was achieved as much by what they left out as by what they included in the final and supplementary reports.

The answer to the 'when?' question was a very firm 'now'. Again, political agendas required an almost instant response in order to support the notion of a radical and innovative government not afraid of change. The TGAT group had to deliberate and finalize their reports in a matter of months, the subject working groups were allocated very short time-frames in which to complete their tasks, and the implementation of the curriculum in schools had to begin at once. Most significantly, the assessments had to be put in place at the first possible date for each Key Stage. This requirement for implementation at breakneck speed has been blamed for many of the problems that subsequently arose, and it is worth remembering that the TGAT group had recommended a period of five years from the Attainment Targets being outlined and agreed to the first assessments (TGAT Report, para. 199). Part of the problem may have been that the politicians, having accepted the TGAT proposals, had little idea of the sheer scale of the enterprise being taken on and the time it should therefore realistically take (Daugherty, 1995).

The final, 'how?' question is also an interesting one. Achieving some sort of consensus that change was needed, and subsequently drafting and steering the legislation through Parliament, was in many ways surprising in the UK context, although critics were by no means silent. An important ingredient in the 'how?'

of the curriculum implementation was undoubtedly the many changes in Secretaries of State for Education during this time. Each had a very distinct style of approach to policy-making and implementation which drastically affected the response of both the education community on the one hand and political friends and foes on the other.

## The early criticisms of the approach to the tests and testing

To say the critics of testing were not silent is something of an understatement. Very early in the debate, Murphy (1987) provided an insightful analysis of the potential problems in the assessment approach being proposed. Even at this point, he was drawing attention to basic questions about the purpose of the tests, the feasibility of creating such tests to meet all the requirements and possible alternative approaches. He voiced the fear that the tests would come to dominate the curriculum delivered in the classroom, rejecting the notion of assessment-led curriculum change and pointing out that the best way to avoid this would be to ensure that the curriculum was fully and properly established before introducing any of the testing. He also foreshadowed many of the points made later concerning the difficulties of having short, benchmark tests to assess a full and rich curriculum, and the danger of the system becoming external to, and divorced from, what goes on in school on a day-to-day basis.

### BERA

The Task Group representing the British Educational Research Association (BERA) also published a critique of the assessment policy (Harlen *et al.*, 1992). They had been invited to suggest alternative ways of providing the information the national assessments were designed to deliver and the result is a document that makes many important (and agreed) general points about the nature of assessment in its various guises, what it can and cannot achieve and its strengths and weaknesses. Its recommendations, though now rather bypassed, are worth summarizing since they raise issues of continuing importance in trying to consider ways forward in the national testing. In summary, the document advocated the following as an alternative approach:

- formative assessment, 'rigorous and reliable' (p. 216) as the bedrock of the system, involving the training of teachers to enable them to increase their present understanding of assessment and the range of techniques available;

- the curriculum to be expressed as overall aims rather than fragmented Statements of Attainment, indicating descriptions of progress that would be more usable by teachers;

- a bank of assessment activities and test items to be used by teachers as a check on their own assessments, and also for APU-like surveys and national monitoring;

- the introduction of a National Record of Achievement, for the reporting of the profile of pupil achievements at regular points;

- the publication of test scores, but with value-added measures published alongside to set the results in context.

These proposals were criticized by others, most notably Black (1992), Blanchard (1992) and Goldstein (1992), each of whom pointed out different problems in these alternatives. Blanchard (*op cit.*) argued that the version of formative assessment outlined missed out the vital ingredient of the pupil, the focus of the intended learning and the vehicle through which improvements in learning will be achieved. Goldstein's criticisms were mainly concerned with the issue of resurrecting APU-type surveys when they had already proved so problematic in technical terms, and with trying to make a formative Record of Achievement into a summative document without fundamentally changing its nature. Most significantly, however, he also criticized the BERA group for ignoring the political realities and agendas of centralized control and marketplace ideology and, in so doing, missing the opportunity to have a genuine voice in the debate.

One of the most trenchant criticisms of the BERA critique, perhaps predictably, came from Paul Black, the chair of the original TGAT group. He saw three major weaknesses in their alternative recommendations: namely, the proposals about summative assessment, the introduction of national surveys and the attention given to criterion-referencing (Black, 1992). He emphasized that the TGAT group had been required to focus on the thorny issues of the links between formative and summative assessment, the need for public confidence in the results and the need for detailed calibration and moderation, and this was precisely what had made their task a difficult one. His main criticism was that to omit the 'certification' function of the assessments was a major flaw: individual pupils needed their scores to be valid and reliable, an outcome unlikely to be achieved through formative assessment, profiles of achievement and 'checking up' through nationally 'banked' assessment activities and questions. These are indeed fundamental matters within the system which politically naïve analyses are unlikely to be able to address with any incisiveness.

## The TGAT proposals: a retrospective

So with the benefit of hindsight and ten years experience of testing, how should we now view the original TGAT vision? Paul Black himself has recently written about the early days of the TGAT group (Black, 1998a). The group was aware both of the ideals, the most innovative and teacher-supportive approaches to assessment, and the realities of trying to ensure that the system proposed had a reasonable chance of being accepted by the politicians . In other words, their commitment was to formative assessment as the best way of achieving this raising of standards, tempered by the recognized need for valid and robust summative assessments.

The response to the report was on the whole positive, although Margaret Thatcher (the UK Prime Minister at the time) later wrote that she had suspicions about it when she heard that it had been welcomed by the National Union of Teachers and the *Times Educational Supplement* (Thatcher, 1993). Over time, as we have seen, the report's basic principles were gradually eroded, most notably in the abrupt change from 'tasks' to 'written examinations' in 1991 (Clarke, 1991), the progressive down-playing of the role of teacher assessment and the virtual abandonment of the idea of a single scale of progression by the move to "Key Stage' specifications in the 1995 review of the curriculum. Why did this happen?

The TGAT group had emphasized the idea that a wide-ranging and detailed assessment system could be put in place, but some of the inherent tensions in this assertion seem to have been overlooked. Daugherty (1995) refers to their emphasis on a seamless web of assessment methods and purposes as being rather too simple but nevertheless sees the approach as 'an honest attempt to reconcile the irreconcilable' (p.179). The criterion-referencing approach was indeed a radical one and, interestingly, both the left and the right (in political terms) took to the idea, the left because it represented an enlightened and educationally defensible approach to assessment, and the right because it seemed that vague and general notions about learning were at last being pinned down into clear statements about exactly what should be known and understood at various points in a child's schooling.

The 10-Level scale has proved to be a rather different matter, however, not least because it was (and is) not age-related. As we have seen, the simple idea of summarizing pupil attainments in a number of grades or categories at the end of each Key Stage seems an attractive and workable one, except for the fact that it does not encourage a wider view of progression across the phases of education, nor does it facilitate communication across the year groups in schools. However, recent studies have suggested that test outcomes and other aspects of pupil records are even now, after many years of the 10-Level scale and now an 8-Level scale, not being passed on and shared between phases (McCallum, 1995). What was not recognized in the early stages, however, was that it might not function well as a vehicle for end-of-Key-Stage reporting, given a limited number of levels and many years of schooling. Perhaps more significantly, it did not seem to be appropriate to answer the straightforward questions posed by the community and politicians alike, namely, exactly how pupils progress throughout their schooling.

These were the major fault-lines that emerged in the system during the first five years, but was the whole approach flawed from the beginning? There is no simple answer to this. There were clearly inherent problems in the proposals that were either overlooked or not addressed during their compiling but many aspects were valid and innovative. The sheer speed at which the curriculum had to be implemented would have put any system under strain, but particularly one so detailed and demanding of teachers. The proposals might also have had a more sporting chance of survival if the curriculum specifications produced by the subject working groups had been more streamlined from the beginning and in keeping with the basic TGAT framework. Perhaps Daugherty's judgement may be the most appropriate one: the TGAT framework was an honest and innovative attempt but it also contained some irreconcilable elements.

## Technical issues in the testing

Good assessment depends upon a clear purpose and full understanding of the three vital dimensions of *reliability* (or *dependability*), *validity/authenticity* and *manageability*. In a criterion-referenced system these three require special consideration. Looking back, much of what has happened in testing can be seen in terms of the balance, or lack of it, between these three, a point also discussed very effectively in Whetton (1997).

Criterion-referencing, while sometimes seen as the acceptable face of assessment by the education community, is not without its problems. Hailed in the early 1960s as a new and more appropriate way to assess, especially in the USA, it was in some ways founded upon a psychological model that had some question marks over it. Stating precise learning objectives and then deciding on ways of evaluating whether or not these have been achieved is not straightforward, since it may lead into over-specification and trivialization on the one hand or unassessable generalities on the other. It also carries with it the danger of only including those aspects of learning, understanding or behaviour that can most easily be specified, thereby potentially missing out some of the most vital dimensions in educational terms. It is also the case that earlier attempts at criterion-referencing in the 16-plus examination system had not been particularly successful

Initially, as the early versions of the National Curriculum were being devised, these matters were not necessarily in the forefront of the minds of the working parties whose job it was to specify the learning requirements at each level. The result, as we have seen, was the vast and complex system of State-ments of Attainment arranged in Levels, within Attainment Targets, within Profile Components, within subjects that prevailed in the late 1980s. The unwieldiness of this system rapidly became apparent and the first of several 'streamlinings' began. However, none of these necessarily eased the job of the test developers who still battled with the range of 'criteria' at some Levels in some subjects, and the ambiguity of many of them.

The earliest assessment activities (tasks) produced at Key Stages 1 and 3, true to the TGAT principles, were varied in content and presentation and response modes. This strengthened validity but at the expense of dependabil-ity in the outcomes. The first evaluations of the Key Stage 1 assessments in 1991 suggested there was not enough standardization in the procedures and scoring to ensure reliability and massive manageability issues were raised. The responses to 1991 sent reverberations throughout the system and it proved to be a period of rapid learning for all, test developers, policy-makers and teach-ers alike. Almost overnight the assessment goal posts were moved, especially at Key Stage 3 where rich assessment 'tasks' became formal written examina-tions. But even at Key Stage 1 the first of many subtle and not so subtle steps were taken to formalize the assessment by moving away from practical tasks and activities towards formal pencil and paper tests. At this point manageabil-ity had triumphed over validity.

### Reliability

But what about reliability? The first assessment activities had some question marks over them in this regard, and the only remedy, had this approach pre-vailed, would have been extensive training of the teachers in order to ensure an acceptable degree of agreement about the assessment judgements being made. Such moderation procedures and agreement trialling might, paradoxically, have brought about more rapid improvement in the standards of teaching and learning, but this is the subject for later sections in this chapter. In the event, the advent of more written tests and mark-based approaches to some extent changed the focus for the analysis of reliability.

As we saw in *Chapter 4*, traditional notions of reliability do not match with a criterion-referenced approach to assessment. In essence, it becomes instead an matter of estimating the dependability of the categorizations derived from the aggregation of the assessment information; in other words, the extent to which the Level awarded to each pupil represents a 'true' placement. The advent of written tests instead of assessment activities made the situation more straight-

forward, since the element of teacher judgement and the variability this introduced into the system was removed. In this new circumstance, some of the
major aspects of reliability become the uniformity of the administration procedures, the accuracy of the marking and the precise way the marks are generated and aggregated. Over the years, especially at Key Stage 3, a variety of
mark aggregation systems has been implemented, including some extremely
bizarre ones. However, the situation with the written test at all Key Stages has
now settled down to a system of simple threshold marks for each level. Such
'cut-score' methods always seem to have an arbitrariness to them, but it is the
same in any grading system: there will always be pupils who just miss the
threshold.

But in what sense is this approach criterion-referenced? Perhaps the QCA
terminology is better used here. The tests are 'criterion-related' in that each
question included in the tests assesses an element of the prescribed curriculum
and the questions as a whole in a test sample the total domain of the Programme of Study. This is one of the only ways of proceeding, since the Programmes of Study are not 'levelled' in the way that Statements of Attainment
were. Each question is therefore criterion-related, but once it has been
included in the test, with the scoring systems as they now stand, the questions
become vehicles for collecting marks, which are then totalled and used (in relation to the thresholds) to locate the pupil at a level for the test. However, we still
need much more research on exactly how pupils score their marks and how
these 'profiles' of scores relate to both the sampling of the curriculum and the
level of difficulty of the questions. It is in this context that questions of validity
again come into play.

As many critics have pointed out (see in particular *Chapter 7* ) it seems
unlikely that two to three hours of a pencil and paper test can adequately
address and sample the broad curriculum of each core subject: written answers
can seldom cover all the skills and understandings required. So are the tests at
each Key Stage valid and authentic (Torrance, 1995)? The answer to this question varies to some extent from Key Stage to Key Stage and the reasons for any
invalidity within them will vary accordingly. At Key Stage 1, the validity problems are more likely to reside in the mode of assessment for such young pupils,
while at Key Stage 2 the problem probably rests partly in the mode of the
assessments and the manner in which the questions are asked and partly in the
sampling of the curriculum. The validity queries at Key Stage 3 seem to be
mainly those of sampling such a wide curriculum in a short series of tests (for
example, Ruthven, 1995). Written tests have no doubt enhanced the reliability
and manageability of the testing, particularly now that administration procedures and marking are more tightly monitored, but at the expense of some
aspects of validity. The uses to which the results are put is also a major element
in the evaluation of validity: in high stakes assessment, where the results have

such significance, the appropriateness and dependability of the outcomes are thrown into even greater relief.

## The uses of the results: parents, reporting and league tables

Informing parents about their children's progress in school is clearly a matter of fundamental importance. Although not so high profile an agenda in the late 1980s when the National Curriculum was being formulated and the legislation drafted, the whole movement was taking place against the backdrop of the 'market economy' ideology of the (then) Conservative government. Parents were significant 'consumers' in relation to the education system and they had a right to information. The 'Records of Achievement' initiatives had made some impact during the 1980s, but the line adopted by the Department for Education was that this should not be required as the national reporting system; instead, the precise form of reporting to parents would be left for schools to determine. By 1991, however, the DES had published a draft 'standard format' for reporting to parents and had also published a leaflet entitled *How is your child doing at school?* (DES/WO, 1991). This leaflet attempted to offer guidance to parents about interpreting the reports they would receive from schools and, significantly, explained the national assessments purely in terms of reporting to parents about their individual child.

Later in 1991, however, the era of 'Charters' began, at the instigation of the (new) Prime Minister, John Major. The document *Education: A Charter for Parents* was published in September 1991 and put considerable emphasis on parents having an entitlement not only to information about their own child's progress but also about the performance of schools as a whole in order to be able to make judgements and choices about where to send their children. This Charter also set out in detail more about the kind of report parents could expect from schools which was to include information about national performance on the tests. Parents were also entitled to a report from school governors that would give information about performance on the national tests for the school as a whole. This brief was subsequently added to in various Circulars (1992), which gradually made it clear that the core subjects were to be the main focus.

All this necessarily implied that national data about performance would be collected and published, a process that had begun (in the national testing) in December 1991, when the first Key Stage 1 results were published, LEA by LEA (but not school by school), much to the dismay of LEAs who had been told that 1991 was to be an 'unreported run' for the tests. Once begun, this procedure accelerated so that we now have a situation where not only are A level and GCSE examination results published school by school but also the Key Stage 2 test results. The publication of the results for Key Stages 1 and 3 was ended in 1993. Ironically, this means that the Key Stage 2 tests take on a very high profile indeed, despite the fact that they were the last to come on-stream.

Whether parents welcome this information and make use of it is not clear. One study in the early days of the Key Stage 1 testing (Holden *et al.*, 1993) suggested that parents were satisfied with their children's education but that they were not entirely clear about the format of the national tests. A scant majority (51per cent of a sample of 120 sets of parents) thought testing was a good idea, many saying that it showed up their children's strengths and weaknesses in a useful way. However, about a quarter of the sample were against the idea of testing, arguing that the children were too young. Just under half the sample (47per cent) agreed with the idea of publishing the results, most saying it allowed them to compare schools. On the other hand, a quarter of this sample were against the idea of publication, seeing it as potentially misleading information.

We have already reviewed the matter of league tables (see *Chapter 6*) and suggested that this is still an area where further research and investigation need to be carried out. Raw data on the scoring outcomes of individual schools are indeed misleading, but the problem at the moment, in both practical and theoretical terms, is to find a measure of 'value-added' that is sensitive enough to reveal the required 'adjustments' to the raw scores but not so unwieldy as to make the system unworkable. A cynic might, however, point out that publishing these league tables has become big business for national and local newspapers: listings sell newspapers and so, whether they need it or not, parents and the community are bombarded with this information during the 'league-tables season'.

## Teacher assessment and the national tests

The TGAT report had outlined a two-pronged national assessment system, combining moderated teacher assessments and national Standard Assessment Tasks. In this system, teachers were supposed to carry out formative assessments across the curriculum (underpinned by sound record keeping) and to reach summative judgements at the ends of the Key Stages. This demanded careful planning and detailed recording in relation to both the curriculum requirements and the learning needs of individual pupils, but from the beginning teachers were offered little guidance about these procedures (Owen, 1991). Moderation, the means of bringing assessment judgements into line and ensuring consistency of standards, was stressed by TGAT as a vital piece in the jigsaw of the national assessments. In policy terms, however, teacher assessment and the related aspect of moderation seem always to have been seen as being of secondary importance, and the gradual moving of the assessment goal posts in the early 1990s increased this trend.

In the early days of national curriculum implementation, the extent of the curriculum specifications, even in the core subjects alone, meant that teacher assessment was likely to play a role. Not all Attainment Targets could be assessed in the SATs, so teacher assessment scores were included in the final aggregation process at Key Stage 1. However, where a Teacher Assessment (TA) score and SAT score were different for the same Attainment Target, then the test score over-ruled the teacher's judgement, unless a clear case was made by the teacher. The first year (1991) brought many discrepancies between the two sets of scores, but these were rapidly ironed out in the subsequent year as teachers learned the rules of the game and as Teacher Assessment scores could be decided after the testing had been carried out (Shorrocks *et al.*, 1992 ; 1993).

Teacher assessment as such received little direct support from the centre. In 1990 (SEAC, 1990) the famous Teacher Assessment books were published to a mixed reception and at later points SCAA published several guides for teachers at all Key Stages exemplifying the required standards for each Level (see for example, SCAA, 1996b). The funding and resource, however, basically went into the testing and the procedures that supported it (Black, 1994).

From the early days also, moderation procedures had been put in place to try to ensure some consistency of standards across teachers, schools and regions, although the matter of a national audit seemed to be overlooked. These procedures took different forms. At Key Stage 1, it was the responsibility of the LEAs and took the form of school clusters, agreement trials and moderation audits. At Key Stage 3, however, LEAs shared the responsibility with the examining boards, with the LEAs being responsible for administration and training and the examining boards for moderation arrangements, the quality audit. The advent of the written tests made this distinction even more clear.

When the crisis emerged in 1993, the unmanageability of the teacher assessment demands was a significant part of the argument. The Dearing review offered guidance that teacher assessments and record keeping should be drastically cut back, a move in any case facilitated by the streamlining of the curriculum. Teacher assessment was to be recognized for what it was –a very different approach to assessment, covering many more dimensions of pupils' work on many more occasions than the tests. It was to be recognized more formally by being reported separately to parents, with these important differences explained.

Teacher assessment has therefore had a chequered history in the national testing, beginning as a central issue in the original conception but never being given the same high profile or recognition as the tests (Gipps, 1995). Lip service has been paid to it, but it has attracted neither the attention nor the resources of the tests. Yet there is a paradox here. There has always been a school of thought in education circles (for example, Harlen, 1992) that the most effective teaching can take place when integral formative assessment is part of teacher strategy in the classroom. In other words, careful tracking of what pupils can and cannot do should give rise to more focused teaching and hence better learning. This was the touchstone of the TGAT approach and one important way in which the quality of teaching could be improved and standards raised (Black, 1998a).

A recent survey of the research on the effects of formative assessment (Black and Wiliam, 1998) shows that the frequent, constructive feedback to pupils that such an approach implies yields substantial learning gains. This seems to be especially relevant for disadvantaged learners and low-attaining pupils, the very group where attainment in a national context needs most improvement. The paradox is that a government policy on effective teacher assessment of a formative nature might have produced better and faster gains in performance than the present emphasis on using testing to raise standards. This is speculation, but it is interesting speculation and a topic to which we will return at the end of this chapter.

## Testing, falling standards and school improvement

The issues of falling standards and school improvement strategies could each be the subject of a book in themselves in order to do them justice. It is not the intention here to go into much detail on either of them but rather to signal the links between these various aspects of national policy and to try to reach some final conclusions.

From the earliest days of its inception, the raising of 'standards' (however defined and measured) was always one of the central purposes of the National Curriculum. This embodied both a raising of standards through clarifying what was to be taught and also through monitoring whether it had been learned via the assessment system. The assessment agenda, both hidden and overt, was that the testing would of itself lift performance in schools, particularly if the results were made public. This was very much the ideology of the first five years or so of the implementation. Questions were raised about making over-simplistic links of this kind (see for example Shorrocks *et al.*, 1992 and others) and almost encouraging the extensive coaching and 'teaching to the test' kind of school response that would be the very worst of outcomes. Fears abounded, as we have seen throughout this book, that the assessment tail would wag the curriculum dog in completely unacceptable and unproductive ways.

More recently, however, the central government emphasis appears to have moved towards school improvement approaches, alongside the continued school-by-school publication of the test results at Key Stage 2. This seems to be a step in the right direction, since the problem with relying on the 'stick' of the league tables is that it provides schools with absolutely no guidance about rectifying problems and improving the quality of teaching and learning – the real driving force for improving standards (Desforges, 1992). Of course, there now exists a formal system of school inspections (through OFSTED), in England and Wales, which is another potential channel for bringing about change and improvement. There can be, however, tensions between these two forces for change (the national testing outcomes and the school inspections) as witnessed by a recent report (*Daily Telegraph*, 14.7.98) that showed that one of the highest performing schools in the Key Stage 2 league tables had received a poor inspection report. They were judged to be failing their pupils in important ways and offering poor quality teaching, ill-matched to the potential of the pupils. This example points up both the importance of value-added measures in the league tables and also the inappropriateness of relying on the test outcomes as a measure of the quality of the teaching and learning going on in a school.

So how can schools be improved and what role could and should the testing play in this? This is not the place to detail the vast international literature that now exists on the subjects of both school effectiveness and school improvement (but see, for example, reviews by Brown 1994; Reynolds, 1995). The key message seems to be that 'input–output' measures and performance indicator approaches may have a role to play in the analysis, but it is by examining processes and strategies within schools that the greatest insights are likely to be gained. At the level of the school, organizational and management strategies are important but as Black and Wiliam (1998) argue, we also need to investigate the 'black box' of the classroom and the teaching and assessment strategies deployed there.

The central government response, the somewhat revised one of the last few years, has moved into this arena in a limited way by their benchmarking and target-setting initiatives. From September 1998, all schools, primary and secondary, will be required to set targets for their test outcomes at the relevant National Curriculum levels for the next few years. Schools will also be able to compare themselves and their 'outputs' with other schools with similar catchments and intakes (benchmarking). Both these strategies are interesting ones, but once again they focus on 'product' rather than 'process'.

In relation to target setting, the vital question is *how* a school sets its targets. It is perfectly possible for schools to draw figures out of the air, as it were, or to apply a formula like adding a small percentage each year. Approached in this way, performance may or may not rise to meet these targets, since no thought has gone into the school and classroom issues which affect outcomes. More enlightened Local Education Authorities and schools have approached the issue in a different way (see, for example, DfEE, 1996). They have used the opportunity to consider past test results in detail, for instance looking at the performance of boys and girls or the performance of the highest and lowest attaining groups of pupils, and then evaluating these against wider aspects of school organization and classroom teaching strategies. In other words, this approach requires schools, as an organization, to sit down, think and discuss. If anything is likely to improve the quality of what goes on in schools it is this emphasis on the process of professional self-evaluation and open-minded discussion. The test results may therefore indeed improve over the years, and the national targets may be met, but this will have been achieved through a process that is professionally productive in both the shorter and longer term.

## So what of the future?

The title of this book contains the word 'future', so what is the answer to this particular question? In a sense it has been implicitly answered in most chapters, since by outlining the history and pointing out the strengths and weaknesses of the present situation, there have been implicit implications for what could happen. However, it will not be educational professionals who decide, it will be the politicians. Such matters are far too important to be left to the professionals (Ball, 1990)!

The political commitment to raising standards in all schools suggests that the national testing and monitoring programme will continue, with all schools and all children in each of the relevant age groups being involved. In principle, of course, this is not the only way to proceed even with a similar political agenda: national sampling of performance could replace it, but this is a very different approach, where testing could become more lengthy and detailed because only a national *sample* of schools and pupils would be involved. This would potentially increase the validity of the testing itself and the manageability issue would be less of a problem since only a limited number of schools would be involved each time. The issue of constructing equivalent tests for each occasion would, in theory, be no more challenging than at present, although the equating procedures (statistical and more qualitative) would probably need to be reconsidered and sharpened up. However, the phrase 'similar political agendas' was very deliberately used earlier in this paragraph. This survey approach would not require the accountability of *all* schools each year, and hence it would not meet other aspects of the agenda.

The present assessment system is a product of both this particular agenda and of a series of *ad hoc* government decisions, often taken at great speed and without sufficient evidence or reflection. As such, it is the very opposite of the rational and planned system that the original TGAT proposals envisaged, and which, no doubt, the politicians too held as an ideal. It is rather like the story of the traveller seeking directions who is told not to start from here. The present testing has its flaws, many of them discussed in these pages, and if we had the opportunity to start again we would surely approach the task very differently. This at least would avoid the confusion, rescinded decisions, teacher stress and in-fighting that have characterized the past decade. Whether the end products would be very different, however, is a most interesting question to pose.

# Glossary of acronyms

| | |
|---|---|
| APU: | Assessment of Performance Unit |
| AT: | Attainment Targets |
| BERA: | British Educational Research Association |
| CAI: | Common Assessment Instrument |
| CATS: | Consortium for Assessment and Testing in Schools |
| DES: | Department for Education and Science |
| DfEE: | Department for Education and Employment |
| EAL: | English as an Additional Language |
| ELMAG: | East London Monitoring and Assessment Group |
| FUR: | First Unreported Run |
| GCSE: | General Certificate of Secondary Education |
| HMI: | Her Majesty's Inspectorate |
| ILEA: | Inner London Education Authority |
| LEA: | Local Education Authority |
| MCT: | Minimum Competency Testing |
| NAEP: | National Assessment of Educational Progress |
| NAS/UWT: | National Association of Schoolmasters/Union of Women Teachers |
| NEA: | Northern Examinations Association |
| NFER: | National Foundation for Educational Research |
| NFER/BGC. | National Foundation for Educational Research/Bishop Grosseteste College |
| NICC: | Northern Ireland Curriculum Council |
| NISEAC: | Northern Ireland School Examinations and Assessment Council |
| NUT: | National Union of Teachers |
| OFSTED: | Office for Standards in Education |
| PC: | Profile Component |
| QCA: | Qualifications and Curriculum Authority |
| SAT: | Standard Assessment Task |
| SCAA: | School Curriculum and Assessment Authority |
| SCCC: | Scottish Consultative Council on the Curriculum |
| SEAC: | School Examinations and Assessment Council |
| SEB: | Scottish Examination Board |
| SEN: | Special Educational Needs |
| SOA: | Statement of Attainment |
| STAIR: | Standard Tests and Assessments Implementation Research |
| TA: | Teacher Assessment |
| TGAT: | Task Group on Assessment and Testing |
| WGMET: | Working Group on Measurement and Educational Testing |
| WO: | Welsh Office |

# References

Alexander, R. (1984). *Primary Teaching.* London: Holt, Rinehart & Winston.

Alexander, R. (1992). *Policy and Practice in Primary Education.* London: Routledge.

Alexander, R., Rose, J. and Woodhead, C. (1992). *Curriculum Organisation and Classroom Practice in Primary Schools.* London: DES.

Angoff, W.H. (1971). Scales, norms and equivalent scores. In R.L Thorndike (Ed.) *Educational and Psychological Measurement.* Washington, D.C.: American Council on Education.

Ausubel, D. P., Novak, J. D. and Hanesian, H. (1978). *Educational Psychology: A cognitive view.* New York and London: Holt, Rinehart &Winston.

Ball, S. (1990). *Politics and Policy Making in Education.* London: Routledge.

Balogh, J. (1982). *Profile Reports for School Leavers.* York: Longman

Barnes, A. (1993). Key Stages in the development of the Key Stage 3 SATs. *English in Education, 27,* 4–9.

Bartlett, D. (1991). SATs for some but not for all? *British Journal of Special Education, 18,* 90–92.

Bennett, S.N., Desforges, C., Cockburn, A. and Wilkinson, B. (1984). *The Quality of Pupil Learning Experiences.* New York: Lawrence Erlbaum.

Birnbaum, I. (1993). Averaging out, *Education, 181,* 390.

Black, H., D. and Dockrell, W., B. (1984). *Criterion Referenced Assessment in the Classroom.* Edinburgh: The Scottish Council for Research in Education.

Black, P. (1990). APU Science – the past and the future. *School Science Review, 72,* 13–29.

Black, P. (1992). Assessment policy and public confidence: comments on the BERA Policy Task Group's article 'Assessment and the improvement of education'. *The Curriculum Journal, 4,* 421–427.

Black, P. (1994). Performance assessment and accountability: the experience of England and Wales. *Educational Evaluation and Policy, 16,* 191–203.

Black, P. (1998a). Learning, League Tables and National Assessment: Opportunity lost or hope deferred? *Oxford Review of Education, 24,* 57–68.

Black, P. (1998b). *The Black Box: Raising standards through classroom assessment.* London: Kings College, London.

Black, P. and Wiliam, D. (1998). Assessment and Classroom Learning. *Assessment in Education, 5,* 7–73.

Boaler, J. (1994). When do girls prefer football to fashion? An analysis of female underachievement in relation to 'realistic' mathematics contexts. *British Educational Journal, 20,* 551–564.

Blanchard, J. (1992). A critical commentary on the BERA Policy Task Group's article 'Assessment and the Improvement of Education'. *The Curriculum Journal, 4,* 115–119.

Brennan, R.L. and Kane, M.T. (1977). An index of dependability for mastery test. *Journal of Educational Measurement, 14,* 277–289.

Broadfoot, P. (Ed.) (1986). *Profiles and Records of Achievement: A review of issues and practice.* London: Holt, Rinehart & Winston.

Brown, S. (1994). School effectiveness research and the evaluation of schools. *Evaluation and Research in Education, 8,* 55–68.

Byers, R. (1994). The Dearing Review of the National Curriculum. *British Journal of Special Education, 21,* 92–96.

Callaghan, J. (1976). 'Time and Chance'. Speech given at Ruskin College, Oxford, reprinted in Cox, C. B. and Boyson, R., *Black Paper* 5. London: Critical Quarterly Society.

Campbell, R. J. (1993). The broad and balanced curriculum in primary schools: some limitations on reform. *The Curriculum Journal, 4,* 215–229.

Clarke, K. (1991). Letter to the School Examinations and Assessment Council, January, 1991.

Clarke, K. (1991a). Speech to the Secondary Heads Association, March, 1991.

Clarke, P. and Christie, T. (1996). Trialling agreement: a discourse for change. *British Journal of Curriculum and Assessment, 6,* 12–18.

Close, G., Furlong, T. and Swain, J. (1996). The Key Stage 3 tests and tasks: Headteacher opinions on their impact, effect on the curriculum, teaching and learning and teachers' assessments. *British Journal of Curriculum and Assessment, 6,* 19–25.

Close, G., Furlong, T. and Simon, S. (1997). *The Validity of the 1996 Key Stage 2 Tests in English, Mathematics and Science.* London: Association of Teachers and Lecturers.

Colwill, I. (1996). Intentions and perceptions: a review of the first year of monitoring the school curriculum in England. *British Journal of Curriculum and Assessment, 7,* 33–37.

Conway, S (1992). An assessment of the damage done to Bradford by the publication of the Key Stage 1 league tables in 1991. *Education, 13th, March, 10.*

Cooper, B (1993). Testing National Curriculum mathematics: some critical comments on the treatment of 'real' contexts for mathematics. *The Curriculum Journal, 3,* 231–244.

Cox, C.B. and Dyson, A.E. (1969). *An Open Letter to Members of Parliament.* In C.B. Cox, and A.E. Dyson (Eds), Black Paper 2. London: Critical Quarterly Society.

Daily Telegraph (1998) *'Top school criticised by Ofsted'.* article by John Clare (Education Editor), 14.7.98.

Daniels, S., Shorrocks-Taylor, D. and Redfern, E. (1999). Starting summer born children earlier at infant school can improve their National Curriculum results: or can it? *Oxford Review of Education*, in press.

D'Arcy, J. (1994a). Assessment and testing in schools: a Northern Ireland perspective. *The Curriculum Journal, 5 ,* 43–53.

D'Arcy, J. (1994b). Setting reliable National Curriculum standards: a guide to the Angoff procedure. *Assessment in Education, 1,* 181–199.

Daugherty, R. (1995). *National Curriculum Assessment: A Review of Policy 1987–1994.* London: Falmer Press.

Dearing, R. (1993). *The National Curriculum and its Assessment: Final Report.* London: School Curriculum and Assessment Authority.

Department of Education and Science / Welsh Office (1974). *Educational Disadvantage and the Educational Needs of Immigrants.* London: HMSO.

Department of Education and Science/Welsh Office (1980). *A framework for the School Curriculum,* London, DES/WO

Department of Education and Science/Welsh Office (1982). *Mathematics Counts* (The Cockcroft Report). London: HMSO.

Department of Education and Science/Welsh Office (1985). *Better Schools.* London: HMSO.

Department of Education and Science/Welsh Office (1988). *National Curriculum Task Group on Assessment and Testing: A Report.* London: DES / WO.

Department of Education and Science/Welsh Office (1991). *How is your child doing at school?* Leaflet. London: DES/WO.

Department of Education and Science/Welsh Office (1995). *Assessing seven and eleven year-olds in 1995.* Circular 21/94. London: DES.

Department for Education and Employment (1996). *Looking at National Curriculum Assessment Results: What LEAs are doing.* London: DfEE.

Desforges, C. (1992). Assessment and learning. *Forum, 34,* 68–69.

Donaldson, M. C. (1987). *Children's Mind.* London: Fontana Press.

Dutta, K. (1992). The SATs experience: an individual teacher's perspective. *Multicultural Teaching, 10,* 24–27.

Ebel, R. L. (1991). *Essentials of Educational Measurement.* Englewood Cliffs, N.J.: Prentice Hall.

Elliott, J. (1991). Disconnecting knowledge and understanding from human values: a critique of National Curriculum development. *The Curriculum Journal, 2,* 19–31.

Enright, L. (1993). Testamania. *Education, April,* 323.

Fairbrother, R. (1993). Reliability, validity and manageability of national tests. *British Journal of Curriculum and Assessment, 4,* 7–13.

Fairbrother, R., Dillon, J. and Gill, P. (1995). Assessment at Key Stage 3: teachers' attitudes and practices. *British Journal of Curriculum and Assessment, 5,* 25–31.

Ferriman, B., Lock, R. and Soares, A. (1994). Influences of the National Curriculum on assessment in Key Stage 3. *School Science Review, 76,* 116–120.

Forbes, R.H. (1982). Testing in the USA. *Educational Analysis, 4,* 69–76.

Galton, M. and Simon, B. (1980). *Inside the Primary Classroom.* London: Routledge & Kegan Paul.

Gill, P. (1994). Comparisons of Key Stage 3 pupils' performances in national tests in Science and Mathematics: a question of validity. *British Journal of Curriculum and Assessment, 4,* 12–15.

Gipps, C. and Goldstein, H. (1983). *Monitoring Children: An evaluation of the Assessment of Performance Unit.* London: Heinemann.

Gipps, C., Steadman, S. and Blackstone. T. (1983). *Testing children: standardised testing in schools and LEAs.* London: Heinemann.

Gipps, C. (1990). The debate over standards and the uses of tests. In B. Moon, J. Isaac and J. Powney, *Judging Standards and Effectiveness in Education.* London: Hodder & Stoughton.

Gipps, C. (1992). Equal opportunities and the Standard Assessment Tasks for 7 year-olds. *Curriculum Journal, 3,* 171–183.

Gipps, C. (1995). Teacher assessment and teacher development. *Education, 3,* 1–8.

Glaser, R. (1963). Instructional technology and the measurement of learning outcomes. *American Psychologist, 18,* 519–521.

Golby, M. (1994). After Dearing: a critical review of the Dearing Report. *The Curriculum Journal, 5,* 95–105.

Goldstein, H. (1992). Improving assessment: a response to the BERA Policy Task Group's report on assessment. *The Curriculum Journal, 4,* 121–123.

Goldstein, H and Nuttall, D. (1986). Can graded assessments, records of achievement, modular assessment and GCSE co-exist? In C.V. Gipps (Ed.) The GCSE: an uncommon exam. *Bedford Way Papers, 29.* London: Institute of Education.

Gorwood, B. (1994). Curriculum organisation and classroom practice in primary schools – can we learn from middle schools? *School Organisation, 14,* 247–256.

Gravelle, M. (1990). Assessment and bilingual pupils. *Multicultural Teaching, 9,* 13–15.

Guy, W and Chambers, P. (1974). Public examinations and pupils rights revisited. *Cambridge Journal of Education, 4,* 47–50.

Hargreaves, E. (1996). Using and applying mathematics: Research into effective assessment in M. Sainsbury (Ed.) *SATs- the inside story: the development of the first national assessments of seven-year-olds, 1989-1995.* Slough: National Foundation for Educational Research

Harlen, W., Gipps, C., Broadfoot, P. and Nuttall, D. (1992). Assessment and the Improvement of Education. *Curriculum Journal, 3,* 215–230.

Harlen, W. and Malcolm, H. (1994). Putting the curriculum and assessment guidelines in place in Scottish primary schools. *The Curriculum Journal, 5,* 55–67.

Harding, A. and Naylor, J.A. (1980). Graded objectives in second language learning: a way ahead. *Audio-Visual Language Journal, 17,* 169–174.

Harris, M. and Coltheart, M. (1986). *Language Processing in Children and Adults.* London: Routledge & Kegan Paul.

HMI (1985). *The Curriculum from 5 to 16.* London: HMSO.

HMI (1992). *Assessment, Recording and Reporting: A Report by HMI on the Second Year, 1992–93.* London: HMSO.

Holden, C., Hughes, M.and Desforges, C. (1993). What do parents want from assessment? *Education, 3–13, 3–7.*

Inhelder, B., Chipman, H. and Zwingmann, C. (1976). *Piaget and His School: A reader in developmental psychology.* New York: Springer-Verlag.

Iven, H. (1992). Testamania: the proposed Key Stage 3 pilot tests. *Education 3–13, 3,* 30–33, *179,* 323.

Jackson, C (1996). *Understanding Psychological Testing.* Leicester. British Psychological Society.

Jones, G.E. (1994). Which nation's curriculum? – the case of Wales. *The Curriculum Journal, 5,* 5–16.

Light, P. (1979). *The Development of Social Sensitivity.* Cambridge: Cambridge University Press.

Macintosh, H. (1993). Referencing in assessment. *British Journal of Curriculum and Assessment, 4,* 24–26.

McCallum, B. (1995). The transfer and use of information between primary and secondary schools. *British Journal of Curriculum and Assessment, 6,* 10–14.

McCallum, B. (1995). Marking the marking: External marking of Key Stage 2 English 1995. *British Journal of Curriculum and Assessment, 6,* 15–17.

Meadows, S. (1993). *The Child as Thinker.* London and New York: Routledge.

Messick, S. (1980). Test Validity and the Ethics of Assessment. *American Psychologist, 35,* 1012–1027.

Mortimore, P. and Mortimore, J. (1986). Secondary school examinations: the helpful servants not the dominating master. *Bedford Way Papers, 18.* London: Institute of Education.

Moon, B. (1990). A child's curriculum for the 1990s. *Curriculum Journal, 2,* 5–17.

Murphy, R. J. L. (1986). The emperor has no clothes: grade criteria and the GCSE. In Gipps *et al.,* The GCSE: An Uncommon Exam. *Bedford Way Papers 29.* London: Institute of Education.

Murphy, R. J. L (1994). Dearing: a farewell to criterion referencing? *British Journal of Curriculum and Assessment, 4,* 10–12.

Murphy, R. J. L. (1987). Assessing a national curriculum. *Journal of Education Policy, 2,* 317–323.

Murphy, R. J. L. (1988). National testing: assessing the damage, *ACE Bulletin, 23,* 10–12.

Murphy, R. J. L. (1996). Drawing outrageous conclusions from national assessment results: where will it all end? *British Journal of Curriculum and Assessment, 7,* 32–34.

National Curriculum Council (1990a). *The National Curriculum Information Pack No. 2*. York: NCC.

National Curriculum Council (1990b). *Curriculum Guidance: The Whole Curriculum*. York: NCC.

National Union of Teachers (1996). *Key Stage 2 Test and Teacher Assessment Results: The case against league tables*. London: NUT.

Nickson, M. (1996). What is the difference between a pizza and a relay race? The role of context in assessing KS2 Mathematics. *British Journal of Curriculum and Assessment, 7*, 19–23.

Nuttall, D. (1980). Will the APU rule the curriculum? Supplement to *Education, 155: 21*, ix–x.

Nuttall, D. L. (1988). The implications of National Curriculum Assessments. *Educational Psychology, 8*, 229–236.

Nuttall, D. and Goldstein, H. (1984). Profiles and graded tests: The technical issues. In *Profiles in Action*. London: Further Education Unit.

Owen, P. (1991). The case for teacher assessment. *Education, 3*, 30–33.

Piaget, J. (1954). *The Construction of Reality in the Child*. New York: Basic Books.

Piaget, J. (1970). *Genetic Epistemology*. New York: Columbia University Press.

Pole, C. (1993). *Assessing and Recording Achievement*. Buckingham: Open University Press.

Pollitt, A., Hutchinson, C., Entwistle, N. and De Luca, C. (1985). *What makes an exam question difficult?* Edinburgh: Scottish Academic Press.

Popham, W. J. (1987). Two-plus decades of educational objectives. *International Journal of Educational Research, 11*, 31–41.

Qualifications and Curriculum Authority (1997). *Assessment and Reporting Arrangements, Key Stage 2*. London: QCA.

Qualifications and Curriculum Authority (1998a). Unpublished information on the performance of boys and girls at Key Stages 2 and 3.

Qualifications and Curriculum Authority (1998b). *Standards at Key Stage 3 English: Report on the 1997 National Curriculum Assessments for 14-year-olds*. London: QCA.

Qualifications and Curriculum Authority (1998c). *Standards at Key Stage 3 Mathematics: Report on the 1997 National Curriculum Assessments for 14-year-olds*. London: QCA.

Qualifications and Curriculum Authority (1998d). *Standards at Key Stage 3 Science: Report on the 1997 National Curriculum Assessments for 14 year-olds*. London: QCA.

Qualifications and Curriculum Authority (1998e). *Standards at Key Stage 2, English, Mathematics and Science*. London: QCA.

Qualifications and Curriculum Authority (1998f). *Standards at Key Stage 1, English and Mathematics*. London: QCA.

Reynolds, D. (1995). The future of education: the highly reliable school, *Education Review, 9*, 48-51.

Richards, C. (1993). Implementing the National Curriculum at Key Stage 2. *The Curriculum Journal, 4*, 231–328.

Richardson, K. (1991). *Understanding Intelligence*. Milton Keynes: Open University Press.

Robinson, C. (1988). Assessment and the Curriculum, *Educational Psychology, 8*, 221-227.

Ruthven, K. (1995). Beyond common sense: reconceptualising National Curriculum assessment. *The Curriculum Journal, 6*, 5–28.

Scardamalia, M. and Bereiter, C. (1986). 'Writing'. in R.F. Dillon and R.J. Sternberg (Eds) *Cognition and Instruction*. New York: Academic Press.

Schagen, I. and Hutchison, D. (1994). Measuring the reliability of national curriculum assessment. *Educational Research, 36*, 211–221.

Schneider, W. and Pressley, M. (1989). *Memory Development between 2 and 20*. Berlin: Springer-Verlag.

Schools Council (1982). *Profile Reports for School Leavers*. York: Longman.

School Curriculum and Assessment Authority (1995a). *Review of Assessment and Testing: Report from the School Curriculum and Assessment Authority to the Secretary of State for Education and Employment*. London: SCAA.

School Curriculum and Assessment Authority (1995b). *Evaluation of Key Stage 2 Assessment in England and Wales 1995*. London: SCAA.

School Curriculum and Assessment Authority (1995c). *Evaluation of the External Marking of National Curriculum Tests in 1995*. London: SCAA.

School Curriculum and Assessment Authority (1995d). *Standards at Key Stage 2, English, Mathematics and Science*. London: SCAA.

School Curriculum and Assessment Authority (1995e). *Consistency in Teacher Assessment: Exemplification of Standards (Mathematics), Key Stages 1 and 2*. London: SCAA.

School Curriculum and Assessment Authority (1996). *Consistency in Teacher Assessment: Exemplification of Standards (Mathematics), Key Stages 1 and 2*. London: SCAA.

School Curriculum and Assessment Authority (1996b). *Consistency in Teacher Assessment: Exemplification of Standards, Key Stages 1, 2 and 3*. London: SCAA.

School Curriculum and Assessment Authority (1997a). *Evaluation of Key Stage 2 Assessment in England 1996*. London: SCAA.

School Curriculum and Assessment Authority (1997b). *Evaluation of Key Stage 3 Assessment in 1995 and 1996 at the University of Exeter*. London: SCAA.

School Curriculum and Assessment Authority (1997c). *The Value Added National Project: Report to the Secretary of State*. London: SCAA.

School Curriculum and Assessment Authority (1997d). *Assessment and Reporting Arrangements*, London, SCAA.

School Examination and Assessment Council (1990). *A Guide to Teacher Assessment: Packs A, B and C, a Source Book for Teacher Assessment*. SEAC/Heinemann Educational.

School Examination and Assessment Council (1991a). *School Assessment Folder*. London: SEAC.

School Examination and Assessment Council (1991b). *The Pilot Study of Standard Assessment Tasks: a report by the STAIR Consortium*. London: SEAC.

School Examination and Assessment Council (1991c). *A Pilot Study of Standard Assessment Tasks for Key Stage 1: a report by the NFER/BGC Consortium*. London: SEAC.

School Examination and Assessment Council (1991d). *A Pilot Study of Standard Assessment Tasks for Key Stage 1: a report by the CATS Consortium*. London: SEAC.

School Examination and Assessment Council (1992e) *Key Stage 1 Pilot 1990: a report from the Evaluation and Monitoring Unit*. London: SEAC.

Sebba, J. and Byers, R. (1992). The National Curriculum: control or liberation for pupils with learning difficulties? *The Curriculum Journal, 3* , 143–160.

Shan, S.-J. (1990). Assessment by monolingual teachers of developing bilinguals at Key Stage 1. *Multicultural Teaching, 9*, 16–20.

Shorrocks, D., Daniels, S., Frobisher, L., Nelson, N. , Waterson, A., and Bell, J. (1992). *The Evaluation of National Curriculum Assessment at Key Stage 1: Final Report of the ENCA 1 Project*. London: Schools Examination and Assessment Council.

Shorrocks, D, *et al* (1993). *Report on the 1993 pilot in mathematics assessment at Key Stage 2.* Confidential Report to the Schools Examination and Assessment Council.

Shorrocks, D. (1993). Whither Key Stage 1 assessment? *British Journal of Curriculum and Assessment, 3,* 2.

Shorrocks, D. (1995). Evaluating National Curriculum Assessment at Key Stage 1: Retrospect and Prospect. In P. Broadhead. *Research in Early Years Education.* Clevedon: Multilingual Matters.

Shorrocks-Taylor, D. and Daniels, S. (1999). A comparison of the multi-level modelling outcomes produced by the Value-Added National Project and the Leeds Longutudinal Study. *Oxford Review of Education,* in press.

Siegler, R. S. (1998). *Children's Thinking.* Englewood Cliffs, N.J.: Prentice Hall.

Simon, B. (1993). A return to streaming? *Forum, 35,* 36–37.

Simon, J. (1979). What and who is the APU? *Forum, 22,* 7–10.

Sizmur, S. and Burley, J. (1997). *Assessment in the Core Subjects in 1996: Key Stage 1 Evaluation Report.* London: School Curriculum and Assessment Authority.

Sizmur, S. and Sainsbury, M. (1996). Criterion referencing and level descriptions in national curriculum assessment. *British Journal of Curriculum and Assessment, 7,* 9–11.

Taylor, T. (1995). Movers and shakers: high politics and the origins of the National Curriculum. *The Curriculum Journal, 6,* 161–184.

Thatcher, M. (1993). *The Downing Street Years.* London: HarperCollins.

*Times Education Supplement* (1995). Anger intensifies over English marking. *TES,* 30.6.95.

Torrance, H. (1991). Evaluating SATs – the 1990 pilot. *Cambridge Journal of Education, 21,* 129–140.

Torrance, H. (1995). Teacher involvement in new approaches to assessment. In H. Torrance *Evaluating Authentic Assessment.* Buckingham: Open University Press.

Wallace, I. (1994). The Northern Ireland Curriculum – solving actual problems. *The Curriculum Journal, 5: 1,* 32–42.

Weinstock, A. (1996). League tables – for better or for worse? *British Journal of Curriculum and Assessment, 7,* 13–15.

Welsh Office for Education (1995). *Assessing 7- and 11-year-olds in 1995.* Circular 51/94. Welsh Office for Education.

Whetton C. and Sainsbury, M. (1992). *An evaluation of the 1991 National Curriculum Assessment. Report 4: The working of the Standard Assessment Task.* London: SEAC.

Whetton, C. (1997). The psychometric enterprise – or the assessment aspiration. In , S. Hegarty (Ed.) *The Role of Research in Mature Education Systems.* Slough: National Foundation for Educational Research.

Wiliam, D. (1992). Value-added attacks: technical issues in reporting national curriculum assessments. *British Educational Research Journal, 4,* 329–341.

Wiliam, D. (1993). Validity, dependability and reliability in National Curriculum Assessment. *The Curriculum Journal, 4,* 335–350.

Wiliam, D. (1994). Once you know what they've learnt, what do you teach next? A defence of the National Curriculum ten-level model. *British Journal of Curriculum and Assessment, 3,* 19–23.Wiliam, D. (1996). National Curriculum Assessments and Programmes of Study: validity and impact. *British Educational Research Journal, 22,* 129–141.

Wiliam, D. (1995). It'll all end in tiers! *British Journal of Curriculum and Assessment, 5,* 21–24.

Wiliam, D. (1996). National Curriculum Assessments and Programmes of Study: Validity and Impact. *British Educational Research Journal, 22,* 129–141.

Wiliam, D. and Black, P. (1996). Meanings and Consequences: a basis for distinguishing formative and summative assessment. *British Educational Research Journal, 5,* 537–48.

Wolf, A. (1993). *Assessment Issues and Problems in a Criterion-based System.* London: Further Education Unit.

Wood, R. (1982). Educational and Psychological Measurement: Further Efforts at Differentiation. *Educational Analysis, 4,* 120–134.

Wood, R. (1987). *Assessment and equal opportunities.* Text of a public lecture at ULIE, November, 1987.

Wood, R. (1988). The Agenda for Educational Measurement. In D. Nuttall (Ed.) *Assessing Educational Achievement.* London: Falmer Press.

## Further reading

Black, P. (1997). *Testing: Friend or Foe?* London: Falmer Press.

Gipps, C.V. (1994). *Beyond Testing.* London: Falmer Press.

Gipps, C.V. and Murphy, P. (1994). *Assessing Assessment series,* series ed. H. Torrance, *A Fair Test? Assessment, achievement and equity.* Buckingham: Open University Press.

Gipps, C.V. and Stobart, G. (1997). *Assessment: A teacher's guide to the issues.* London: Hodder and Stoughton.

Gipps, C.V., Brown, M., McCallum. B. and McAlister, S. (1995). *Assessing Assessment series,* series ed. H. Torrance, *Intuition or Evidence?: Teachers and National Assessment of Seven Year Olds.* Buckingham: Open University Press.

# Index

Compiled by Mary Kirkness

Please note: tables and figures are indicated by italics unless there is related text on the same page